Women Who Ride
the Hoka Hey

Women Who Ride the Hoka Hey

Enduring America's Toughest Motorcycle Challenge

ABAGAIL VAN VLERAH

McFarland & Company, Inc., Publishers
Jefferson, North Carolina

ISBN (print) 978-0-7864-9585-6 ∞
ISBN (ebook) 978-1-4766-3611-5

LIBRARY OF CONGRESS AND BRITISH LIBRARY
CATALOGUING DATA ARE AVAILABLE

© 2019 Abagail Van Vlerah. All rights reserved

No part of this book may be reproduced or transmitted in any form or by any means, electronic or mechanical, including photocopying or recording, or by any information storage and retrieval system, without permission in writing from the publisher.

Front cover images: *inset top to bottom* Debby Pearson, Kelly Quinn a.k.a. Throttle Girl, Wendy Battles; *background* the author rides into a sand storm on the 2012 HHMC. Photographs courtesy of the subjects.

Printed in the United States of America

*McFarland & Company, Inc., Publishers
Box 611, Jefferson, North Carolina 28640
www.mcfarlandpub.com*

Mitakuye Oyasin
("For All My Relatives")

Acknowledgments

I am eternally grateful to the women who took time out of their lives to share their stories with me. I channeled them as I rode and as I wrote. Building myself in their image makes me a stronger person.

I am also thankful to my family and friends who pushed me to complete this manuscript. You know who you are; I could not have done it without your love and support.

Finally, I am indebted to my Hoka Hey family. Most importantly, I am grateful for Jim Red Cloud and Beth Durham for allowing me into their home and family.

Table of Contents

Acknowledgments	vi
Preface	1
Introduction	3
Motorcycle Culture	4
A Brief History of Women in Motorcycling	5
1. The Hoka Hey Motorcycle Challenge and Sport	11
The Hoka Hey Motorcycle Challenge	12
Motorcycling as Sport	37
2. On the Problematic Nature of the Hoka Hey	42
Problems with Ethnographic Research	43
Motorcycling, Sport and Masculinity	45
Motorcycling and Whiteness	49
Native American Ties and Cultural Appropriation	52
Jim Red Cloud Durham	64
2010 Hoka Hey Motorcycle Challenge	65
3. An American Girl: The Women of America's Toughest Motorcycle Challenge	69
Eula "Junie" Rose	71
Tristica Kendall	74
Sheila Hoehn (and Trixie)	76
Carla Dubois	77
Kristin "Jersey Pearl" McKelvey	79
Bryana Mason	80
Kelly Quinn a.k.a. Throttle Girl	81
Debra Langley	83
Wendy Battles	84
Jane Bixby and Schatzi Brown	86

Debby Pearson	88
Eden Mailloux	90
Sherie Newell	91
Abby Van Vlerah	92
Conclusions	97

4. Feminist Ethics of Care and Intrinsic Motivation — 98

5. I Can Do Anything: Finding Empowerment Through the Hoka Hey — 119

6. She's Got Bigger Balls Than Most Men, They're Just on Her Chest: Gender, Identity and Change — 142

7. I Cried All the Way Home: The Difficult Reality of Leaving the Road — 167
- Accidents and Wrecks — 173
- Personal Health and Safety — 174
- Familial Duty — 177

Conclusion — 185
Chapter Notes — 191
Bibliography — 197
Index — 203

Preface

The Hoka Hey Motorcycle Challenge (HHMC) is a multi-thousand-mile endurance motorcycle challenge designed to raise awareness about the Lakota Sioux and the Pine Ridge Indian Reservation in South Dakota. Few women participate in this challenge; typically, the participants are 90 percent men and 10 percent women. However, women finish the challenge at a higher percentage rate than men. The success of the women who ride the Hoka Hey offers a lens through which to re-examine our interpretations of motorcycling and sport. Further, this project investigates the experiences of women who participate in the Hoka Hey, the potential challenges they face in this masculine environment, and if they change perceptions of women riders or the attitudes of their male counterparts. Interdisciplinary literature from sport and leisure studies and motorcycle studies grounds this book; my background in feminist cultural studies gives it academic framework. Sport scholarship and feminist cultural studies influence my work through the following premises: 1) understanding how women are marginalized through the dominance of masculinity in sport; 2) recognizing that women are socialized to participate differently in sport than men; 3) finding sport as a source of empowerment for women; and 4) advocating that these sources of empowerment can build potential for transgression either through altering perceptions of women riders or through challenging opinions of male riders.

This work is what Laurel Richardson describes as a "pleated text" in her work "Skirting a Pleated Text: De-Disciplining an Academic Life" (2). Throughout the text I weave together interpersonal stories, narratives, composite narratives, blog posts, and narrative non-fiction with textual and theoretical analysis. The sections including theory and analysis are largely in regular type font whereas the narrative sections are set apart with italics. While I wrote many of the narratives in the first person, most are composite narratives, which knit individual quotes from various interviews into one voice. Although not always marked with quotation marks, endnotes follow the direct quotes to indicate which unique storyteller is speaking. As Richardson suggests, "the pleats can be spread open at any point, folded back, unfurled" (2). By using this method, my hope is to create a dynamic, accessible story; and, I invite the reader to play with this text. Feel free to skip around, pick up and put down various sections and enjoy.

This book also unapologetically uses words that may seem strong or offensive to some. I include these in my own words, in the analysis, and in the words of the women who spoke them. Sometimes, when you are in an extreme situation, you just need to swear. Further, using vulgar or crude language can align women in hegemonically masculine environments with their male counterparts. Many women use this language to distort lines of traditional gender performance. I respect their choice of words. I also overlook the stringent use of grammar in some narrative sections to make the text accessible and conversational.

Introduction

Close your eyes and picture in your mind a person who rides a motorcycle. Look from his black boots up his leather-chapped legs to his chain-drive wallet beyond his protruding stomach to his hairy white-skinned arms extending from his body and hanging loosely away from his large torso and dragon-emblazoned shirt. Your eyes travel from the bit of hair poking from the collar of his black t-shirt to his scraggly beard and deep-set eyes. Tough and hard, his skin has the appearance of pockmarked leather. His balding head and tufts of remaining grey hair show his age. Now, envision an athlete. You may still picture a man, but he is likely clean cut, well built, and wearing some kind of sporting uniform. His smooth skin accentuates his muscular frame. Loose-hanging sport shorts extend to his knees and he wears huge high top sneakers that show the massive size of his appendages. Perhaps if you played a sport at some point in your life you imagine a person in this exact sporting garb; but still, a clean, lean, strong figure appears in your mind.

If you are one of the few who pictured a woman in each scenario, kudos. For everyone else, your brain likely conjures these images based on culturally constructed stereotypes and presumptive ideas about each subculture. For sport, you likely pictured someone who participates at what sport scholars call the center of sport.[1] The complex concept of the center of sport—in which scholars show the sporting world revolving around cultures of masculinity and heterosexuality—puts the sports you see most on TV at the center. Thus, they are more valuable than other sports. The NFL mega-conglomerate highlights this concept. Despite its issues (such as lauding a culture of violence) the NFL remains one of the (if not *the*) most popular sport leagues in the United States. Billions of dollars annually pour into this machine while other sports (like women's rugby) receive no airtime, no funding, and few fans. Society values sports at the center of sport as most important—men's sports football and basketball in particular. However, feminist cultural studies,[2] the theoretical foundation of this book, challenges these preconceived images and conceptions of what western cultures deem "best." The exercise of envisioning both a motorcyclist and an athlete shows the cultural divide between the two groups. When asked to think of an athlete you likely did not picture someone on a motorcycle. When asked to think of a motorcyclist you likely did not think of a woman. These images are emblazoned on our minds because of largely accepted and unquestioned social and cultural constructions of each group. Feminist cultural studies, and this book, asks you to challenge those notions. Erase those images. If we erase those traditional images from our mind's eye, we can see motorcyclists as both athletes and women.

People who identify as women and ride motorcycles choose to exist and participate in a traditionally masculine culture. Similarly, women athletes share experiences with women motorcyclists—as do women engaging in other masculine cultures, such as the military. These shared experiences speak to the ways in which women create a specific gender performance to either align or distance themselves from their male counterparts. This book explores the ways women in one masculine space perceive their experiences to be different from men's. Participating in masculine environments can challenge women, but it also has the capacity to empower them. By expanding their comfort zones to include masculine bodily experiences, female athletes push themselves and find empowerment through blending their masculine and feminine attributes. In short, women in sport and motorcycling show an ability to blend feminine and masculine traits to become better competitors.

Motorcycle Culture

Motorcycle culture can include a vast array of cyclists: riders of café and sport bikes (e.g., European- or Japanese-style motorcycles), weekend warriors who only ride during nice weather, outlaw clubs, endurance racers, and many more. Throughout this work, I use the term motorcycle culture to refer to the culture surrounding endurance motorcyclists in general and, most specifically, the culture surrounding the Hoka Hey Motorcycle Challenge. This includes a subset of the larger motorcycle culture involving riders of American touring motorcycles. Because of popular media representations of motorcyclists, these are "bikers" in the eyes of the public. While these popular representations may illustrate participants as enormous, burly, bearded, tattooed white men clad in black leather, in reality (and as you will see throughout this work) many different types of endurance riders exist.

Endurance motorcycle racing encompasses a culture of its own. Within this world, the Hoka Hey stands as the most grueling challenge. The Hoka Hey bills itself as the longest, hardest race in existence. Alongside other endurance rides, like the Iron Butt Rallies, American Legends Motorcycle Rallies, and the Cannonball Run, the Hoka Hey stands out as the outlaw of this group.m American Motorcyclist Association—the governing arm of the motorcycle world—denied the Hoka Hey sanction, aligning the challenge with the outlaw club mentality. Outlaw motorcycle clubs are collectives that seek approval from no one. Outlaw motorcycle clubs and the Hoka Hey tend to embody a "take it or leave it, this is who we are" attitude. Because the Hoka Hey advertises itself as the "toughest competition in history for the toughest men in history," women who participate in the ride must negotiate their femininities while adopting the rough masculine attitude of the ride.

A Brief History of Women in Motorcycling

While motorcycle culture clearly began at the advent of the machine, societal perceptions of motorcyclists have changed greatly over time. Invented in 1876 by German engineers, the first two-wheeled motorcycle was not more than a bicycle with an attached engine (Alford and Ferriss 19). Subsequently, the motorcycle industry moved to America and grew in popularity with the founding of today's largest American motorcycle corporations—the Indian Motorcycle Company in 1901 and Harley-Davidson in 1903. Born of the bicycle industry, early motorcycle companies associated their products with simplicity, physicality, power, and speed. Advertisements for Indian Motorcycles from 1909 described the machine with sayings like "Like a Flash," "the simplest ever made," and "more power for size than anything built" (Alford and Ferriss 23). During the late nineteenth and early twentieth centuries, the country was experiencing a boom in bicycling. Women, in particular, used the new machines for transportation and exercise. The bicycle craze became a catalyst for changing women's fashion (from wearing skirts to the greater acceptance of pants) and women's roles; with women's participation in bicycling came a change in our place in society from the private to the public sphere. As bicycles evolved into motorcycles, women played a consistent role in early motorcycle sales and advertising.

Advertisements for motorcycles and motorcycle-related products during the 1920s often utilized female models. Steven Alford and Suzanne Ferriss's book *Motorcycle* describes some of these early advertisements, citing a 1917 advertisement for Excelsior, which appeared in *Motor Cycle Illustrated* (100). The full-page ad depicts a woman in a full-length dress working on the engine of her motorcycle—illustrating even women can fix a motorcycle, it *is* that simple! Used as another selling point, motorcycle columnists boasted motorcycle riding as healthy for women. An article in the *Evening Standard* from 1928 stated, "Girls will find motor-cycling brings health. It will give them honest, fresh-air complexions. It will make them hardy and strong" (Alford and Ferriss 101). However, universal acceptance did not accompany these images, articles, and advertisements. Also during this time, Social Darwinists, whose ideas were founded in Charles Darwin's theories of evolution, gained popularity and multiple "scientific studies" purportedly proved that women are more fragile than men. Studies such as these prompted questions about women's participation in motorcycling. Their much weaker bodies supposedly could not support the motorcycle and would be subject to injury or, worse yet, their reproductive capacity would be inhibited by motorcycling (Alford and Ferriss 99). Regardless of their position for or against women motorcycle riders, these popular images, articles, and advertisements laid the foundation for women's participation in early motorcycling.

Commonplace in early motorcycling, endurance racing enhanced motorcycle corporations' abilities to advertise their machines. Racers would traverse the country, making stops in towns to speak about their bikes. Perhaps surprisingly, women participated in these early rides. In fact, a rich history of female endurance riders and racers dots the cultural past of motorcycling. Ann Ferrar's work *Hear Me Roar: Women, Motorcycles, and the Rapture of the Road* discusses the first transcontinental female motorcycle trip completed by Effie Hotchkiss in 1915. Her mother, Avis, thinking it improper for a young woman to travel the country alone, accompanied Effie in a sidecar. Their cross-country trip atop Effie's Harley-Davidson took them from New York to San Francisco and paved the way for women's distance motorcycling (Ferrar 20). A year later, sisters Augusta and Adeline Van Buren rode across the United States on separate motorcycles to prove women's ability and aptness to serve as military couriers. They report the trip took "great physical and mental stamina" as their adventure made them the first women to cross Pikes Peak in Colorado atop motorized vehicles (Ferrar 22). While their efforts proved unsuccessful in garnering positions for women as couriers, they contributed to a lasting legacy of women motorcycle riders.

Early endurance races and rallies served as grounds for women to show their motorcycling prowess. In 1907, Clara Wagner participated in a 365-mile endurance race from Chicago to Indianapolis at only eighteen years old. Although she earned a perfect score, race officiates denied her a title and deemed her "unofficial" because she was a woman ("True Pioneers"). Later, Dot Robinson challenged race operators and participated in the Jack Pine Enduro competition in 1937 (Alford and Ferriss 104). Race operators, including American Motorcyclist Association secretary E.C. Smith, attempted to bar women from the 1937 race; however, Dot secured enough signatures to override the rule and win women's right to participate in Enduro races (Ferrar 27). Enduro races traversed dangerous natural terrain as participants rode through swamps, rivers, and sand. These races tested motorcycles and their riders for their ability to ride on multiple surfaces. Putting these skills into practice, early motorcyclists engaged in informal distance rides in which women actively participated. The first person, either male or female, to cross the African continent on a motorcycle was British motorcyclist Theresa Wallach. She completed the 7,500-mile north-south course towing a trailer behind her motorcycle and sidecar (Alford and Ferriss 104). These stories published about women in motorcycle and other popular magazines show women's riding was not an anomaly.

Throughout the 1920s and '30s, women motorcyclists gained acceptance and, during World War II, opportunities opened for women to continue riding motorcycles. The Motor Maids, a women's motorcycling organization started by Dot Robinson, sought to assist the war effort by volunteering for dispatch riding. Dot Robinson herself supported the war effort riding as a motorcycle courier. Similarly, Bessie Stringfield, the most well-known African American female rider, "joined a motorcycle dispatch unit and rode as the only woman in a unit of six other African American riders" (Alford and Ferriss 106). Stringfield's earlier days as a motorcyclist gained her notoriety as the "Motor Queen of Miami." Despite encountering both racism and sexism, Stringfield made multiple cross-country trips for the war effort. Later, she founded the Iron Horse Motorcycle Club and was inducted into the Motorcycle Hall of Fame. During the war, women on motorcycles were common and they assisted the war effort through riding. Much like women on the factory lines, female motorcyclists received little cultural backlash and received acclaim for aiding the war effort.

However, Alford and Ferriss and Ann Ferrar note post-war anxieties changed the landscape of women riding motorcycles. The scholars note the post-war return to traditional notions of femininity and domestic life kept women on the road from cultural acceptance (Alford and Ferriss 106). During these years of economic and social rebuilding, women were expected to be demure wives and cautious mothers—not motorcycle riders. Despite the strides toward gender equality in the workforce made during the war, post–World War II America was unsettled and in search of a national culture. As men returned from war, women left positions in factories and returned to lives as housewives. Men returning from war desired a complete restoration of their pre-war lives and likewise, supportive women returned to their familial duties. This return to the home and men's simultaneous return to lives as primary breadwinners reinforced traditional views of male and female divisions of labor. The resurgence of the ideals of domesticity created a culture that valued tradition, family life, and hegemonic conceptions of femininity and masculinity. Markers of hegemonic femininity include colors, behaviors, and attributes traditionally associated with women or the feminine (e.g., wearing pink, donning makeup, cooking, physical weakness, fragility, and prettiness). Adopting markers of femininity became commonplace and continue to permeate even modern society. Not only did this result in women being reverted to their pre-war lives as wives and mothers, it also left little room for female participation in masculine arenas, including motorcycling.

While the return of men from war made motorcycling more difficult for women, it did not entirely stop women's participation. In the post-war years, Dot Robinson's Motor Maids sustained themselves as an organization by adopting traditionally feminine cultural markers, like pink jackets and lipstick holders affixed to their motorcycles to compensate for their association with the masculine space (Ferrar 26). The Motor Maids rode pink motorcycles and kept demure, respectable, and "ladylike" attitudes toward male riders. This transformation of the Motor Maids from dispatch couriers for the war effort to women riders donning pink was "carefully crafted in an image of women motorcyclists that conformed to, rather than challenged, conventional expectations for femininity" (Alford and Ferris 106). Via fashion, accessories, and their motorcycles, the Motor Maids and other female riders kept women motorcyclists on the road but also forever changed the cultural acceptance of women riders and athletes.

Because women in sport are seen as "less than," some women choose to alter their identities in order to fit in. In her article "Queers Even in Netball?: Interpretations of the Lesbian Label among Sportswomen," Kate Russell describes both positive and negative experiences of women in sport and their relationships to being labeled lesbian. Pertinent to my research, Russell points to the ways in which sportswomen negotiate their identities to accommodate for perceptions of sports in which they "should" or "should not" participate. Like female motorcyclists, these athletes must justify their participation in sport because of gendered stereotypes. Further, Russell suggests that women decline to discuss their sport in certain situations when their choices may come under scrutiny. For example, women who participate in "masculine sports" such as hockey may choose not to mention their participation in the workplace so as not to bring their gender identities into question. As Russell states, "the fact that these women are constantly expected to justify their participation shows that people believe it to be an unexpected activity which, in turn, reflects stereotype formation and maintenance" (112). Catherine Roster's article "Girl Power" mirrors these findings. In this work, she describes how many women withhold information about their motorcycling identities to friends and family. Specifically, female motorcyclists from Roster's study chose not to identify as motorcyclists when they felt they might be labeled as unfeminine, such as when they identified as mothers or wives. As a female motorcyclist, I understand this predicament; in my personal life, motorcycling is an identity marker I choose to reveal only when necessary or to people whom I trust. Roster describes how labels can be limiting to the interpretation of femininities, stating, "here there is only one definition of femininity as meaning 'not manlike' which prevents any other possible expression of femininity"

(117). As Roster suggests, adopting notions of dominant femininity only serves to further limit the overall interpretations of female motorcyclists. Through their disassociation, the female athletes and motorcyclists in these studies unknowingly perpetuate the marginalization of women in their respective arenas. This highlights the irony that often women within sport or motorcycling are the ones who prevent inclusiveness.

Despite these myriad challenges, women continue to participate in sport and motorcycling. Because these arenas remain dominated by men, women often adapt to feel comfortable within these environments. By doing so, women athletes do not discard their femininity. Rather they utilize all aspects of themselves (masculine and feminine) to become more complete people and challengers. Their ability to be gender chameleons in turn makes them feel empowered. Their presence and success in these masculine spaces then alters common perceptions about what it is to be an athlete or motorcyclist.

1

The Hoka Hey Motorcycle Challenge and Sport

An imposing Native American man sits atop a bright yellow Harley-Davidson motorcycle. He wears the same sundrenched, yellowed Hoka Hey tank top and jeans I saw him wear so many times on the Hoka Hey. His tanned skin makes his large tattoos difficult to decipher. His is a familiar face—deep smile lines around his mouth, his rose-colored glasses perched just below his billowy eyebrows. A source of comfort from the ride, his was the face I looked to many times for strength and advice throughout my 6,000-mile journey. I press play on the embedded YouTube video, giddy with the thought of seeing my friend come to life, if only on my computer. He begins talking to the camera, uncomfortable and with a tinge of awkwardness as he clearly reads from a script: "Hi, I'm Jim Red Cloud, founder of the Hoka Hey Motorcycle Challenge."

"Hi, Jim," *I think and wink at the small digital image of my friend and mentor. He continues the endorsement video for event sponsor Cee Bailey's windshields. As the short video progresses, I cringe as the words come out of his mouth:* "So if you're looking for a windshield that's been tested by the most toughest motorcycle challenge in history, and the toughest men in history, then you wanna look towards Cee Bailey. Toss me a Rockstar." *The can of energy drink flying in from the right side of the scene hits the Cee Bailey windshield like his words hit my heart. The toughest MEN in history? What about the women? What about us? Thanks for reminding me that this culture lauds masculinity above all else. Despite its comical nature, the advertisement video reinforces that I, and my fellow women riders, play in a man's world.*

Scholars describe the motorcycle as the perfect vehicle (Holbrook Pierson). However, a motorcycle is also an American cultural icon. Films, television series, advertisements, and fashion form cultural constructions that situate the motorcycle, and its surrounding culture, as a white, working class, masculine space. These deep cultural roots create a potentially off-putting space for many would-be riders. While members inside the culture may perceive it differently, these cultural constructions contort the social mindset about motorcycles and motorcyclists. Similarly, some motorcyclists choose to perpetuate these cultural constructions through actions, attitudes, and gender performances. As such, the surrounding culture of masculinity, class, and whiteness creates a specific space that women riders must strategically navigate.

Historically, both motorcycle culture and sport glorify masculinity. The Cee Bailey/Hoka Hey endorsement video highlights the invisibility of female participants in the Hoka Hey Motorcycle Challenge. While these sentiments may not reflect the actual opinions of challenge operators, they mediate the public and female participants' interpretations of motorcycle culture and the challenge's environment. In this chapter, I describe the roots of the HHMC in Native American culture and the social justice aspects of the conditions of the challenge, as well as the event itself. As part of my ethnographic findings, I utilize documents and artifacts from the HHMC and my personal experiences to characterize the challenge. In addition, I critically examine historical and contemporary media representations of motorcycling and its cultural associations. The analysis of motorcycle culture and the Hoka Hey documents converge to offer a thorough understanding of the HHMC within the context of motorcycle culture. What emerges from this interpretation is a site of layered masculinities, race, and class where challenge participants constantly interact. Consequently, the culture this chapter highlights is what women face when they choose to participate in the Hoka Hey. Within this cultural context, women constantly negotiate their standpoints as women riders.

The Hoka Hey Motorcycle Challenge

Blog Post: The Hardest Thing I've Ever Done
  The Hoka Hey is the hardest thing I've ever done. Period. It was a mental challenge (following the directions and negotiating difficult rides) and physical challenge (not eating, not sleeping, and being outside for 11.5 days straight). Much like running a marathon, it doesn't seem bad (now that it's over); but I'm trying not to lose sight of everything we've been through. It was demoralizing every day (missing a turn would easily knock down your momentum/confidence). Every day the road threw things at you that you thought you couldn't handle. Pushing through those moments is what the Hoka Hey is about.
  We were worn down physically and part of the ride became about fighting fatigue (after we discovered Five Hour Energy, this improved/became easier—my dad is hooked). The first few days of the trip we had to stop often to regain some energy (stopping at gas stations and briskly walking the parking lot or doing a few yoga stretches on the side of the road). I couldn't believe that it was possible to doze off on a bike. It's possible. And scary. For me, between not running and riding so long, my

1. The Hoka Hey Motorcycle Challenge and Sport

The 2012 Hoka Hey Motorcycle Challenge logo. Over time, the group changed the tag line from "It's a good day to die" to "It's a good day to ride." (Courtesy Hoka Hey Motorcycle Challenge.)

energy levels were zapped. My dad was worn down because of the heat. On about the fourth day of the trip he (finally listened to me) put his sun shirt on, and was able to stay awake longer during the heat of the afternoon. On top of being tired, we slept in parking lots, which didn't allow for much sleep. At night my dad often got leg cramps and we didn't get back on the ground after he was up and the cramp subsided. During a leg cramp, it was all I could do to pull him up off the ground and try to get him walking again. It was also difficult because I could tell he was in excruciating pain. In all, we only slept a max of six hours a night on the trip (and that was only once ... at the end). Mostly we had only two to four hours each night.

On top of that, I don't have a windshield on my bike (the only one on the ride to go without). Perhaps I'm stupid, but I really just didn't know any better. Without a windshield the wind pounds on your chest. I had my bags behind me on the seat to lean up against—without my packs I'd have a core workout in which I'm not interested. The ride itself made your arms tired from leaning the bike back and forth. My right hand (throttle hand) is numb. I literally can't feel my middle finger. I think it's from the vibrations and keeping on the throttle all day, every day. The feeling is starting to come back now that I'm not on the bike.

The mental challenge was greater than the physical challenge. I was the only one on our team capable/willing/who knows of reading and understanding the directions while we rode. I would memorize two lines of the directions at a time (L 219 4.2 miles; R 321 43.88 miles) and repeat that over and over in my head. When we made a turn, I'd memorize another line (R 321 43.88; R 341 5.6). At first I was doing the mileage math in my head. I needed to track how many miles I went on a tank of gas and would keep a running tally of how many miles we needed to go on each road. Say I started at twenty miles; I knew that when my trip odometer reached (around) 24.2 we needed to make a right turn onto 321. The mileage on the directions was sometimes right, sometimes close, and sometimes WAY off. The math was only reliable to a certain point. Couple that with riding, looking for signs, and making sure that the two people following you were still upright and following made for a stressful trip to say the least. Then I would get "yelled at" for not going fast enough or not knowing if my headlights were producing white or yellow light. Bottom line, I was a mess. I only cried four times (almost a miracle). Somehow my dad didn't think the ride was "stressful" (he doesn't like to admit that he's stressed) but he also wasn't trying to follow the directions.

I don't think you can do this ride with only one person. I wouldn't want to do it with anyone other than my dad. But at the same time, it was unnerving to see (or not see) him in my mirror or in front of me. Sights of him wrecking, running off the road, and being hit by a car flashed in my mind each time we turned a corner. It was a stressful and straining trip for eleven and a half days. Right now I'm thankful for our safe arrival and already looking forward to our next ride.

Overcoming those challenges and pushing through is what makes the Hoka Hey empowering. Despite laying my bike over twice, I kept going. This is not an easy ride. It's not for fair weather or novice riders. It's tough. Purposely tough. Not everyone finishes. Not everyone survives (2 riders killed in year 1; this year one rider is in ICU in Missouri). We ran our own race and we were able to finish. I'm pretty proud of our team—neither of us could have done it without the other [Blog Posted 17 August 2012 by Abby Van Vlerah].

Women who participate in the Hoka Hey describe it as simultaneously one of the most difficult and most rewarding things in which they have ever participated. While the challenges faced by each rider vary, many common threads exist among the experiences. Like other lifestyle sports, the element of risk--coupled with successfully overcoming the challenges encountered--produces a feeling of elation and accomplishment. On the road, women tackle physical barriers (safety, fatigue, and sickness), emotional obstacles (fear, the desire to prove themselves, and regret), natural factors (weather, animals, and exposure), and man-made problems (mechanical issues, wrecks, and the difficulty of the ride and its directions). To overcome the myriad of issues they face, the riders bond together and dig deep within themselves to find ingenuity, perseverance, and strength. Because of their ability to face and overcome challenges, riders express a newfound sense of accomplishment once they've completed the challenge.

1. The Hoka Hey Motorcycle Challenge and Sport   15

Abby's bike in line before the 2012 HHMC. Each year the challenge begins before dawn with a ceremony and blessing for the riders. Challengers must adorn their bikes with some sort of HHMC logo. Riders earn patches (as pictured here) by completing challenges. (Author photo.)

The Hoka Hey Motorcycle Challenge celebrated its inaugural run in 2010. Intended to raise awareness for the Lakota Sioux reservation in Pine Ridge, South Dakota, the challenge takes riders across the country on "the longest and most grueling motorcycle challenge on earth" (Hoka Hey). Challenge organizers intend for riders to sleep outside to understand homelessness and, as a result, speak to the public about the substandard living conditions on the Pine Ridge reservation. This challenge therefore becomes part outdoor adventure, part motorcycle challenge, and part social justice event. While the challenge course changes each year, the overarching qualities of the Hoka Hey remain relatively consistent. Standard markers of the Hoka Hey include turn-by-turn directions, the utilization of only secondary roads, checkpoints, the difficulty of the ride, and the specific period of time in which riders must complete the challenge. Challenge organizers design these elements to make the ride intentionally difficult.

The Hoka Hey organizers and those most familiar with the culture adamantly use the term challenge—not race—to define the Hoka Hey. Clearly, the terms race and challenge differ, with race indicating a sense of competition against other participants and challenge insinuating a personal competition. However, in my opinion, the level of competition associated with the Hoka Hey is both that of a race and a challenge. During the 2010 event, organizers used a first-to-the-finish-line model in which only one person won prize money. In subsequent years, they focused on the challenge aspect of the event and created a "window" for finishing to win prizes. Organizers intended this change to create a more inclusive environment in which participants only competed with themselves. While organizers encourage participants to compete only with themselves, the presence of other riders makes it almost impossible to not pit yourself against someone else at one point or another along the ride. To respect the Hoka Hey culture, I use the term challenge to describe the ride throughout this work.

Set during the warm summer months most common for motorcycle riding, the challenge takes place anywhere from June to August. Because of the length of the ride, which varies between 6,000 miles to 14,500 miles, participants remain on the course for anywhere from five days to a month—or as long as it takes to finish. Despite hosting the event during the summer, the distance and cross-country nature of the ride create temperature extremes. The challenge traverses anywhere from Alaska to the Southeastern United States. The variety in topography of the event makes for cold days, hot nights, tornadoes, rain, sleet, snow, and everything in between. Riders must prepare for any situation while understanding that it is not possible to foresee everything the road and course will bring. This element of the unexpected is part of what makes the Hoka Hey so challenging.

While riding a motorcycle always implies an element of risk, the difficulty of the ride and allotted time frame give challengers reason (or excuse) to participate in dangerous behavior. Speeding is common, with the hardest riders going at speeds upward of 110 miles per hour. Two challengers lost their lives during the 2010 event and 2012 left a 70-year-old man in critical condition in a Missouri hospital. In total, over the span of seven events, five people have died. After the first event, challenge organizers went to great lengths to dissuade participants from being careless, riding under sleep-deprived conditions, and competing with one another. Before the start of each challenge, riders sign waivers absolving challenge operators of any impending fault. The first lines of the "Terms and Conditions" speak to organizers' desires to create a fair and safe event. They state:

1. The Hoka Hey Motorcycle Challenge and Sport

HOKA HEY MOTORCYCLE CHALLENGE™ (the "Event") is a challenge of endurance, navigation, long distance riding skills and the ability to execute those skills safely and in strict compliance with all state and federal laws, while adhering to all of the Terms and Conditions of the Event. Applicants ("you") must not compete in any manner with other participants. You must only challenge yourself. You must NOT place any bets or wagers of any kind in relation to the Event. You must drive safely and abide by all motor vehicle laws and provisions in each State. You must drive with proper courtesy to all other participants and members of the public. This event is not a race or competition to arrive first at any location (1).

Stipulations of not placing wagers and abiding by motor vehicle laws intend to keep participants safe. Betting with other participants increases the intensity of the competition and creates a dangerous culture. Despite best intentions, this statement does not keep challengers from betting with one another and altering the sense of competition—changing from a personal competition to a competition with whoever made the wager. It is important to note that no women whom I interviewed discussed making any wagers regarding the challenge. As such, wagering on the challenge becomes a typically masculine act. Many participants encourage new challengers to "ride your own ride"; however, some challengers will violate safety laws, enact dangerous behavior, and compete with one another.

Other challenge rules and regulations varied throughout the many years of the competition. For example, the regulation stipulating that riders must sleep outdoors changed in 2012 and rules about traffic violations (e.g., whether any speeding or moving violation will result in disqualification) alter from year to year. These changes result directly from actions and suggestions of participants in previous years. Other regulatory changes include the variation of speeding rules and competition style. The willingness of race organizers to alter the event shows the detail, desire, and attention given to hosting the best event possible. As the challenge continues to evolve, so do its challengers. The constant flux of the challenge brings additional riders into the fold but also alienates others.

Women on the Hoka Hey indicate a fear for their personal safety while being on the road alone. They often pair up with other riders to combat this issue. Rules of the challenge indicate that you should sleep outside by your motorcycle. The women interviewed express specific concern for their safety when sleeping outside. While this may not actually cause problems, it does create an element of fear for women who choose to ride solo. In reality, it causes problems for some women who experience robberies, sometimes at gunpoint, and who struggle to find safe places to sleep. While men may encounter these same problems, the socialization of women and real issues of sexual assault and violence lead women to fear more greatly for their safety. Again I point to government institutions and schools, as well as film, media, and news outlets, which discourage women from walking alone at night for fear of sexual assault rather than discouraging men from committing these acts. These types of scare tactics fail to focus on the real problem (the men who perpetrate sexual assaults) while placing blame on women and victims. Despite this, women who participate in the Hoka Hey do sleep outdoors, sometimes alone. Women riders develop ways to cope with their fears which, in turn, leads to feelings of empowerment. It is important to note that while overcoming fears may lead to empowerment, it does not eliminate risk.

Women specifically felt a sense of unease and fear surrounding the idea of sleeping outside. Sleeping on the road was not easy for everyone and the fatigue and loneliness often brought on fear. Sheila spoke of hiding herself because she was a woman: "Bein' a single woman you're not gonna go out in a sleepin' bag on the side of the road and invite yourself to have problems. You know, so I know outta sight outta mind is the way to be."[1] Similarly, Kelly noted, "Typically you see a bike on the side of the road and you're going to assume, and there's somebody in a bedroll, you're going to assume it's a big burly tattooed motorcycle dude. Just like the stereotype. Not so much. Obviously as a woman out there on the road that is my biggest concern."[2] Sleeping on the side of the road alone was Junie's main concern as well: "Three years in a row I've hooked up with people because of my lack of confidence in myself. Each year I've let myself hook up with somebody because you know, I don't like sleepin' out there by myself. I'm afraid at night."[3] Sherie also mimicked this feeling of vulnerability, stating, "That was one of the hardest things about the Hoka Hey was finding somewhere that I felt safe to sleep 'cause I was on my own."[4] Wendy agreed, "I quickly found out that I don't like riding alone. That was scary. That was, you know, but I was facing my own fears, my own demons. You know a man can go out and camp and ride alone and he's relatively safe. You put a female out there and it ain't so safe anymore. And I quickly found out."[5]

The women constantly deal with fear felt on the road. Motorcycle stories often include overcoming a fear—the fear of riding for the first time, riding after a wreck, or your safety on the road; women riders experience, challenge and overcome fears daily. The length, difficulty, and uniqueness of the Hoka Hey exacerbate fearful feelings. Fear on the road is specific to women, who are more likely than men to feel threatened by being alone. Motorcycle scholar Liz Jansen describes how, through riding, women are "coming face to face with fears" which can lead to feeling powerful (110). She states, "By boldly staring down that fear and calling upon skills they've discovered through riding, they've become aware of even greater power extending far beyond themselves and their circles" (110). In the HHMC, overcoming fears and obstacles enable women to feel empowerment. Not only are women harnessing the power of their machines to overcome fear, they take on power structures which preclude them from feeling safe.

Fear is a common technique used within hierarchies to establish and maintain power. By understanding and feeling fear, people are discouraged from performig certain dangerous or risky behaviors. For example, rather than addressing our culture of violence in which it is acceptable to rape, women are taught to fear walking alone at night in order to "protect" themselves from potential dangers (such as rape or theft). This reinforces the hierarchy, which keeps women reliant on men. An alternate response (and one that would challenge the hierarchy) would be to address the culture of violence prevalent in the United States. Here, disciplinary structures, such as those present in patriarchal societies (i.e., propaganda and media outlets), discourage women from participating in certain events (such as endurance motorcycle challenges) by instilling fear. In other words, society socially conditions women to fear the unknown and feel unsafe, which can keep them from participating in events such as the Hoka Hey, or going anywhere alone as a young woman. In part, this reifies our femininity. Fear disciplines women into succumbing to their accepted gender roles. Put another way, social institutions force women to feel the need to be with a man to ensure their safety or that they would be safer if they were men. However, these social institutions do not always produce their intended outcomes. Women overcoming fear and embracing feelings of power exemplifies this. Women who participated in the Hoka Hey, rather than not participating in the event because of fear, overcame their fears and felt empowerment. Fear did not keep them from engaging in dangerous or risky behaviors; rather, doing so reinforced the human ability to turn feelings of fear into an empowering experience.

One reason for its heightened sense of competition and dangerous behavior is the time frame within which challengers must complete the route. Each challenge asks riders to complete the ride within a given time frame to earn the title "challenge finisher." There are three places for challengers—contenders, finishers, and arrivals. Contenders complete the challenge within a specific window of time and are eligible to win prize money. However, contenders may not receive prize money if they fail to follow the rules properly. Finishers complete the challenge within a longer time period, typically prior to the post-challenge end of the road party and awards ceremony. Arrivals are those who cross the finish line any time after the awards ceremony. Event organizers determine the time frame for each challenge by assigning an official rider to test the route each year. The amount of time in which the official rider completes the route then determines the window for winning prize money. Unlike foot racing, the course never closes. Instead, organizers vow to stay at the finish line as long as they know riders remain on the course. While the allotted time frame for each challenge differs, typically riders must average approximately 1,000 miles per day. For example, in 2012, riders needed to complete the 6,000-mile course in seven days. During this challenge, the finish line was open for a thirty-six hour window between the sixth and seventh days of the challenge. Operators considered anyone who crossed the finish line during the given period a contender and split the prize money equally among them. In addition to challenging participants to move rapidly through the course, the window of time the finish line is "open" keeps riders on the road for longer than may be necessary. For example, the finish line may not open until the seventh day of the challenge even though some riders may finish the challenge in only five days. Because the challenge operates without a large support team, this allows organizers time to cross the country but also intends to keep the safety of the riders in mind.

We are STILL in Arkansas. My mind drifts with the phone still next to my ear. I stare despondently down at the Rand McNally map deemed useless by the big rig driver who helped us at our last stop. His deep laugh faded in my head as I replayed his unintentionally condescending words, "Yup, Rand McNally never been to Arkansas." My eyes darted from directions to map. We were only halfway through the course. We've been on the road for five or six days. My brain trying to sort out what day it was and how long we'd been riding. The days, hours, and miles blurred together like a dream you wake up from disoriented and covered in sweat. I snapped back into reality as I hear my mom's voice on the other end of the phone. "Ok. I love you too. Talk to you later, Momma. Thanks for the information." Aggravated and exhausted I hang up the phone and slump my head between my bent knees, sitting on the gas station curb. Nothing feels good at this moment. My body aches. My mind remains cloudy and the fatigue of the trip begins to set in.

Grimacing from exhaustion and a saddle-sore ass, I muster the energy to stand up, stretching my body as much as possible in my riding boots and full body gear. It feels good to move. What I wouldn't give to strip down and do some yoga now. No time for that. I release the stretch and amble toward my dad. A deep sigh erupts from my body like a geyser, "She said someone's already at the finish." I drop my head in an unconscious sense of shame as the words fall out of my mouth. "It's on the tracker. Someone's just sitting in New York." I pictured in my head a computer screen with the GPS system and familiar yellow numbered tags next to a small motorcycle icon in a parking lot. Just sitting. It was too early to cross the finish line but we were still so far away. A rider had completed the course with days to spare and we were still not to the second checkpoint. Stunned. Tired. Confused at the possibility. Our trek was only beginning. Despite a sandstorm, hail, and four thousand miles, our journey had barely launched while someone else's had already come to a close.

"Hhhuh. Whhhaa…. But the finish line doesn't open for two more days!" my dad shouts. The quotidian twisted smile of bewilderment flashes across his face as he laughs at the possibility. His tan-knuckled hands, filled with a can

of Pepsi and a lunch-size pack of Oreos unfurl into the air. "Guess that's why they said take your time." *His comment about the organizers' suggestion that it was an easy ride felt like a punch in the gut. It was not an easy ride for us.*

And you didn't think it was possible," I jibe back, shooting him my best I-told-you-so glance.

"Well, they have to be cheating," he said emphatically as he took another drink of his pop and made another cookie disappear under his greying mustache.

"Well, they certainly weren't sitting by the side of the road in Arkansas drinking Pepsi and eating Oreos." We laugh at ourselves. We aren't cut out for this ride, but we're determined enough to finish it, I thought as we climb laboriously back onto the bikes without another spoken word.

A turn-by-turn challenge requires riders to follow a specific preset route. Each rider follows the same course; the rules for the Hoka Hey specify riders must not deviate from this route. While most races (including foot races) are turn-by-turn, the Hoka Hey does not provide markers along the route to indicate turns. It would be virtually impossible to mark the massive cross-country route. Instead, riders must read and follow the directions perfectly. Specifically, the challenge Terms and Conditions packet indicates, "Participants must adhere to the prescribed route as written in the driving directions that will be provided. If you find that you have strayed from the route, you must backtrack or circle around to the place you left the route and continue from that point" (1). Printed on standard-size paper with a standard font size, directions are difficult to read on a motorcycle. They indicate which direction (left or right) riders must turn, onto which road, for how many miles riders stay on a particular road, and the total number of miles traveled. While challenge organizers call this a map, there is no pictorial representation of the route.[6] Increasing the difficulty of the ride is the face that the routes only utilize secondary roadways. Over the course of its years in operation, the Hoka Hey changes the style of directions. Always on a Microsoft Excel-like document, the way operators indicate turns and mileage changes. Now, rather than producing "exact" miles between each turn, the directions indicate less than, about, and more than X miles to the next turn.

Turn Right onto NW 62nd Street, go 4.99 miles to NW Humphrey Road then turn Left onto NW 66th in .52 miles. The directions continue like this on alternating green and white lines for the remaining third of the page. It seems like an endless grocery list filled with items you can't locate in the store. Your brain wanders down each aisle searching for the right ingredient but fails each time. But this part should be easy, Humphrey Road and 66th HAVE to be big streets, well-marked signs through a town. And again I am reminded this is the Hoka Hey and it isn't going to be THAT easy. Despite the numbering and naming of the streets, we are still riding through cornfields. No well-marked street

Las Vegas, NV to Kirkwood, MO

LAS VEGAS HARLEY-DAVIDSON
2605 S. EASTERN AVE. LAS VEGAS, NV 89169

Turn	Onto	Ride	Total
	Las Vegas Harley-Davidson		
R	Karen Ave	0.00	0.00
R	S. Maryland Pkwy	1.00	1.00
R	NV SR 589 – E. Sahara Ave	0.26	1.26
L	NV SR 612 – S. Nellis Blvd.	4.06	5.32
R	NV SR 147 – E. Lake Mead Blvd	13.58	18.90
L	NV SR 167 – Northshore Rd	2.85	21.75
S	Becomes NV SR 169 – Northshore Rd.	41.69	63.44
L	Merge with NV SR 12 – Moapa Valley Rd.	21.15	84.59
L	I-15 S / US 91 / NV SR 6 - Ramp	0.05	84.64
R	Exit 91 Glendale Blvd Ramp	2.25	86.89
L	E. Glendale Blvd	0.25	87.14
R	W St Hwy 168 / N NV 168	0.67	87.81
R	US 93 / NV SR 7 / Great Basin Hwy	23.98	111.79
L	NV SR 318 / SR 375	54.46	166.25
L	NV SR 375	0.61	166.86
L	NV SR 6	98.70	265.56
R	Merge with US 95 / Erie St / Main St @ Tonopah	49.25	314.81
R	US 95 @ Coaldale Jct	40.66	355.47
R	NV SR 362	62.34	417.81
R	US 95 / NV SR 3 / Veteran's Memorial Hwy	1.37	419.18
L	US 95A / Yerington Cut-Off / Veteran's Memorial Hwy	32.73	451.91
L	Ramsey Cutoff	51.10	503.01
L	US 50	3.45	506.46
R	NV SR 79 / Six Mile Canyon Rd	14.28	520.74
L	Mill St. @ Virginia City	7.44	528.18
R	NV SR 341 / C St / Geiger Grade Rd	0.49	528.67
R	US 395 B / NV SR 430 / Virginia St	11.94	540.61
R	Longley Ln @ Reno	4.20	544.81
R	NV SR 659 / S McCarran Blvd	1.67	546.48
L	Victorian Ave	0.13	546.61
R	NV SR 445 / Pyramid Way / Pyramid Lake Hwy	0.65	547.26
R	NV SR 446 / Sutcliffe Hwy	29.90	577.16
R	NV SR 447	13.25	590.41
L	NV SR 427 / Main St @ Fernley	14.93	605.34
L	US 50A / E Main St	3.19	608.53
L	US 50 / Reno Hwy	18.35	626.88
S	Merge with US 6 & US 93 @ Ely	268.46	895.34
S	US 6 / US 50 Utah State Line	63.40	958.74
L	UT SR 141 / S. State St. @ Santaquin	155.80	1114.54

Continued on Page 2

Directions from the 2012 HHMC. Directions for each leg of the challenge are given at the checkpoints. In 2012, the directions gave exact mileage between turns, which became a challenge as odometers differ slightly from motorcycle to motorcycle. (Author photo.)

signs or towns emerge. Occasionally a small house or sprawling farm dots the landscape but essentially, we are alone on country roads. The signage is typical for any country road, small and usually tipped over or leaning from having been hit by a car or knocked over by teenager pranksters. Sometimes we encounter a stop sign but largely the roads just turn into one another without notice. It is a Right, Right, Left, Straight, Left, Left, Right scenario that confuses me and makes me think we are just riding in circles. Of course, you can only turn left so many times in a row before you're just back in the same place, right? It is a feeling of endlessness and exhaustion I had not before experienced. Just get through this to Rossville and we'll find a place to stop, I thought in my head between repeating lines of the map.

Prior to this point, my dad and I had been conferring on directions. We'd stop at an intersection, think about which way to go, and agree before taking off. We'd confirm we were going in the right direction and had listened to the other's opinion. But this time it is too hot to stop. The heat index continues to climb as a cloudless sky blazes the relentless sun down on our unprepared skin. We had started wearing long sleeves but hadn't yet figured out the beauty of a UPF 50 sun shirt. As we roll on the throttle and away from the intersection, I can feel my dad starting to wear down behind me. He is falling back. His engine rattles in the distance, sounding farther and farther behind. I have to get him off the road, I think as we continue down the straight country road. The reflection of his face in my mirror looks more like a purple dot than his normal mustachioed features. His skin looks purple. He doesn't do well in the heat. Then, just as the eternity of left-hand turns beings to seem unending, my consciousness shifts. I don't know if it is the heat, or the exhaustion, or a survival instinct to get off the road, or just that I am in the right frame of mind, but somehow I saw the roads coming before they were there. I know where the next turn will be. I can estimate the mileage ahead of me and know if we are one or two roads from the next turn. I finally get the directions. It feels AWESOME. Confidence and adrenaline surge through my body. "Fuck yeah," I yelled to no one and the world. "I finally GET IT!" I don't need to stop to ask my dad if we were going in the right direction. It is like I rode through these cornfields all my life and I am on my way home from work. I know Humphrey Road will be the next right. I don't need help and I am not questioning myself. About six miles into the series of half-mile- followed by two-mile stretches, he starts to fall behind. I put my feet down and feel the rubber soles melting into the pavement as I wait for him at a stop sign.

He finally pulls up beside me with a confused and overwhelming look on his face. "You see where we are?" I yell over the roar of our engines. He looks back at the directions then at the road sign then at me. "We're down here," I point excitedly to my directions about three fourths of the way down the page from where his hefty fingers hovered. "Oh," he says flatly. "I was looking for

66th." 66th was a few miles back. He was looking for a road we'd been off of for miles. I start to explain the directions to him. His face and arms are turning a deeper shade of purple from the sun. There isn't any time to explain, I thought to myself. I need to get us out of this heat. Just a few more miles to Rossville.

"Just follow me. I get the directions now." I take off down the road, his bike following me as if pulled by an invisible chain.

Later, my dad stands by our bikes and fills them with gas. He doesn't speak much. He is despondent and tired. "I totally nailed those directions!" Seemingly his opposite, I am excited. I jump, fist pump, and let my emotions show. This is one of my greatest moments of triumph throughout the trip. My dad admits he was confused by the directions. I thought it was just because it was too hot for us to be outside. Our brains literally fried. I only later realized my greatest moment of triumph was simultaneously my dad's first moment of defeat. He thought the directions proved I didn't need him anymore.

One of the hallmarks of the Hoka Hey is that riders travel the country only on secondary roads. The routes specifically avoid highways and even larger secondary roads. Instead, riders traverse county, state, and back roads throughout the country. Despite efforts to remain on paved roads, occasionally the route deviates into gravel or dirt. Likewise, road conditions vary from state to state, forcing riders to dodge potholes and other adverse road conditions caused by a lack of funding; state and federal monies are poured into highways, taking away from the upkeep of secondary roads. Although these roads are intentionally difficult to ride, they offer riders opportunities to see a vast area of the country. The back roads generally twist through state or national parks, Native American reservations, and small towns. One rider notes in a promotional video for the Hoka Hey, "I just saw the amber waves of grain. I'm looking at purple mountains. The redwood forest we'd already gone through." Another states, "I had no idea what I was missin' as much riding as I do. When you see this country from this perspective. Why people drive on freeways? Crazy" ("The Movement"). Scenic byways, historic transportation corridors, and cultural trails are common avenues for the route. The women of the Hoka Hey describe how they became one with nature and engaged their senses while riding. As Schatzi noted, "[W]e take a lot for granted. But we really, we saw some exquisite scenery. And a lot of times you remember it, but like why didn't I have my camera out at that point in time?"[7]

There were animal stories. Elk. Deer. Buffalo. In her interview, Sheila listed all the animals she saw: "we had a wolf, some big horn sheep, just on the side of the road!"[8] The amount of wildlife encountered on the Hoka Hey is expansive, although not all viewed safely from a distance. Carla describes the darker side of wildlife and motorcycling. "I had an altercation with a buffalo. That's another thing. Ugh. I came up on Custer Park just around supper

SPOKANE VALLEY, WA to MEDICINE PARK, OK

Turn ID	Distance	Turn	Road	@ Miles
		Start	Depart Lone Wolf Harley-Davidson	
		Turn Right	E Cataldo Ave	
D 1	< 1	Turn Left	N Barker Rd	
D 2	< 1	Turn Left	I-90 E - ENTER IDAHO	
D 3	@ 30	Keep Right	Exit 22 ID-97 ramp	
D 4	< 1	Turn Right	ID-97	
D 5	@ 35	Go Straight	ID-3	
D 6	@ 25	Keep Right	ID-6	
D 7	@ 25	Turn Left	ID-9	
D 8	@ 15	Turn Left	ID-8 (2nd Ave)	
D 9	< 1	Turn Right	ID-3 (Wyoming St)	
D 10	@ 15	Turn Left	Cedar Ridge Rd	
D 11	< 1	Turn Right	Southwyck Rd → 215 Rd (Old ID-7)	
D 12	@ 25	Go Straight	ID-7 (Cavendish Hwy)	
D 13	< 4	Turn Right	Michgan Ave (to US 12)	
D 14	< 1	Turn Left	US-12 (ID-7)	
D 15	@ 30	Turn Right	ID-13 (N Main St)	
D 16	@ 25	Turn Left	US-95	
D 17	> 75	Turn Left	ID-55 (Virginia St)	
D 18	> 75	Turn Left	Banks Lowman Rd (CR 17 | FR 24)	
D 19	@ 35	Turn Left	ID-21 (Ponderosa Pine Scenic Rte│FR 25)	
D 20	> 50	Turn Right	ID-75	
D 21	< 100	Turn Right	US-20	
D 22	< 100	Go Straight	ID-51 (**No Sign** - @ I-84) (American Legion Blvd)	
D 23	< 100	Go Straight	NV-225 - ENTER NEVADA	
D 24	@ 100	Turn Right	Merge onto I-80W	
D 25	@ 20	Keep Right	Exit 279 to NV-278 (Bush St)	
D 26	< 1	Turn Left	NV-278 (Bush St)	
D 27	< 100	Turn Left	US-50 (Lonliest Hwy | Great Basin Blvd)	
D 28	@ 100	Turn Right	US-93 (Great Basin Hwy)	
D 29	< 125	Turn Left	NV-319 (Main St)	
D 30	@ 20	Go Straight	UT-56 - ENTER UTAH	
D 31	< 75	Turn Right	N Main St (I-80 BL | US-130)	
D 32	< 1	Turn Left	UT-14 (E Center St)	
D 33	< 50	Turn Left	US-89	
D 34	@ 20	Turn Right	UT-12	
D 35	@ 125	Turn Right	UT-24 (E Main St)	
D 36	< 50	Keep Right	UT-95	
D 37	@ 125	Turn Right	US-191 - Enter Arizona	
D 38	@ 50	Turn Left	US-160 - (pass thru NM) Enter Colorado	

Continued on Page 2

Directions from the 2018 HHMC. In later years, challenge operators changed the directions to offer estimates of mileage between turns using "less than," "greater than," and "about" symbols. (Author photo.)

time, dinnertime, ... just as I went up over the pass I was in the middle of the herd. Well, when I get up in there and there's the mommas and the babies and the daddies. Oh, I could feel the emotion and the ... the stress in the air. Like an aura; it was just overwhelming."[9] Similarly, Tristica experienced the raw power of nature through the buffalo: "I'm cruising along and there's like a freakin' heard of buffalo in the road. And it's like one of those things, that's like, Oh, Shit! You know and there's like a *house* in front of me. But you know, you slow down and just find a path through them and just ride through 'em and hope that they don't get ticked off."[10] Like our country, the buffalo are both bucolic and bellicose and the Hoka Hey reminds riders of that duality.

Like animal encounters, riders of the Hoka Hey often speak of weather affecting the ride. As they traverse the country, riders encounter sandstorms, hail, rain, heat, cold, tornadoes, and hurricanes. From one extreme to another, challengers understand the ride as a test of how much exposure we can handle. Some riders, out of their home state for the first time, express surprise at the temperature differences our nation offers. Wendy from Florida felt the weather in her body: "I have never been out West or up North or in extreme conditions. So I didn't realize that elevation, and rain, and heat, and cold, would affect your body so much."[11] Debra recounted the extremes by illustrating the temperature differences on one road, saying, "[you're] on the top of them mountains lookin' at snow and then when you'd get down the mountain you'd be pullin' your clothes off you'd be so hot. And uh goin' around the mountain all of a sudden you'd hit where there was hail. And I was like, 'Well, where'd that come from?'"[12] Sheila described the severe cold riding through Alaska on the 2010 ride: "You know, it was just crazy and it was just freezing. And I mean, beyond freezing cold. And I was just thinking, good thing I got this heated seat and these heated grips. You know, it's helping. But it's just so freezing cold. And I mean two weeks before it was so hot"[13] Byranna recounted a similar aversion for the Canadian and Alaskan weather: "[We had] twelve hours of straight sleet, rain, snow, hail crap thirty minus degree weather."[14] Of course, nothing shields you from the rain and cold on a motorcycle. There is no protective bubble, heat, or windshield wiper. Instead, raindrops feel like a million tiny needles peppering your skin.

As emphasized in the quotations above, women Hoka Hey challengers describe the appeal of exposure to nature. This sentiment mirrors and expands on both motorcycle and sport literature, both of which also indicate the appeal of nature for participants. In her introduction to *Understanding Lifestyle Sports,* Belinda Wheaton describes lifestyle sports as "occurring in a non-urban environment" and asking participants to "become one with nature" (12). Likewise, motorcycle scholars such as Jansen, Joans, and Mullins describe exposure to nature as a key element of motorcycling. Specifically,

Jansen states, motorcycling "appeals to our basic nature, satisfies primal needs and brings out our strengths ... riding outside of urban areas is a spiritual experience" (9). Through encounters with animals, weather, and natural beauty, the HHMC exposes challengers to the physical grandeur of the United States and Canada, and pushes challengers outside of their traditional, more urban environments. However, while this exposure takes challengers out of urban landscapes, it reminds us that the urban/natural binary no longer exists. We've killed nature by putting roads, hotels, gas stations, and homes in its midst.

Exposure to the natural world while on a motorcycle challenges and deconstructs the oppositional forces of urban/rural. Riding a motorcycle epitomizes post-industrial, capitalist society. Riding the Hoka Hey highlights the push and pull of man versus nature. No longer are motorcycles used as workhorses for delivery vehicles, symbolizing a retreat from industrial necessity to a post-industrial capitalism in which we use machines for pleasure rather than purpose. In other words, our society has evolved into one where the motorcycle is a leisure vehicle rather than a work vehicle. However, while we are on this man-made leisure machine, we specifically choose rides that will put us closer to nature. While participating in the challenge or other lifestyle sports, feeling as though you're one with nature in an attempt to reclaim a more primal existence. We take the long way home, we climb mountains, and we visit national parks and forests. Here we have the two pulls—a man-made machine and the landscapes with which we long to connect.

This idea is reminiscent of Leo Marx's 1964 work, *The Machine in the Garden: Technology and the Pastoral Ideal in America*, the quintessential American Studies myth and symbol text deconstructing literary works that expose this dichotomy.[15] The juxtaposition between these two forces blurs as the industrial enters nature, not only through the motorcycle but also through the roads on which challengers travel, gas stations at which they purchase items, and rest stops at which they relieve their bodies. Encountering animals or feeling the raw power of a storm reminds challengers they are mere visitors in all landscapes and environments. By riding through sandstorms or seeing wild animals, Hoka Hey challengers connect with the natural world while atop an unnatural machine. Being on a motorcycle in the middle of a sandstorm (as I was on the 2012 ride) felt unreal, surreal, and real all at the same time. Our machines propel us into the impending cloud of inescapable dust. We find ourselves in a place we arguably should not be when exposed to nature.

Similarly, the natural element of the challenge blurs the native/nonnative binary as challengers uncover their connection to the natural world. The myth that Native Americans are more in touch with nature than their colonizers comes into question through white challengers' recognition of the natural world. Challengers break down and embody the plural as they cross the country. Riders take on hegemonic characteristics of both the native and nonnative by becoming increasingly comfortable in the natural environment while still not reaching total immersion. As they become both more and less comfortable in their element riding through unknown environments, riders take on markers of both white and native cultures. Simply put, we both try to become one with the nature around us and panic in the sandstorm. We sleep outside, exposed to the elements, but we still carry cots, tents, and sleeping bags. While we make attempts at breaking down the differences between white and native cultures, we fail to embody fully one limited definition of either trope. We are still in between.[16] While on the ride, Hoka Hey challengers feel this conflict between natural and urban, white and Native American—a pull exposing the real messiness and complications of living in a seemingly dualistic world. When we place ourselves into these unlikely arenas, we add to the multiplicity of our identities and tap into our ability to rupture ourselves, thus turning the Hoka Hey into a life-changing experience.

In addition to the use of secondary roads and exposure to nature, the difficulty of the ride is a crucial element of each Hoka Hey. Challenge organizers bill the ride as the "toughest ride" for the "toughest riders on earth" through "some of the most technical roads in North America" (Hoka Hey). A technical road includes multiple twists and turns, and requires a great level of riding skill to navigate. Routes typically traverse mountain ranges and other areas the interstate highway system specifically avoids. Commonly called "twisties" by riders, 270-degree turns, "piggy-tails" (turns which look like a spiral) and S-curves abound on technical roads. These roads require riders to understand their machines and know how to avoid "over-steering" the bike. Instead of using their arms to turn (a technique that quickly leads to fatigue), skilled riders use their bodies to lean into curves. In addition to navigating curves, riders must know how to ride on incredibly steep grades. This includes slowing the bike with the engine by downshifting so as not to "burn up" the front brakes, and using the clutch to regulate speeds. One of the most amazing stories recounted from the women riders is Eden's tale of traversing a mountain to Lukachukai. I add an extended quote here to show in her own words the difficulty of the ride. The bolded sections are my own emphasis.

> I dumped my bike three times on the first one. More or less because I managed to be a little bit stubborn at the time. There was one stretch between New Mexico and Arizona where we were supposed to find Highway 13, Red Rock Highway. I'd been up and down one section of the freeway, or highway, like three times could not find this bloomin' road. I asked three of, who I thought were residents, two of them said take this road. One of them said, oh you need to go further north. So I figured two out of

three, go with the majority. I should have gone with the third. It started off, the road started off asphalt. Then it went to gravel. And we were told in the pre-ride meeting, be prepared for gravel. Ok. I thought no biggie. Then it got into dirt roads. I was like, **well, they said it was going to be a challenge**. And so I'm on the Indian reservation and I finally come across this lone little trailer with two, a little Indian couple here. And I ask them, "Is this the road that goes over the mountain to Lukachukai?" And they said yes. They nodded. And I'm looking at the road going, "OK...."

So yeah, I'm going up this jeep road. And after **I've dumped the bike three times, fully loaded, I managed to pick it up. The fourth time I dumped it, I was too exhausted**. It was late in the day. I mean my arms I was shaking all over. And I couldn't pick it up. And I was like, alright, I brought tie downs. Brand new, brand new, I hadn't even taken them out of the little packages, I think. But they weren't threaded. I was going to tie down one end to a tree, one end to the rear and work a lever system and get the bike up. 'Cause the bike didn't roll on its side. No, it rolled over on a rock. So it was flat. Even with the engine guards, it was straighter than flat. [LAUGHTER]

And yeah, it was leaking fuel. Finally, the fuel stopped and I was going, oh crud. I even called my hubby to try and help me figure out how to put the tie downs, the ratchet systems, in correctly. 'Cause every time I did it, it would wind to where the tie down would just wrap on itself until you got this great big ball and then it wouldn't do it anymore. I could not figure out how to properly wrap it. So I called him. He could not figure out how to properly tell me how to do it over the phone. And I even had to hike up the hill in order to get a signal. And I was down to like a quarter bar. And I was like, "Honey, if you don't hear from me in a couple of days, I'm somewhere between Arizona and Lukachukai."

I was like, yeah, 'cause there's a cliff right next to me. And all the way down there's a valley. It's like yeah, ok, if something goes wrong I'm toast. [LAUGHTER] It will be a recovery not a rescue.... But anyway, I managed to dump that bike so many times on that dirt road it was horrid. I was sore for several days afterwards. Just because the bumping and the rocks.... It was a total of ten hours and thirty-six miles.

And this point, going downhill, it was where I finally figured out after dumping my bike several more times that I had to unload my bike and leap frog. Where I would haul my gear down about a hundred yards, walk back up to the bike, ride my bike down ... bump, bump, bump, bump, bump, bump, bump ... take the stuff down another hundred. Ride my bike down ... bump, bump, bump, bump ... oh my god. Finally I heard cars in the distance. And couldn't see any roadway. And in the mountains, I've done enough hiking to where just because you hear something doesn't mean it's necessarily close. 'Cause you can have echoes off the canyons and such. So it could have been a quarter-mile away that I heard cars or it could have been another ten miles away. And it was like, "Ok, don't get too excited," but I couldn't help myself. And then it was like, I did, it was only like a quarter-mile more and there was asphalt. I literally got down on my knees and I didn't kiss the asphalt, thank you. But I did do one of those kneeling [praying] motions like "YEAAAHHH!" And it was like, oh yeah, it was funny.[17]

She laughed as she gave this description. It seemed impossible that she could laugh about this, but having rode the Hoka Hey myself, I understand the use of laughter as a way to meet and overcome the challenge. If you did not catch the nuances of Eden's ride, I will break it down for you: This tough-as-nails, petite woman rode only thirty-six miles in ten hours. As she traversed a dirt road (that she was not even supposed to be on), her bike tipped over four times. Only after the third time lifting her bike off the ground by herself did she set up an ingenious pulley system to help her lift the weight of the bike. Then, on the way down, she took to unloading the packs from her bike, walking them down the hill about a hundred feet, and then going back to get the bike. Moreover, the whole time she was thankful, positive, and laughing.

Eden's unbelievable ride over the mountain reveals motorcycle accidents and breakdowns as a frequent occurrence along the Hoka Hey due to the difficulty of the ride. By overcoming her fears of being alone, of taking on the great challenge of climbing the mountain, and by making mistakes, Eden shows the capability of women to overcome the social mores of women and girls in Western society. Negotiating the space of uncertainty lying between one side of the mountain and the other, Eden metaphorically and literally challenges the society that tells her not to go anywhere alone. When she moves out of the space of fear and reclaims her position as a woman rider, she takes on full responsibility for what happens to her. Other riders, men, and society can no longer protect her. Through this process, she gained the utmost confidence and became a woman living outside the confines of her gender expectations. If navigated safely and skillfully, the technical roads on the Hoka Hey route can be executed without trouble. Although nothing as traumatic as Eden's experience, my own ride brought exposure to seemingly insurmountable roads.

Frustrated at how many times we drove around the same block looking for County Road 22, we finally pulled into a gas station. After dismounting, my dad pushed me toward the police officer's car. "Go on, Ab. Go ask." I thought about how silly it was that my lady bits unquestionably made me the designated person to ask for directions as I stretched my legs and ambled toward the patrol car with a kind-eyed man inside. He had no clue where County Road 22 was. An internal sigh of relief that made me feel better about my skills with the directions. The police officer got out of his car and consulted thick three-ring binders in his trunk. He looked in the index of his maps for County Road 22 and Dekalb Avenue—our designated intersection. He flipped effortlessly through the thick binder pages to the proper map. Black and white dashes and solid lines ran about the plastic-covered pages. He explained that the map indicated which roads were paved and which were gravel—gravel indicated by black and white dashes and pavement by a solid black line. I loathed the prospect of the dashed lines.

"God. Are they sending you down a gravel road?" His southern drawl had an air of astonishment. Looking pensively up at the sky he shook his head and

concluded, "No, I think they paved that last year." Clearly these roads weren't traveled very often, even by locals. The officer must have been thinking the same thing. "We don't even go down these roads. That's one hard ride they have you on." He chuckled and eyed me for size and stature. I didn't take the bait but instead looked with dread at the map. My dad—the direction asking complete—joined us to peer at the pages laying out the Arkansas countryside. The line at the end of the policeman's finger didn't even look like a real road. It was a black-and-white checked zigzag on the page, end over end sharp corners creating a series of sideways Ms. It was like there had been a break in the road and the crisscross line was what they did to fill in a gap. It couldn't be that bad, I told myself to muster the courage to move on. We thanked the officer for his help and climbed back on the bikes.

Later, we took a hard right onto Center Street/County Road 22 (which wasn't marked as County Road 22 at all). The map didn't lie. Center Street/County Road 22 was a zigzag. Thankfully, as the officer thought, the county HAD paved it. There was no time to think about how hard the riding was. After we turned onto the road it quickly rose in elevation. The curves were the tightest switchbacks we'd seen and the incline the steepest. It was the equivalent of making a U-turn inside a ten-by-twelve room and increasing in height from the floor to the ceiling through the turn. And then it turned back the other way. This continued through about six different turns—back and forth, increasing in elevation each time. The pavement on the road was built up thickly. In the center of the curve there was a gutter-like hole and steep two-foot drop, the crevasse filled with dirt and gravel. If you went off the road to the right, made too sharp of a turn, you'd be done. You could not get your bike out. To the left, there was only the tree-covered side of the mountain. There were no lines on the road and it wasn't wide enough for two cars or even a car and a motorcycle to pass one another. One lane. Our bikes pulled to each side of the road as we leaned though the tight curves. Thankfully, no one else in the county was stupid enough to take this road. "Just keep going. Just keep going," I chanted to myself. "Look through the turn." I gripped my handlebars so tightly my knuckles whitened. I pulled my body forward on the bike. I could feel every pound of my motorcycle between my legs chugging up the road. I stayed in a low gear to make the ascent. Chug Chug Chug—I could hear my bike laboring up the hill. Chris was in the lead, me in the middle, and my dad taking up the rear. I concentrated on the turns and whenever I could, looked in my mirror to see if my dad had made it up the hill. My thoughts quickly flipped between focusing on getting myself through this road and thinking of how heavy my dad's bike was and how difficult he said it was for it to go up hills. After the switchbacks the road evened out a bit and we continued to climb the mountain. There was no time to think about what had just happened. We all made it through and it was time to focus on the road ahead.

Checkpoints serve as destinations throughout the ride. Upon reaching each checkpoint riders receive directions to the next checkpoint and so on until they complete the route. Typically, checkpoints are Harley-Davidson dealerships sponsoring the challenge, and they offer riders a place for respite and motorcycle servicing. Checkpoints remain open twenty-four hours a day in case riders arrive through the night. At each checkpoint, riders must check in and designated officials verify rider credentials, which includ a rider card and coin. As the Hoka Hey Terms and Conditions stipulate, "Failure to check in at any checkpoint during the course of the Event will be subject to automatic disqualification and you will forfeit any award as well as any entry fees paid" (5). Race officials also include secret checkpoints to verify riders stay on course. These are unnamed, unmarked points along the course. Organizers verify entry into a secret checkpoint using the GPS tracking systems installed on each motorcycle. Time spent at each checkpoint varies from rider to rider. Some use these locations as places to sleep for the night; others simply check in, receive the directions, and quickly continue on the route.

We finally made it out of the Louisiana swamp to Renegade Harley-Davidson, our second checkpoint, around 6:00 p.m. We were on the road so long our bikes and minds desperately needed a servicing. The sun was still high in the sky but the store had closed an hour earlier. We were too late for the 48-hour open period described by the challenge. I knew it was going to be close. We missed it. Secretly thankful for the possibility of having to be off the road until they opened again the next day, I dismounted my bike. By the time we arrived, I felt a keen sense of closeness with the store clerks. Beth gave them my phone number because she knew we were close. All day, I told them how we would be there soon. All day my estimation increased. The roads were harder and longer than I expected. As I pulled off my goggles, I saw the door swing open. The amazing team at Renegade waited for us, knowing we were on the way. The checkpoint operators tracked us all day on the large flat screen monitor outside the service bay. A small-built, extremely beautiful woman with sandy brown hair and a sweet Southern accent greeted us outside the store. You couldn't help but feel an attraction to her—a result either of her looks or my desperation. She escorted us inside, out of the heat, and immediately made us feel at home. As she wrapped her delicate arms around me, her soft envelopment brought tears to my eyes. I was so thankful to be there, surprised we survived this long. I realized I hadn't talked to another woman in days and her delightful accent and kind words made me miss my mom and every woman I know. She was wonderful, empathizing, sympathizing. She told me how fantastic it was I was doing this trip with my dad. She had been watching us and was proud of what I'd done. I felt an indescribable sense of comfort just being near her. I wanted to pack her in my bag and keep her with me for the rest of the ride.

She quickly pulled out the next set of directions from behind the counter and started crossing out things in red pen—the directions were wrong leaving Renegade. Her Southern drawl turned from a sound of comfort to confusion as she flooded my head with "take this road, not what's written down." Just as fast as the relief came, it was gone again. I was confused and overwhelmed. The security I felt quickly changed to exhaustion and I wanted to cry, this time not from joy but from an overwhelming sense of what was to come. I found out we were going to ride the Tail of the Dragon, a road so hyped up I'd been dreading it since Nebraska. "You're gonna do it, girl," she said to me as she grabbed my shoulders and shook me back into the moment. I didn't want to believe her. We asked how far it was to the next town where we could grab a bite and hunker down for the night. We learned that we wouldn't make it there for another six hours. That would put us in past midnight. Chris and I decided it wasn't worth it to push that hard. We were already so far behind the rest of the pack. At this point we just wanted to finish, alive and together. We would stop in Alexandria for the night. Feeling the relief of a break flood back to me, I savored a beer while my bike disappeared into the service bay.

The Hoka Hey limits riders to riding American-made motorcycles with V-Twin engines only. A V-Twin is the standard motorcycle of most American companies. These include Harley-Davidson, Indian, Victory, and custom-made motorcycles. Focusing on touring bikes rather than racing bikes allows for a more level playing field for competitors. This rule keeps racing bikes designed for speed out of the competition. To create further equity among riders, the Terms and Conditions specify gas tanks must not be larger than standard 6.2-gallon tanks (the largest size available as stock on most machines) and riders must not carry additional fuel cells. Additional fuel sources are an advantage because along the prescribed route, gas stations are often few and far between. Here, knowing when your bike will need gas becomes part of the challenge. These rules attempt to ensure riders do not have advantages of speed or timesaving devices. Motorcycle inspections occur prior to the start of the race to be sure.

The first Hoka Hey, in June 2010, took riders from Key West, Florida, to Homer, Alaska. Other than sleeping by their bikes and the start and end of the route, participants knew little else about what to expect on the first challenge. Upon arrival in Key West, the organizers hosted a rider meeting to explain further the details of the race. During the first meeting, organizers informed participants of the rules, including not using hotels and disqualifications for speeding. There were few rules during the first year. Rather, the event was hosted and billed as a race and subsequently became incredibly competitive. The organizers offered one cash prize of $250,000 to the first rider to reach Homer, Alaska. Because of the large cash prize and organizers spending two years advertising the race, over 700 riders registered for the 2010 Hoka Hey. Due to the high-stakes competition during this sporting event, participants in the lead allegedly removed road signs along the route and enacted incredibly dangerous behavior such as placing tacks on the road to create tire blowouts or other accidents.

Increasing the difficulty of this race was the lack of driving distance between turns in the directions. Riders of the 2010 race noted a greater necessity for attention to detail, as riders could have been on a designated road for less than a mile or over two hundred miles. The total distance traversed for the ride was approximately 10,000 miles and took some participants nearly a month to complete. One of the most notable challenges for participants was the extreme temperature variation of the 2010 Hoka Hey. Riders experienced more than a one-hundred-degree change in temperature as they moved from the Arizona deserts to the northern extremes of Canada. Riders encountered rain, snow, and extremely hot temperatures throughout the trip. Of the 700 riders, fewer than 200 completed the challenge and arrived in Alaska.

The 2011 challenge increased in mileage to become the longest endurance challenge ever hosted. Traversing 14,500 miles and crossing two countries, the 2011 challenge reached all lower 48 United States in only sixteen days. Many participants of this race were on the road for over a month. The 2011 challenge began in Arizona and ended in Nova Scotia, Canada. Because challenge operators intended for the 2010 challenge to be the first and only competition, they did not have a great deal of time to advertise and raise money for the 2011 challenge. The decision to have another challenge in 2011 was made at the 2010 challenge's finish line and left less than a year to advertise for the next event. Because of this last-minute decision, the entries for the 2011 challenge were significantly fewer at only about 200 participants. The competition model for this challenge changed as well. During this challenge, organizers offered a pool of money to divide among all contenders who completed the ride within a given time frame instead of offering one prize. Theoretically designed to lessen the sense of competition among riders and focus on the Hoka Hey as a personal challenge, altering the competition model did not dissuade individuals from breaking competition rules or state and federal laws. Participants still wagered with one another, frequently exceeded the posted speed limits, and received assistance from outside sources regarding directions.

During the 2011 challenge, rules stipulated participants must not speed. According to participants, challenge operators used polygraph tests when contenders reached Nova Scotia to ensure their truthfulness. Eleven contenders crossed the finish line during the open time window in 2011. When confronted with the polygraph test, most admitted to breaking speed limits. Allegedly, the HHMC gave no prize payouts during the 2011 challenge because of this behavior. This dispute, however, led to the alteration of the rules moving forward. In 2012, the rules stipulated that a moving violation, rather than speeding, would result in disqualification. A strong majority of the contenders made an agreement with challenge organizers and settled the dispute, resolving they would roll any prize money into next year's challenge instead of "cashing out." One contender chose to sue challenge organizers for defamation of character. The incident and lawsuit greatly affected the organizers' ability to advertise for the 2012 season, their time and money spent defending a lawsuit instead of attending rallies and promoting the challenge.

Additionally, feedback from the 2011 race indicated the contest was too long. In response, race organizers made the 2012 route less than 6,000 miles. This allowed a new group of participants to enter the event, since it required less time to complete. The shorter 2012 race allowed less time to be taken away from jobs, families, and lives outside the Hoka Hey. Challenge organizers intended for the shortened challenge to result in increased participation; however, only 89 participants began the 2012 race, their smallest contingent of competitors. The challenge began in Las Vegas, Nevada, extended across the country through eighteen states, and ended in the sovereign nation of the Seneca Native Americans within the state of New York. Called the "United We Stand" ride, the 2012 challenge was the first to bring together multiple tribes of Native American people. A number of rules changed for the United We Stand event based on previous experiences. For 2012, the rules "discouraged" but did not prohibit challengers from sleeping indoors. In another change to the 2012 race, organizers stated they would allow law enforcement officials to dictate challenger safety instead of telling participants how to be safe by banning speeding. Consequently, the speeding ban changed from requiring participants to obey the law to simply asking participants to prove they did not receive a moving violation. As the Terms and Conditions state, "Any moving violation, speeding (ANY speed, NO exceptions, regardless of the fact that YOU may only have been trying to pass a slower moving vehicle), failure to signal, improper lane change, etc. will be grounds for automatic disqualification from eligibility to receive awards" (1). Moving violations of any kind were grounds for disqualification.

Because of its shorter route, an unprecedented number of contenders actually completed the race and qualified for money. Approximately 30 riders completed the 6,000-mile journey within the allotted seven-day window. Some riders finished within five days but were warned, via mass text by race organizers, they should not cross the finish line too soon. Doing so would result in a disqualification. During the 2012 Challenge, organizers tracked riders using GPS devices attached to their motorcycles. These devices linked to a website, which updated rider locations every three seconds. With GPS tracking devices located on each motorcycle, race organizers could tell some contenders reached the area surrounding the finish line days prior to the window. The contenders who finished prior to the finish line opening (the first arrived merely five days after the start of the race) remained just outside the limits of the Seneca Nation until the prescribed time. Views from the GPS tracking site showed the motorcycles of some contenders in a parking lot at a bar in a neighboring town. The riders who blatantly disregarded the rules of the competition (e.g., obeying the speed limit, arriving within a certain time frame) angered and frustrated many other challengers. After the challenge, organizers utilized the GPS systems to verify each rider's route to ensure accuracy.

A fourth challenge took place in 2013 and began the end of the Hoka Hey's first phases. Specifically, Jim Red Cloud planned to not participate in the arrangement of future challenges and instead focus additional time on his law practice. Challenge organizers hoped to pass the race to another nation in need of assistance and awareness. Called "Wolakota," meaning "Walk in Peace" in Lakota, this race displays Native American cultural significance overtly. The Hoka Hey website calls our current period the time of the Seventh Generation, a time described in a prophecy as the point at which all people must come together. As the website states:

> A Lakota prophecy was given during the hard times of the 1890s. The Sacred Hoop—the tie binding the Seven Fires of the Lakota, Nakota, Dakota Nations—had been broken by massacres, starvation and campaigns to eradicate the Buffalo Nation. The Lakota Nations are direct descendants of the Buffalo and their way of life, culture and Spirituality are dependent on this relationship. The prophecy says, in part, *that the Seventh Generation would come together to Mend the Sacred Hoop, restore the Spirit of the Nations and unite all Nations to heal our Mother Earth.* **Now is the time of the Seventh Generation** (Hoka Hey).

While challenge operators advertised the 2013 ride as a healing year, all Hoka Hey challenges ask riders to embody the warrior spirit and exhibit Native American cultural significance.

The Hoka Hey did not end with the 2013 ride. The ride continued in 2014 with a return ride from Key West to Alaska, albeit on a different route. Called "Unfinished Business," the challenge continued with its traditions of extreme riding and again involved a relatively small group, drawing approximately 100 riders. At the 2014 ride, organizers announced a new structure. In 2014, a group of interested riders took over the Hoka Hey and as a committee chose the fate of the challenge. Now, the Hoka Hey only runs a longer challenge every other year. On the off year, challengers come together for smaller rides, as indicated by the 2015 ride starting from the geographical center of the United States and riding to the Sturgis Rally and Races near Pine Ridge, South Dakota. Despite the original organizers being less involved, the challenge continues because its riders feel so passionately. While we do not know what the future of the challenge holds, participants will carry the spirit of the challenge well into the future.

The icons of the HHMC include a Native American band of brothers, the warrior spirit, and motorcycles ridden by the toughest men in history. These images conjure thoughts of Western mythology and beg riders to take on insurmountable feats of the past. They also surround women riders as they attempt the challenge of the Hoka Hey and its hegemonic masculinity. The layered masculinities of motorcycle culture and sport combine to create a sustained environment that looks upon women as substandard competitors. By blatantly ignoring women riders in any iconography, discussion, and advertising, the Hoka Hey bills itself as a challenge for men. Despite this fact, women riders not only take on the challenge but also experience success and empowerment, and create change in its wake.

Motorcycling as Sport

It is important to take a short detour here to explain why I view the Hoka Hey as a sport and describe more about this specific kind of sport. My understanding of motorcycling and endurance challenges as sport builds on the concept of lifestyle sports. Many scholars consider these sports outside the center of sport. Belinda Wheaton's edited work *Understanding Lifestyle Sports: Consumption, Identity, and Difference* informs my definition of lifestyle sport. Alternative models of competition and achievement, reliance on consumerism, and added elements of risk characterize lifestyle sports. In some cases, lifestyle sports are also known as extreme sports. Wheaton describes lifestyle sports as "anything that doesn't fit under the western 'achievement sport' rubric" (3). While some scholars might argue that lifestyle sports are "forms of play" rather than sports, Wheaton argues we should reject the play/sport binary and suggests we move beyond dichotomies to understand lifestyle sports' "meaning" (3). I agree with Wheaton in that we should consider lifestyle sports (e.g., snowboarding, skiing, and motorsport) as sports with equal value among other forms of sport. Wheaton and other scholars (Rinehart; Wheaton; Midol and Broyer) suggest that lifestyle sports are sites that have the potential to subvert traditional ways of understanding sport—including "traditional rule-bound, competitive, and masculinized dominant sport cultures" (3) similar to the ones the athlete in your mind's eye may play. Wheaton's volume highlights adventure racing, snowboarding, skiing, and other lifestyle sports that, like motorcycling, add an element of risk. It is my belief that the risk assumed in lifestyle sports transcends the risk associated with other forms of sport. For example, extreme skiing or surfing could lead to more perilous disasters (e.g., life-threatening avalanches or shark attacks) than those associated with team sports such as football or basketball. Of course, there is an element of risk in any sport (as shown by the increasing dialogue surrounding concussions in football players). That said, getting a concussion is not exactly the same level of risk as falling off a mountain or being attacked by a shark. Lifestyle sports specifically rely on risk as a part of their culture, creating a unique atmosphere for participants.

Lifestyle sports pair well with the possibility for seeing the race and class implications of sport. According to Wheaton, lifestyle sports entwine with postmodern consumer culture. Lifestyle sports are a commodity sold to consumers—who tend toward privilege, whiteness, masculinity, and the middle class—as a complete package (Wheaton 6). Consumerism in lifestyle sport not only takes the form of the sport itself in a pay-to-play environment, but also through the deeply important lifestyle package. Thus, lifestyle sports not only are costly—requiring entry fees and travel to specific locations—but also require a certain level of capital in the form of time. Further, Wheaton argues that lifestyle sports create space for identity politics, "a politics that is expressed around competing and passionate claims about the right to belong and to be recognized" (9). Because of the political and identity associations around lifestyle sport, participants must be able to fit into the culture both racially and socioeconomically to become full participants. Lifestyle sports value those participants who are able to pay their way into the sporting identity. In other words, it is not enough to be able to pay for participation lifestyle sports; people must also look and act the part. Acting the part includes taking on a tough, masculine attitude. Although lifestyle sports do not regularly address issues of gender—in fact, some sports allow or require men and women to participate together—, I argue that lifestyle sports value masculinity over femininity, which is evident in the reliance on risk. While *Understanding Lifestyle Sports: Consumption, Identity, and Difference* does not include specific chapters on motorcycling or endurance challenges, I believe both of these sports fit within Wheaton's definition, specifically through their commercialization, competition style, and racialization.

Participants in the Hoka Hey specifically must pay an entry fee of $1,000. Add to that the cost of a motorcycle, 10,000 miles worth of gas, gear (rain suit, map holders, tank bags, camel backs for water, tent, bed roll, helmet, boots, and any number of other items), and the time it takes to cross the country on secondary roads and you have a very costly pastime. Further commercializing the challenge are the patches, shirts, and other paraphernalia sold to riders. The sense of competition, which tells riders to challenge themselves and not race against other riders, exemplifies the non-Western style of competition made real through lifestyle sport. The level of risk involved (again, five people have lost their lives on the challenge courses) also aligns the Hoka Hey with other lifestyle sports. Additionally, the largely white population of riders signifies the traditional racialization of lifestyle sport. The gendered experiences of women who participate in this culture also mirror lifestyle sports.

Lifestyle sport literature suggests that sport remains gendered and women's experiences remain marginalized even in the environments that profess to transcend gender by asking men and women to play on the same field (Pflugfelder). Scholars Joans, Pflugfelder, Kay, and Laberge study women's marginalized experiences in lifestyle sport. According to these authors, women's participation in these sports is essential but constantly negotiated through their femininity. Through gender expression, gender nonconformity, and the reality of their sexed bodies, the gender of female athletes comes into question even in lifestyle sport. This literature shows that although lifestyle sports profess that gender does not matter (i.e., allowing women and men to compete against one another), the experiences of female athletes prove otherwise. Consequently, through gendered discourse surrounding these sports, the female body mediates experiences for athletes and participants. In "'Mandatory Equipment': Women in Adventure Racing," Joann Kay and Suzanne Laberge find that, while the adventure racing discourse supports women's equality of strength to men, the actual practice suggests that women's perceived natural (in)capabilities make them less valuable competitors. Adventure racing places multi-gendered teams against one another across multiple natural terrains where each team bikes, swims, kayaks, and hikes/runs to the finish. In their research, scholars found men describing their female teammates to be "mandatory equipment" rather than competitors. Similarly, Pflugfleder's article, "Something Less than a Driver: Toward an Understanding in Gendered Bodies in Motorsport," argues that despite the supposed gender egalitarianism in motorsport, the discourse surrounding women's performance retains notions of gendered power relationships. For example, Pflugfelder notes the ways in which the media and other racers attribute Danica Patrick's (the most successful female open-wheel racer in history) successes to her smaller female body rather than her competencies as a driver. Similarly, Joans contends motorcycle culture discourse relegates women to positions that are "necessary but peripheral to the biking world" (139). These experiences lead women to negotiate their femininity in order to make space for themselves within these cultures.

Many theorists, notably R.W. Connell and Messner, cite competitive sports as important sources for conceptions of Western masculinities. Throughout these spaces, men and boys learn behaviors and actions that support ideas and sentiments of masculinity. Sentiments such as "you throw/run/hit like a girl" permeate the sporting world and teach boys and men they are better/stronger/faster than their female counterparts who are less than/weaker/slower. These learned behaviors create a divide between men and women while simultaneously essentializing (perceived or real) gender differences. Through this derivation, we are taught all girls are weak while all boys are strong. Scholars, such as L. Walker, point to automotive culture generally as a site that enacts collective conceptions of masculinities. By spending time in mechanic shops or garages and around cars or motorcycles, men and boys learn it is okay for them to get dirty, use tools, and engage in other hegemonically masculine behaviors, such as driving fast, engaging in risky situations, drinking alcohol, and making bodily noises. Simultaneously, these characteristics thrive because the masculine space of automotive culture does not invite women to participate. Here a "boys will be boys" mentality is not only accepted but also encouraged.

Like sport, automotive culture can create a "boys only" environment in which women are "othered" (meaning they are not part of the dominant group) and/or made to feel unwelcome. Motorcycle culture, as part of automotive culture, similarly serves as a collective repository of masculine behaviors. Both sport and motorcycle culture are spaces in which women are "othered" because of this reliance on and promotion of hegemonic masculinity. In situations such as the HHMC that combine both sport and motorcycle culture, the masculinities of each environment layer upon one another. I argue the masculine attitudes associated with each culture create an additive property in which the sum of the whole is greater than the individual parts. When layered, these constructions of masculinities create difficult environments for women to negotiate. Retaining components of both sport and motorcycle culture, endurance motorcycle challenges therefore become heavily masculinized spaces.

Layered masculinities reflect sites of compounding oppression that emerge when multiple masculine institutions converge. For example, masculinities associated with military and science fields converge for female astronauts and racecar drivers when they face oppression from both sport and automotive cultures. Endurance Motorcycle Challenges exist simultaneously in sport and motorcycle culture. While sport and motorcycle culture are different entities, masculinity steeps both. However, when combined, the two laud masculinities both separately and together. Women's participation in events such as the HHMC is especially difficult because of layered masculinities. Here sport and motorcycle culture combine, creating a space in which women hear they "should not" participate because they are not equal competitors to men (sport) and also "should not" ride motorcycles (motorcycle culture). The elements of risk and competition converge to create an atmosphere perceived to exclude women from participation. Often seen as loving caregivers rather than ruthlessly competitive risk-takers, women entering this culture become "othered" not only from the hegemonic masculinity of motorcycle culture, but also the hegemonic masculinity of sport.

The Hoka Hey retains aspects of sport through competition, physicality, and the necessity for skilled riding. While the organization works hard to make the Hoka Hey a "challenge" instead of a "race," there remains elements of competition which support the idea of winners and losers. Here the sense of competition, the difficulty of the ride, performance and challenge conditions, and overall attitude surrounding the challenge promote masculinized elements of sport. These masculine elements include physical strength, strength of will, grit, and necessary training. Newsletters, blogs, and the website remind riders that fortitude, strength, and toughness—traits associated with masculinity—are all necessary character traits for completing the Hoka Hey. However, the Hoka Hey is not an ordinary sporting event as it is also rooted in motorcycle culture. The duality of the challenge as both a sport and motorcycle event compound the masculine environment in which women challengers contend.

Clearly a motorcycle challenge, the Hoka Hey retains aspects of motorcycle culture traditionally associated with hegemonic masculinity. Most of the participants are men and technical riding is key to the challenge. This event is not for "fair weather" riders (those who enjoy short weekend rides); instead, the Hoka Hey is a difficult feat for even skilled riders. It promotes itself as an experience only for those who are "real" or "true" riders. Because of the skill required, it requires previous association with motorcycle culture, and all its perceptions, to participate. Thus as both a sporting competition and a motorcycle event, the Hoka Hey Motorcycle Challenge is a site of layered masculinities, creating additional obstacles for women to conquer.

2

On the Problematic Nature of the Hoka Hey

That I dedicated an entire chapter of this book to the ways in which the Hoka Hey Motorcycle Challenge poses issues for a cultural studies scholar might suggest I should have found a different topic of research. The duality of this event continues to stun me. On the one hand, the Hoka Hey does amazing things for women's empowerment; and on the other hand, I find ethical and cultural problems not only within the HHMC but also with motorcycle culture more generally. It can be difficult to look past some of the racist, sexist, and insensitive aspects of the challenge and its participants. As you will see, many possible points of contention exist within this work. I choose to lay them out here, address them, and then move on to the real work of telling the women riders' stories. Throughout this chapter, you will read about motorcycle culture's history steeped in whiteness and masculinity. You will hear more about the challenges with my chosen methodology; read speculative controversy about the Hoka Hey's founder Jim Red Cloud; and follow an attempt to unpack the cultural appropriation of indigenous cultures. It is important to bring these issues to the forefront of the discussion in order to represent accurately the challenge and its challenges, but I hope after all of that, we can move forward and reveal the real stories of the women of America's toughest motorcycle challenge.

Throughout this research, I connected with the Hoka Hey community. In part, this came through my participation in the event but also through the process of researching and writing this book. Because of my status as a participant and researcher, many members of the community allowed me special access to certain situations and information. Specifically, I became friends with the Hoka Hey Challenge operators, Jim Red Cloud and Beth Durham, as well as the women I interviewed. They are my friends, my mentors, and my family. However, my desire to represent accurately this faction of motorcycle culture, its participants, and the challenge outweigh the affiliations I assumed because of my participation. To ensure the accuracy of my research I did not alter any challenge-related texts or conversations in order to portray these people or their experiences in a more positive light. As will be evident from this chapter, I have not mitigated the negative aspects of the culture; rather, I expose and question them in order to hopefully make the event and culture more inclusive.

Problems with Ethnographic Research

Ethnography enables researchers to gain firsthand knowledge of lived experiences of various subcultures. Typically, researchers gain this knowledge by attempting to see the culture from the lens of a participant, commonly known as participant observation. The researcher tries to get to know the participants and the culture from a very detailed and intimate level. Through connections, researchers gain access to groups and situations to which others may not have the ability to experience. In this case, my riding the Hoka Hey allowed me to make connections from the standpoint of a cultural insider. Perhaps these women would have talked to another researcher who did not participate in the Hoka Hey, but my position as a fellow female challenger certainly opened doors. After gaining access to a population, ethnographers conduct interviews with cultural participants, listen to their stories, and attempt not only to tell their stories but also to draw larger conclusions about cultural effects. Ethnographers pride themselves on telling otherwise untold stories of the real world. These individual stories weave together a quilt that becomes the connective fabric of society. Still, like all research methods, ethnography is not without flaws.

There are many common arguments against ethnography as a valid form of research. Some argue that ethnographers often overlook basic facts in their research, opting instead to take the participants' experiences as fact. We look no further than what our participants say to either credit or discredit participants' claims. Recently, Steven Lubet published a book, *Interrogating Ethnography,* which argues just that. Other arguments against ethnographic research suggest that the studies look at too small a population to make a difference— that their n is too small. These arguments contend that without more subjects from which to draw information, no clear conclusions can be drawn. Additionally, critics of ethnography contend researchers become too close to their subjects through participant observation. This closeness, some argue, makes researchers less objective and taints perceptions. These are all valid arguments and issues ethnographers regularly confront in their research. While it is possible to fall subject to these common flaws, ethnographers pride themselves on remaining objective and telling individual stories that can be an end in themselves. Small subsets of populations can mimic the story of larger groups. The experiences of some allow us to infer conclusions about the larger culture. That said, it is also possible to find value in ethnography simply from the individual stories we tell. Value exists in telling all lived experiences.

Conducting ethnographic research requires preparation and interaction with people and their everyday lives. It is a personal endeavor—for both me as a researcher, and for the women who participate in my research. My feminist cultural studies epistemology, here constructed through the methodology of feminist participatory research, requires me to situate myself as an equal with my research participants.[1] In feminist participatory research, I understand that I am not the expert on this subject and that together the women of the Hoka Hey *and* I tell a story. For me, this is a shared process where all have equally valuable knowledge to convey. Through this process of interviewing and creating new knowledge, I hope the women riders are able to share their stories and feel empowered by having their valuable knowledge recognized. I certainly feel empowered by, and learned greatly from, their experiences, as I hope they have from sharing in this work. I strive to create equality in my interviews and eliminate the antiquated, positivist notion of an investigator/subject hierarchy. I understand ethnography as a process of mutually creating knowledge. In the space of ethnographic research, we all have something to learn from one another.

My feminist methodology requires me to reflect on my own subject position and biases. For this project, reflexivity informs my interpretation of motorcycling culture as well as my interpretations of femininity and womanhood. As a feminist cultural studies scholar, I am aware of gender biases and specifically look for gender imbalances in communities of which I am a part. I am a heterosexual female in my thirties and have been a part of the motorcycling community since I was a child. This position as woman, rider, and scholar allows me different vantage points from which to interpret motorcycle culture. Within this culture, I position myself as a rider first and scholar second; but my standpoint changes based on how I position myself in different situations. For example, when I was on the road during the challenge I first established myself as a rider by entering the competition and later revealed that I was conducting research. In that situation, I was rider first and scholar second. However, when I am in a professional setting, I consciously suppress my identity as a rider because it is less valued than my identity as a scholar. I do not feel that this changes the respect I receive in either culture; rather it enables me to be chameleon-like and adapt fluidly to the different cultural spaces.

As a researcher, I understand reflexivity requires more than listing identities. As such, I understand that my subject position as a researcher may influence the atmosphere of the challenge. Participants could feel uncomfortable being a subject of study or guard what information they share with me because they know I am conducting research. While I did not hide my level of education (I was in the process of earning a doctorate at the time of the challenge) or position as a researcher, I intentionally situated myself as an insider in the culture rather than an outsider. While my position as a researcher offered me a level of power, that I was a first-time participant of the Hoka Hey meant I had a great deal to learn from the past participants. In 2012, I was one of only two women new to the challenge; the other four women were returning participants. While participants of the Hoka Hey may have viewed me as a researcher, my position as a "newbie" in the Hoka Hey culture made this power balance more egalitarian.

I am constantly aware that my research position is dependent on my subjectivity as a woman rider. This essential identity allows me access to the community and allows me to understand the cultural context that comes from being an insider. While I understand that my experiences may be different from those of the other female participants, from my position I am able to see, feel, and understand women's positions as "other" in this culture. However, utilizing feminist cultural studies makes me hyper-vigilant of gender inequities in the culture. Thus, other women challengers and I might not find the same things as misogynistic, offensive, or oppressive. Though I advocate feminism, I did not outwardly identify in this way to my fellow participants so as not to distance myself from the group in any way. However, when asked my political affiliations, I did not mislead the group. Because of this desire for transparency, during the interview process, I remained cognizant of not misinterpreting or misrepresenting the women's voices.

Gaining access and building trust are integral components of conducting ethnographic research. For the purposes of this project, being a member of the motorcycling community and participating in the Hoka Hey gave me access to the community, established me as a legitimate rider, and built trust with the women I later interviewed. Had I not been a rider or participated in the challenge, I may not have gained the same level of access to the community. Like many subcultures, motorcyclists are leery of being subjects of "study." Trust and respect are required tools to enter the culture. Positioning myself as a part of the culture and as a Hoka Hey participant alleviated some of the potential hesitancies of the women. During interviews, women riders commented on my ability to participate in the challenge and associated with me as a fellow Hoka Hey challenger.

Motorcycling, Sport and Masculinity

Despite the early days of motorcycling when women were active and equal participants alongside men, motorcycle culture developed into a cult of masculinity. Breaking into this "boys club" is part of the challenge for female riders. Perpetuating a culture that supports hegemonic masculinity can be a problem; however, it is important to understand how this came to be before we automatically assume it a negative aspect of the sport.

Post-World War II, motorcycling was an outlet for our insecurities about masculinity and the desire to care for "our boys" returning home. This added to the cultural repudiation of female motorcyclists. The resurgence of traditional gender roles in post–World War II America not only created a cultural acceptance of traditional femininity, but also created an increasing need for exclusively masculine spaces. Soldiers found comfort during the war in one another by creating community in military units. The mental and physical strain of war left men, once home, desiring the same level of camaraderie among other men. Thus, spaces traditionally reserved for men, like motorcycling, became common respites from their new lives and spaces for male bonding. As William Dulaney notes in "A Brief History of 'Outlaw' Motorcycle Clubs," this desire allowed motorcycle clubs to grow in popularity as men returning from war sought the camaraderie they left in the field. Veterans not only sought companionship but also specifically desired the companionship of other men in community. Motorcycle clubs created spaces for men to reinforce their masculinity at home after the trying circumstances of war (Dulaney).

To satisfy the need for post-war camaraderie, veterans who joined motorcycle clubs gave rise to motorcycling as an emotional outlet and identity marker as opposed to simply a mode of transportation. Delaney notes American motorcycles were particularly engaging to returning vets, "largely due to the high level of performance and excitement the cycles offered a rider, as well as for the relatively antisocial characteristic of loud exhaust pipes and the large, imposing size of the bikes" (par. 15). This desire for size and loudness reaffirms masculinity by establishing power and dominance as necessary components to riding a motorcycle. Similarly, these clubs often profess masculine ideals of independence and brotherhood stemming from post-war alienation. Motorcycling's background in bicycling and physicality coupled with the surge in post-war motorcycle clubs marked the sport as a culturally masculine space. Consequently, because motorcycle clubs embody notions of hegemonic masculinity, such as strength and power, we begin to understand these groups as exclusively masculine. Thus, despite the rich history of female motorcyclists, men's clubs took the lead in post-war America as the primary icons of motorcycling.

While outlaw motorcycle clubs of the 1940s and 1950s were primarily geared toward men, women's clubs also existed. Exclusively for women, clubs such as the Motor Maids, Women in the Wind, and Women on Wheels allowed female motorcyclists the opportunity to engage with one another and find camaraderie on the road, as was the case with their male counterparts. However, men's and women's clubs were inherently different. Men's clubs typically associated themselves with an outlaw mentality, living and riding against the confines of society and the motorcycling community at large. They rode motorcycles in packs and generally failed to conform to the expectations of Cold War American society (e.g., providing for a nuclear family, holding a steady job, and attending weekly church services). Men's outlaw clubs did not seek the approval of any authority, including motorcycling authorities. Alternatively, women's clubs fell well within the purview of the American Motorcyclist Association. In fact, the Motor Maids, known as the women's organization of the AMA, received its first charter in 1940 (Ferrar 28). Like the men's groups, female clubs perpetuated the association of motorcycling with masculinity. In an effort to set themselves apart from men, female motorcycle clubs made conscious efforts to promote femininity by being "dedicated to volunteerism and to promoting a positive image of the sport" (Ferrar 28). Female club slogans often promoted a "'positive image of motorcycling' directly relating to the newly formed outlaw mentality of many men's motorcycle organizations" (Ferrar 108). Many female motorcycling organizations today, including Women in the Wind and Women on Wheels, retain some of these sentiments. Clubs reminded members to be ladylike at all times. By creating an us/them binary, women motorcyclists inadvertently assert motorcycle culture as masculine. Showing women's clubs as "other" affirms the male-dominated space within motorcycling. This post-war turn toward outlaw clubs as the popular notion of motorcycling allowed motorcycling to become inherently masculine. If men's clubs created an outlaw image, women's clubs intended to show the public motorcyclists were good people, too. However, media representations of motorcycling did not focus on law-abiding, fundraising women's clubs; instead, contributing largely to the notion of motorcycling as masculine, were popular articles and American films (e.g., *The Wild One* (1954), *Wild Angels* (1966), and *Born Losers* (1967)) focusing on outlaw clubs.

Recent television series (e.g., *Sons of Anarchy, Full Throttle Saloon,* and *American Chopper*) further perpetuate popular interpretations and understandings of motorcycle culture. The popular FX television series, *Sons of Anarchy*, chronicles the fictitious life of a California outlaw motorcycle club. Maintaining the stereotypes of outlaw clubs, the Sons take part in various illegal activities and affirm racist, sexist, working-class portrayals of motorcyclists. In their five seasons, the group transitions from producing pornography and transporting guns for the IRA to running a brothel and transporting cocaine for a drug cartel. As a front for their illegal activity, the group runs a mechanic shop, a typically blue-collar form of employment. This choice of profession aligns motorcycling as a working-class activity. Each episode portrays motorcycling as a masculine space, as no women ride. Throughout the show, women are treated as commodities, are unable to make decisions for their families, and certainly are never shown riding motorcycles. Rarely are women even seen as passengers—the motorcycle remains limited to men. The sign hanging in the Sons' clubhouse, "Can't Ride, Can't Lead," associates being physically able to ride a motorcycle with being able to lead the group. Viewed not only as a commentary on the culture's view of women as weak (evident in the lack of female motorcycle riders), this mantra also supports able-bodyism. These media representations color our own impressions of motorcyclists and perpetuate the link between motorcycling with masculinity.

It is important to take a moment here to highlight some of the ways certain cultures marginalize women. In other words, how exactly do we arrive at a place where it seems normal to assume women should not ride motorcycles? As in popular media representations, motorcycle culture and sporting attitudes marginalize women of the Hoka Hey. Western cultures typically link sport with masculinity.[2] Further, sport lauds hegemonic masculinities over other masculinities. Specific to sport, hegemonic masculinity is the notion that characteristics typically associated with masculinity (e.g., strength, power, and toughness) are valued and expected in the sporting world. Western cultures define these characteristics as masculine. Specifically, hegemony is the notion that discourses remain unquestioned and binaries (which you can think of as opposites—male/female, strong/weak) continue to be unequally valued; consequently, we are complicit in their existence. In other words, if something is hegemonic it means we go along with and accept it without asking why. A simple example of this is the assumption that pink is a color for girls and blue is a color for boys. Through media—television, films, and popular magazines—and consumerism—the toy aisle in any store—, we come to associate specific colors with each gender. Pink equals feminine. Blue equals masculine. Further, the idea of hegemony understands that one of these (seemingly) inconsequential markers is privileged over the other—blue being a "better" or more acceptable color than pink. Think about it: How many people do you know hate the color blue? How often is it acceptable (or "normal") for men to wear pink, whereas women wearing blue is commonplace? One color is clearly more accepted than the other. These notions of hegemonic femininity and masculinity go unquestioned and are accepted widely. But hegemonic gender expectations are far more than just colors.

Hegemony tells us what is threatening to our "normal" way of life. Through these learned historic gender expectations, we come to "know" as a society what is "right" and what is "wrong" and learn the spaces in which our specific groups belong. By perpetuating notions of hegemonic masculinity and femininity, we build and maintain a status of normalcy and steer clear of disruption. When people, things, or ideas challenge hegemonic conceptions, they actively threaten the norm. Maintaining spaces where men can be men—such as on a motorcycle—safeguards against disruption. Women who ride motorcycles threaten hegemonic masculinity by entering the boys' only club and combining the two worlds.

Because masculine traits are valued over feminine traits, sporting cultures marginalize women. The marginalization of female athletes comes in various forms. In practical ways, women's marginalization exists through women's sports having less representation and fewer funding opportunities than men's sports. For example, the NBA has much more funding and advertising compared to the WNBA. In more subtle ways, gendered socialization that seeks to "protect" women from getting physically hurt marginalizes women. This discourse discourages women from participating in sports under the guise of "protecting" them while really relegating them to inferior positions. Likewise, this discourse does a disservice to men and boys by encouraging the idea that to be masculine you must tolerate and/or inflict pain. For example, women typically are not allowed to play contact sports. Additionally, reliance on masculinity assumes that if women excel at sports they must have male characteristics that imply they are lesbian, a further marginalized social group (Kauer and Krane; Krane).

The discourse surrounding sport, which supports unquestioned masculinity, also exists in the motorcycle subculture. Motorcycle studies scholars (Auster; Joans; Roster; Thompson) point to the gendered experiences of women in motorcycle culture. Within motorcycle culture, marginalization of women comes in the form of labeling women riders as lesbians, telling them they are inferior riders, or viewing them as sexually charged accessories to men's motorcycles (Joans). Additionally, time constraints and family commitments force women to choose between leisure activities; indeed, scholars such as Auster suggest that confronting the gendered experience of female riders also mediates women's choice of leisure activity. Through cultural constraints or reified discourse, women continually are assigned to positions of inferiority, or subjected to the belief that women are weaker than men in (motor)sport. The ways in which motorcycling discourse supports masculinity assumes that women are not riders. Representations of the sexualized female body and derogatory statements about women pervade the motorcycling community. Women's status as riders is often demonized (as is the case with groups such as Dykes on Bikes), marginalized, under represented, or made to seem invisible.

Motorcycling and Whiteness

In addition to being an environment steeped in perceptions of masculinity, some motorcyclists see motorcycling as a sport reserved for white people. This is another problematic aspect of motorcycle culture. People of color clearly exist within motorcycle culture; however, current scholarship, as well as the culture itself, largely ignores this constituency. As motorcycle scholar M. Shelly Connor notes in her history of motorcyclists of color, segregation politics are alive and well within outlaw clubs and other motorcycle organizations. In her article "First Wave Feminist Struggles in Black Motorcycle Clubs," she notes the high attendance of African American cyclists at predominantly black motorcycle events while commenting on the "exclusionary practices" of white motorcycle clubs (par. 3). This segregation allows for a perception that motorcyclists are only white. Within this culture, blatant racism is seen most through the ignoring of race within motorcycling; segregation rather than integration is the norm. Many white riders assume an unspoken us/them division, as evident with Black Bike Week events, which are a response to the racial divide as well as an ignorance of race issues within the culture. While black motorcycle events create safe spaces for their participants in the culture, they should not have to exist. While we aren't there yet, the elimination of these events should not require black riders to "assimilate" but rather require white riders to challenge their own assumptions about race. Creating separate spaces for riders of color and white riders allows racist attitudes to permeate throughout motorcycle culture and reinforces a position of white privilege.

Barbara Joans's book *Bike Lust* speaks to the racial aspects of motorcycle culture. While many motorcycle scholars overlook issues of racism in the motorcycling community, Joans's work is one of the few that addresses race directly. Looking specifically at riders of Harley-Davidsons, she is both critical and cognizant of the fact that some motorcyclists "as a group are racist, anti–Semitic, homophobic, and misogynistic" (242). However, she does not challenge the group for these behaviors, claiming, "Harley riders are not out to end prejudice. Neither are they out to spread it.... They are out to ride" (254). This simplistic examination of race within the motorcycling culture ignores the nuances of race and class within American society and demonstrates the need for further research addressing intersections of class, race, and gender within sport.

Common at motorcycle rallies, and perpetuating racism within the culture, are sales of patches, vests, and jackets with Confederate flags, Swastikas, and other racist insignias. While motorcyclists who purchase and wear these products may not intend to be offensive to specific groups, they profess to the public that motorcyclists hold racist values and mentalities. By donning these markers, riders intend to be bad asses, to be sensational, or to create a reaction, but are simultaneously (likely) ignorant of the racially charged history of such images. The use of intentionally offensive images keeps whiteness at the perceived center of motorcycle culture and allows those not involved in the culture to assume all motorcyclists are racist. The few motorcyclists wearing these offensive images align motorcycle culture with racism; and, while many cyclists may not harbor racist feelings, the separation of races within the culture creates a space for whiteness to go unremarked. In short, wearing offensive images is a negative exclusionary tactic, which maintains the us/them divide between races in motorcycling.

Some motorcycle organizations, such as Harley-Davidson, currently attempt to address issues of race in the motorcycling community by at least acknowledging the presence of riders of color. Marketing specifically to African American and Latinx riders, Harley creates affinity groups for riders of color. The Iron Elite and Harlistas respectively represent these populations. Despite these attempts by motorcycle organizations to acknowledge riders of color, the cultural perception of motorcyclists remains that of whiteness as seen through popular media representations of motorcyclists.

Whiteness is a central theme of the show *Sons of Anarchy* as the club regularly fights for turf and engages in illegal activities with gangs separated by race. Despite offering a representation of African American and Latino motorcycle clubs, the Sons (and the primary story line) remain a group where whiteness prevails, including a brief aside to amending the club by-laws to allow non-white members (in reference to the character Juice who discovers his biological father was African American). Many Americans do not know anyone in a motorcycle club, or perhaps are not familiar with riders, so these images of criminality, masculinity, class, and whiteness continue to permeate popular culture. Hence, media representations of motorcycle culture become the cultural knowledge base of the masses. Media representations reinforce negative stereotypes and these notions remain common perceptions of motorcycle culture.

Negative images and perceived attitudes of motorcyclists become iconic through television, film, and some (unintentional) actions of motorcyclists themselves. These media representations and actions form a cultural construction of motorcycling, which may or may not reflect the lived experiences of motorcyclists today. Popular constructions of motorcycle culture as rooted in masculinity, criminality, working class values, and whiteness create a space within which women riders must contend. In other words, for the culture to accept them as legitimate members, women riders must find a way to balance their own identities and values with these aggrandized and/or constructed notions of the culture. These perceptions may be exaggerated and the culture continues to change and adjust constantly. However, motorcycle culture itself remains a largely masculine space. Like the women riders of the post-war years, women who ride today continue to negotiate their own femininity and struggle for legitimacy as riders. Cultural perceptions and realities of motorcycling's foundation in masculinity and criminality may be reasons women choose not to enter the culture. However, even after women choose to enter the culture, the motorcycling community can subject them to oppression through sexist remarks and attitudes. All of this creates a problematic foundation on which women riders exist. Despite potential preconceptions and instances of oppression, women enter and excel in the motorcycling community.

Part of the reason I chose to study motorcycling and sport is their foundation in these culturally problematic areas. Cultural studies scholars seek to answer the question of why. So, is motorcycle culture problematic? Yes. Is the Hoka Hey problematic? Yes. Is sport problematic? Yes. This is exactly why we need to understand and study them. Investigating how women navigate the problematic and challenging arenas that tell them they are not welcome can help others navigate similar arenas. Telling the stories of women riders who challenge men's understanding of women riders might encourage more women to ride. It may break down barriers between male and female riders. Further, telling these stories and challenging the problematic masculine nature of motorcycling may lead to challenging its roots in whiteness and able-bodiedness as well, thus opening space for more riders.

Native American Ties and Cultural Appropriation

We gathered in the parking lot of Las Vegas Harley-Davidson, the faded yellow lines barely visible in the darkness of the early morning. Wheel to wheel and side-by-side, two long lines of motorcycles heaped with gear snaked through the otherwise empty space. Quick flashes of bright lights briefly illuminated leather-clad men with smiling faces arm in arm and posing for photos and snapping shots of the green and white lined pages of directions. The energy pulsing through the riders' bodies drove the anticipation of the start into a nervous excitement filling the air. Puncturing the energy, staccato shouts of instruction emanating from the race operators told us to gather. It was finally time. Riders created a three-man deep circle around Jim. His hulking body turned in full circle to bring this motley lot into view. The yellow desert sun began to cast shades of pink and orange over the rust-colored mountains to the east, revealing bearded and mustachioed faces filled with anxious anticipation that matched the electrifying feel in the air. My heart pounded all the way to my ears as Jim chanted the blessing for the warriors in Lakota. Then an English translation, far less beautiful but still full of meaning: "Bless these warriors as we ride our steel horses into battle. Keep your heart strong. And God's hands on you. 'Cause by the end of today, you'll be dancing with him. But remember, it's just a dance. Enjoy the ride. And keep us all safe so you can see your families again." Whispers ceased and a deafening silence enveloped the group us as he began to sing. Awk-

ward but reverent heads fell as he closed his song and broke silently through the circle. I stood motionless but skirted my eyes to the other riders for a sign of how to move forward. Largely unaware of what we were just a part of, we began squirming, rocking side to side in our boots. The white faces not knowing how to respond to such a powerful moment. Then, PHEWWWEEET, a lone rider broke the silence with an ear-piercing whistle. The tension broke like an egg and the yolk of our emotions flowed forth, forcing us to an otherwise unprompted roar together, "Hoka Hey!" Riders scattered, moving hurriedly toward our steel horses, ready to accept the challenge.

Perhaps one of the more problematic aspects of the Hoka Hey is also its very purpose. Although the challenge founders intended the HHMC to raise awareness for Native American issues, it struggles to find a balance between challengers associating either too much or too little with the population it tends to serve. As is the case with many charitable organizations that intend to help the "other" speak, the primarily white Hoka Hey challengers tend to spend more time speaking and less time listening and understanding. After highlighting some of the cultural ties to indigenous cultures imbued in the ride, we will look closer at the issues of cultural appropriation and other potential pitfalls of the Hoka Hey. This often peripheral connection to Native American culture is one of the things about the Hoka Hey, with which I struggle most as a cultural studies scholar. I find myself woefully lacking in knowledge about indigenous cultures. I do not profess to be an expert of indigenous cultures or to know much about their lived experiences. My feelings of ineptitude partially stem from my awareness of the proverbial "the more you know, the more you know you don't know" symptom. While I have done some research on the culture because of this work, I still do not know as much as I likely should. When I initially rode the Hoka Hey, I (like many riders) did not fully grasp the intent of the ride. Sure, we were supposed to raise awareness, and I can say living conditions are bad on the reservations across the country, but to fully understand someone else's lived experience requires much more. The vignette below highlights my pre-challenge lack of cultural knowledge.

I stared awkwardly at Jim's conspicuously painted, bright yellow Road Glide in the forefront of the vast desert landscape of rural Utah. A white letter L stood out on a crumbling red-and-blue painted concrete Lincoln Highway marker in a corner of the dusty roadside pull off point, signaling we were on the first transcontinental highway. Wanting only to stop the awkward silence of our leg-stretching break, the words tumbling out of my mouth, I uttered, "Soooo ... is yellow your favorite color or something?" The naïve question seemed innocuous enough to ask but quickly showed Big Jim Red Cloud my ignorance of his culture. "Oh, that bike was donated to me by Harley. But yellow is a Chief's color. That's why your bandanas are yellow." The wisp of cigarette smoke cut through the warm air and followed the path of his hand as he gestured toward the sun-drenched yellow Hoka Hey bandana tied to the back of my bike. "It's important for my people. And meant to protect you and give you power." Jim replied without much more of a thought. "Cool," I said. Really? "Cool?" That's the best I could come up with? What an idiot. My mind tried to catch up with a more thoughtful response. After all, I did profess to be well educated. Feeling too much pressure to elicit some sort of quip from the files in my brain, I added nothing. Embarrassed by such a trite response, my eyes squinted closed and I hung my head in shame, shuffling back toward my bike. I was a cultural voyeur and a bad one at that.

The Hoka Hey Motorcycle Challenge began as an awareness-raising event to bring attention to the conditions of the Lakota Sioux. The Native American challenge organizers sought a nationwide event to bring attention to the plight of our country's indigenous peoples, specifically the substandard living conditions of the Lakota Sioux on the Pine Ridge reservation in the Black Hills of South Dakota. Jim Red Cloud is an attorney, member of the tribe, and life-long motorcyclist who we will explore in more detail later in this chapter. Jim realized the philanthropic power of motorcycle community and the literal ability that motorcycles have to draw attention. Jim's position as a member of the tribe, his legal expertise, his insider status within motorcycle culture, and his desire to serve bore the HHMC. The message each challenger carries is the Sioux warrior cry of "Hoka Hey."

Hoka Hey apocryphally means, "This is a good day to die" (Niehardt). More literally, Hoka Hey means "Let's go," but challenge founder Jim Red Cloud chose to use the former. It is a Lakota Sioux warrior cry most famously used by Crazy Horse during the battle of Little Big Horn. The Oglala Sioux imbued this warrior cry with significance by using the term continually. Hoka Hey insinuates a readiness to die for a cause and simultaneous acceptance of a life well lived. Even today, the cultural significance of this phrase travels across time and space in tribute to all Native American warriors. Hoka Hey is not only the name of a motorcycle challenge but also a guiding principle. Because of its significance to the Oglala Sioux, it is a phrase given to challenge participants to literally wear as a badge of honor. Hoka Hey emblazons each bandana, t-shirt, sticker, challenge coin, and motorcycle associated with the event. For some, Jim's chosen interpretation of the words is problematic in itself. One could argue that using the apocryphal definition of the words cannibalizes the language intentionally sensationalized for the white masculine audience. While the more common interpretation of Hoka Hey means "It's a good day to die," challenge founders changed some memorabilia to read, "It's a good day to ride"; however, challenge coins retain the former interpre-

2. On the Problematic Nature of the Hoka Hey 55

tation. Challenge participants regularly cry the call. Riders shout "HOKA HEY!" before rides, upon their successful completion, and throughout each ride. It is simultaneously a remembrance of those who have gone before us, and a reminder that we must be fully accepting of and at peace with our lives every day, in case it is our day to die. As this moniker ties the motorcycle challenge to Native American culture, numerous other symbols and practices represent the Lakota Sioux culture throughout the challenge.

The Sioux have a traumatic past steeped in war, loss, and devastation. Like many Native American tribes pushed from their land by the American government, many Oglala Sioux now live on a reservation in South Dakota. While clearly intended to limit the land use of Native Americans, officials professed the intention of reservations to allow Native Americans to live independently. However, reservations did not keep out the surrounding white culture, making it impossible for the Sioux to continue many of their traditional cultural practices. The continual influx of whites to the area, the prospecting and extraction of fossil fuels and minerals by outsiders, and the elimination of animal herds forced the Sioux to assimilate into white culture. Unfortunately, the Sioux received little help from the government and the Lakota Sioux living on the Pine Ridge reservation today—one of the largest Native American reservations in the country—fell into a number of devastating conditions. Impoverished from a long history of white power and greed, they suffer from alcoholism, diabetes, and unemployment, as well as high rates of infant mortality, domestic violence, and teen suicide. Many now are homeless and much of the reservation lacks clean running water. These deplorable conditions exist elsewhere in the United States, but are especially ironic under the watchful eyes of Mount Rushmore, a monument dedicated to our nation's early leaders who professed democracy, equality, and justice for all. This is the message Hoka Hey challengers attempt to empathize with and understand as they champion the cause and discuss the lives of the Lakota Sioux on Pine Ridge.

In the first years of its existence, the Hoka Hey challenge organizers made a point of taking the course through the Pine Ridge reservation. At this point, riders were invited into the home of Chief Oliver Red Cloud (grandfather of Jim Red Cloud) and more directly saw the lived experiences of the indigenous culture they were supporting. In more recent years, as the Chief became ill and eventually passed on, the challenge did not ride to Pine Ridge but instead visited reservations of other nations across the lower 48 states. The 2011 ride was one in which the riders were able to meet Chief Red Cloud. This direct interaction with the culture gave a more nuanced understanding of conditions on the reservation and those riders now describe the interaction as positive and transformative. Schatzi, a long-time participant of the Hoka Hey, described the first time she rode through the Pine Ridge reservation. Through her words, it is possible to see that she more fully understood and empathized with the indigenous people. "They really are poor. And not to have running water really is a sin. It is something we take for granted so easily. They don't even have it. So I mean, indoor plumbing is definitely really nice. And for them to use outhouses ... those days are gone. Or should be".

I understand it is problematic to assume the plight of another culture without having a deeper knowledge of that culture. I understand cultural appropriation (when a person from a majority group takes on the image, elements, or resources of an "other" or minority culture) causes offense, destructive feelings, oppression, and a stripping of identity from the minority. As a ride, the Hoka Hey has the potential to enable riders to culturally appropriate both Native American cultures and homelessness. For example, riders are not required to have any knowledge of Native American issues, cultures, or even to know a single indigenous person. Riders don't take an informational course of any kind at the beginning of the Hoka Hey instructing them to be advocates or even sympathizers of Native American causes. They are asked to "speak" for those on the reservations without (in many cases) actually even visiting these places. This is a problem. If challenge operators really want riders to understand the indigenous cultures, they could require or incorporate some sort of educational component to the ride. But rather than formalize any process, riders must seek out this knowledge and experience on their own, if they choose to do so. That said, this ride can take people who knew very little about the systematic oppression of indigenous cultures of the United States and turn them into advocates for this cause.

Organizers ask Hoka Hey challengers to tell the story of today's Lakota Sioux and to raise awareness of the Pine Ridge reservation as they cross the country. While the riders' lack of cultural knowledge is an issue, opportunities for discussing the hardships of Pine Ridge abound. At each stop for gas, food, or facilities, strangers ask participants why they are on the road. In addition, each challenger's motorcycle must don the Hoka Hey logo and many riders affix their Hoka Hey bandana to their bikes or their person, signifying that they are not just on any ride. These symbols serve as invitations for the public to ask questions about the ride and for riders to share the Sioux story. Not only do challengers speak out about the deplorable conditions on Pine Ridge, they also see first-hand the abject poverty of Native American tribes as they cross through reservations across the country. Because the route takes challengers through reservations and other sites of injustice in our country (such as World War II-era Japanese internment camps), many challengers experience consciousness-raising moments during the ride as their own assumptions, values, and worldviews come into question. Most Hoka Hey challengers are white men, a particularly important constituent group in the quest to raise awareness. Historically, white men have held (and still hold) the most power within our nation. Thus, gaining white male allies (both Hoka Hey challengers and other white men encountered along the route) is crucial to progressing social causes. While white men retain the most interest in maintaining current conditions, they also have the power to affect the most change.

During the 2010 challenge, organizers informed participants of the vision of the Hoka Hey. Native American organizers asked (primarily) white challengers to profess the story of Pine Ridge as they rode across the country. At the pre-challenge party, they also asked riders to metaphorically collect and bring home the souls of fallen Native American warriors. Each ride passed through ancient battlegrounds, grazed burial grounds, and wove in and out of reservations. Challenge organizers saw participants as warriors on a quest to bring justice and awareness to the Native American people. The History page on the Hoka Hey website champions this warrior mentality. It describes challengers as "warrior riders" who are "prepared for combat" ("History"). At the outset of the challenge, Native Americans glorify riders with traditional ceremonial warrior blessings. Multiple Native American prayers and songs accompany the starting line rituals. Passing through the various reservations, state parks, and public lands that once made up the pride of Nations reminds challengers of the reason for their participation. If they choose to look for it, challengers can see the grandeur of national parks (formerly Native American land) and how those parks stand in stark contrast to the poverty of current Native American living conditions.

While riding through reservations and along historically significant routes such as the Trail of Tears can bring riders' attention to Native American problems, challenge participants are more voyeurs than students. Challenge organizers do not provide riders with text or explanation of the route surroundings or larger context. Instead, riders must look for signs of Native American history, oppression, and living conditions. This requires interested riders to pay attention to physical signs or historical markers, the landscape of the natural and man-made environment, living conditions, and other sometimes-imperceptible details while also trying to maneuver a motorcycle, read directions, and stay on course. Seeing or understanding the significance of the ride is not a requisite for participation. While riders are largely untrained in sociological observation and analysis, many do see inequities as they cross the country. For those riders, the challenge takes on special significance. Some of the women riders' experiences are articulated through Jersey Pearl's words below:

> Every single turn had a meaning. Now our job was to pass through Indian reservations and um, you know, areas where Indian battles had been. [Her voice pained as tears started to form in her eyes.] And we were.... Supposed to be collecting the souls

of the warriors to carry them home. So, wow.... It was just so.... [The anguish of the ride flooded back into her memory.] And I'm not a spiritual person. But it really was. You know, everywhere you turned you saw something of this country you really took for granted. How we destroy her. And then the next thing you see. We rode through, literally straight through, farms in Alabama almost as if you were riding on someone's property. There was this appreciation of what the earth had.... But we had no idea what Big Jim's actual premise for the ride was until we got to the Challenger's meeting down in Key West. And that is when he told us about carrying the soul home. [Her tears continued to fall as she mustered through the words.] So, we had no idea. And then it like all just clicked. It just clicked. [She wiped the tears from her face, thankful for the ride.] And then it was like a gift. That we didn't expect.

Jersey Pearl's description of the ride's significance shows the level of social consciousness many women riders experience. The ride challenges their interpretation of their own social positions in direct opposition to those on the reservations. Understanding this nuance does not reach every rider. Many complete the course without making any significant connections.

We pull our motorcycles onto the grass at the very end of the long winding stone drive so I don't embarrass myself or my dad by dumping my ride. I don't do well on stones. I knew this was a nicety for me without my dad having to explain. We dismounted and stretched our legs though we rode but a few miles from our temporary home at the Motel Eight in Hot Springs, South Dakota. My family has always been a little awkward with emotional situations and it showed now as we all drew in deep breaths of clear air and shot nervous glances from one another and then up to Beth and Jim's house, fidgeting with removing gloves and stowing items in our bikes that didn't need to be stowed. It was the Friday before the Chief's funeral. Chief Red Cloud (descendant of arguably the most famous and important Lakota chief in written history), a man we did not know personally but knew through Hoka Hey lore and American History. Grandfather to our friend Jim and legend to the Lakota. We were part of a small group invited to the ceremony. I awkwardly wander through the yard behind my mom, my heart still pounding from successfully yet awkwardly navigating the small bit of stone drive and parking my bike at the end of their yard. Unsure of where to go, we stare at the sprawling country home with expansive porch and an overwhelming number of different doors. Studying each quickly to assess which one we should knock on, I thankfully see Beth in the detached garage and avoid the discomfort of choosing a door. She looks up from her work of gathering chairs and a warm smile comes across her small face. As we enter the well-used garage, we open our arms for a round of short hugs. Warm embraces are flushed with the embarrassment of not knowing what to say. We offer our sympathies to our friend and then offer our help. Desperate to be useful, we take the extra chairs and carry them out of the garage and around the house, thankful to have a job. We are always better when we are being handy.

Walking from the garage, I see it. A massive army green tent-like structure fills the yard. Unsure of what it is, we amble toward it carrying our chairs. Jim tends a fire and welcomes us to his home. Though he doesn't explain it outright, I gather from context clues that the structure is a sweat lodge. The social epicenter of the evening. Yes, the sweat lodge. I can't even lie, I had no clue what a sweat lodge was, meant, or felt like. These thoughts make me increasingly insecure with my whiteness, cultural ineptitude. We mill about as Jim fans and sprays a large bonfire with a standard green garden hose. He begins to talk about the large rocks in the fire. They will create the steam inside the sweat lodge. These are special rocks from sacred places. We will sweat to honor Jim's grandfather, as is the tradition in his culture. Inside my head, I question why he shares such an emotional and powerful time with us. This inclusiveness is unnatural to me. Then I feel a tap on my shoulder.

Beth pulls the ladies aside, holding dresses and shirts in her arms. Six of them in all. She looks at us with a sense of subdued excitement. After looking around the gathering of women, she begins, "Jim doesn't normally sweat with women he's not related to. I'm not sure what he'll want to do, he might have us sweat separately from the men, but if you want to participate I have dresses and skirts you can borrow." This is all the explanation we are afforded. I have so many questions to ask that they will not form properly in my head. This does not seem like the time to show myself as more of a cultural outsider than I know I am. Betraying myself as a researcher, I refrain from asking questions so as not to show my ignorance of this culture. "Oh," she turns back slightly and puts her finger in the air to indicate she has one more point. "If you're on your cycle, we ask that you don't participate." She goes on to a perfunctory explanation about moon camps created during Sun Dance and the bad vibes menstruation creates. Thankfully I am not on my moon cycle and am eager to participate in any kind of sweat. I go into the bathroom with my mom to put on our skirts. We remove our riding boots and jeans, talking in excited, hushed tones about their willingness to include us and what this means, unsure if I will ever fully process this experience. We leave our things in the bathroom and scurry back to the rest of the group. We blush as the men take quick jibes at our new clothes. Floral, long, feminine, skirts and dresses very different from how we first presented ourselves.

Seeing our transformation, Jim nods his head quickly and declares, "We'll all go in together." After Beth's warnings, this decision seems momentous. This means Jim thinks we are related. We are family. Hoka Hey family. We enter the sweat lodge with trepidation. Leaning down and crouching to fit into the small door, we file in one by one. Darkness envelopes us as the tarp door flings down and Jim secures it so no light enters through its flaps. Our eyes harshly adjust *from the bright sun-soaked South Dakota sky to the seemingly eternal blackness inside the lodge. Sweat Lodge. Black. Eyes straining for light in total darkness. After some time, we see the sparkling stones of heat at the center of our circle, blazing red and imbued with meaning. Jim's normally booming voice whispers calmly across the darkness. My heartbeat increases rapidly as I begin to feel the effects of the heat. It must be well over 150 degrees inside the tent, like we are inside an oven. We went in willingly, I remind myself. This is important to my friend. Jim explains that we will all find a prayer. We will say it aloud to one another to give it meaning. We will offer these prayers up to those who went before us. We will end each prayer by saying "Mitakuye Oyasin"—"For All My Relatives." I feel like a cultural voyeur as burning sweat drips into my eyes. Each movement seems painfully draining in this heat. Jim goes on; the heat will not bother you if you concentrate on your prayer. I try to forget my pains and concentrate deeply on my prayer. Then he begins to sing and pray as he beats a drum. Praying. Singing. Mitakuye Oyasin—For All My Relatives. Praying. Drumming. Sweating. Faster now. Mitakuye Oyasin—For All My Relatives. Breathing. Praying. Euphoric. Mitakuye Oyasin—For All My Relatives. After all our prayers spewed from our hearts, the beating stopped. Jim declares the sweat complete. Silence. Then a flash of light as the flap of our sweat lodge flies open. Steam and our prayers evaporate in a thick fog. The air hangs deep with the palatable knowledge of what we shared.*

One by one, we emerge from the sweat lodge, drenched in sweat and emotion, panting thankfully for the fresh August air. It no longer feels muggy. Jim points his solid arm and index finger at me, his eyes burning with intensity, "You can put that in your book, Abby. I trust you." I hope I don't disappoint.

Jim's emphasis on trusting me as a writer and scholar stems not only from the relationship we built but also from a history of cultural exploitation. The historic appropriation of Native American culture is not lost on me. I understand that I am in a position to (mis)represent specific people and, tangentially, larger cultural groups. My cognizance of the misrepresentation and cultural appropriation of Native American cultures informs my writing and presentation of material. I made a point to ask permission to print or discuss situations, experiences, and ceremonies associated with the Lakota culture. Likewise, when asked, I refrained from writing about certain ceremonies, as I had access to those in my position as a Hoka Hey family member, not a public researcher. Nearly every time I saw Jim, he encouraged me to "write good words," an affirmation that not only gives me power as a scholar but also challenges me to represent accurately my friends with an air of social consciousness.

With this access comes the possibility of criticism. Are the challengers of the Hoka Hey taking a culture not their own and exploiting it? On the other hand, can we argue there is no cultural appropriation because Jim invited us into these ceremonies and cultural experiences? These are all problematics with which we grapple as cultural studies scholars. The truth, as is the case in most scenarios, likely falls somewhere between these two poles. Was I a culturally voyeuristic tourist when I participated in the sweat lodge? Perhaps, but likely, it also helps me connect with my study and the people of a different culture. It would be a lie if I said I fully understood the meanings imbued in the sweat lodge, yellow as a chief's color, or any of the other aspects of Lakota culture. Similarly, challengers of the Hoka Hey do not fully understand the plight of the Lakota living on the Pine Ridge reservation. They simply cannot understand it unless they experience that life; although events like the Hoka Hey do bring together people of various cultures and help them better understand one another.

This challenge can change a white male's view of Native Americans and come to a new understanding of the cultural exploitation and decimation of indigenous cultures. This is absolutely the case with my dad. Going into the Hoka Hey, he thought little of the Native American plight or its lasting effects on these people. Now, in his own way, he regularly advocates for indigenous rights and helps to tell others the story of how these people have been historically devastated. This might be just one anecdotal example of the Hoka Hey's power to change, but it cannot be the only one. While the challenge is problematic, there is also room for it to be transgressive. Like the limiting male/female binary, the good/bad binary is of little use. When we look past the complexly controversial nature of the challenge, we can find points of real, lasting change.

You can see how there are positive and negative aspects to the white participants taking on the role of cultural advocate for a culture which they do not fully understand. While some participants do take time to learn about the culture, others see the ride as a chance to ride their motorcycles across the country without the need for advocacy. However, another direct result of the Hoka Hey for some women was a newfound involvement in Native American issues. One woman rides a bike painted with the Hoka Hey logo and uses it as a tool to raise awareness for Pine Ridge. She carries and distributes informational brochures about the Hoka Hey and its cause. Another challenger began a blanket drive to support Pine Ridge. She called on other Hoka Hey challengers to participate in raising funds and blanket donations. Last year the drive donated over 4,000 blankets to the people of Pine Ridge. In addition, the continued participation in the Hoka Hey brings greater awareness to the cause. Each time a rider posts a blog or uses social media to speak about their ride, they add to the interest and awareness of Pine Ridge. However, not all women who participated in the Hoka Hey felt such a deep connection to Native Americans, their cause, or their conditions.

While the ride deeply affected some, others saw the ride as a personal challenge and did not necessarily focus on the social justice aspect of the event. Largely, the women who participated in more than one challenge felt an added connection to the Lakota or all Native Americans. This shows the relational aspects of women's participation and post-challenge growth. Their circle of connectivity and ethics of care extends beyond the ride by affecting their desire to be charitable, raise awareness, and build relationships with others. Still, and possibly even more difficult to grapple with, is the very image of white participants as advocates and the tendency to act like the "white savior."

While it is important to include white people (specifically white men) in the fighting of oppression and inequality, it is even more important to do so in an educational context. Without an understanding of cultural and racial nuances, it is possible for white activists to view themselves as, or take on the problematic role of, the white savior. A trope common in film, and stemming historically from periods of American colonization, the white savior narrative posits idealized white Americans are the only hope to save cultural others—here, Native American cultures. (The irony in this situation being Native Americans came to their current positions through white colonization.) Again, a right/wrong binary emerges. This positioning suggests the white/American culture is better and the Native American culture is in need of saving. Often, the white savior trope promotes activism in which white culture promotes what they think/know to be best rather than asking and listening to the needs and desires of non-white groups. This I-know-better-than-you mentality creates division, not unity. Advocacy without education can lead white riders to promote negative aspects of American (and white) exceptionalism. This can take the form of promoting assimilation rather than listening. Often this happens unknowingly as most riders have a genuine desire to assist those in need. The fear of acting like the white savior should not keep riders from advocating for Native American rights, but creating a system of rider education could help mitigate this pit of cultural quick sand.

Perhaps equally challenging about the HHMC is the way in which challenge organizers ask participants to "mimic the conditions of homelessness" on the reservation by sleeping outside next to their motorcycle rather than using hotels. This is another form of cultural appropriation extending beyond the conditions of the reservations and into a socioeconomic dilemma. How can you possibly mimic homelessness while also (ironically) sleeping next to a motorcycle which costs tens of thousands of dollars? While it adds to the challenge to sleep outside and not use the comfort of hotels, challengers *can* make use of these amenities if they need to since they are not actually homeless, financially challenged, or destitute. Quite the opposite of homelessness, the Hoka Hey is a costly challenge to take on and requires a great amount of financial capital to complete. Having both the means and the time to complete the challenge, riders tend to come from working class to middle class backgrounds. They work hard (and deserve) all they have but simply cannot understand the true conditions of homelessness by sleeping outside. That said, the challenge does force riders to see their own experiences and advantages in a different light.

Riders face their own privilege on the challenge. At times, and depending on the rider, this privilege is white privilege or socioeconomic privilege. This is an intended desire of the event as operators ask challengers to mimic the conditions felt on the Pine Ridge reservation by sleeping outside next to their bikes. The women most greatly affected by this were those who had the opportunity to visit Pine Ridge and meet Chief Red Cloud during the 2010 and 2011 challenges or who participated in more than one challenge. They described the "humble" living conditions of the powerful leader and as a result questioned their own ability to contribute to or dismantle the problem. Likewise, many women riders gained a greater perspective on their socioeconomic status as the ride allowed them to appreciate things generally taken for granted. Women riders cited the ability to pay the registration cost as a common indicator of their economic advantages. They also spoke of being privileged enough to see the entire country, something that sets them apart from other members of their socioeconomic classes at home. Many women spoke of learning to "live without" on the Hoka Hey and described themselves as "fortunate." This indicates a confrontation with their advantaged status. As a direct result of the event, many women felt a new burden of socioeconomic privilege and grew in appreciation for what they have.

Despite its intentions, riders cannot actually feel and understand what it is like to be a Native American living on the Pine Ridge reservation just by completing the Hoka Hey. While they may face their own privileges, they remain white men and women with the ability and money to ride expensive motorcycles across the country. Although riders spend a week or two facing their own status, they quickly return to comfortable lives after the event. Albeit short lived, the Hoka Hey does successfully introduce most participants (some for the first time) to their own privileges. While the riders did not necessarily attribute their privilege position to being white, they often altered their perception of social justice in the United States upon completion of the challenge.[3] While most challengers exemplified color-blind racism, many did make a step toward realizing their position of power. In part because of this newfound association with privilege, many spoke of feeling a sense of obligation to help the people of Pine Ridge and some took to increasing awareness by raising funds and other endeavors. This brought their experiences full circle, again articulating an ethic of care.

Jim Red Cloud Durham

James Gregory Red Cloud
April 2, 1955–June 29, 2017

Jim was an artist and an author with works that focused on cultural disparity and inequality. His passion inspired him to create the Sacred Buffalo, a buffalo skeleton with scrimshaw designs depicting the history and traditions of the Lakota People. He was also inspired to tell the story of Christ through scrimshaw carvings on the bones of a human skeleton. He was a profoundly compassionate man who cared deeply about the concerns and issues on Pine Ridge Indian Reservation and became a Tribal attorney in an effort to help improve conditions there. He was an entrepreneur and founder of the Hoka Hey Motorcycle Challenge, a long-distance motorcycle ride established to bring awareness to the plight of Indian people around the Nation. Jim also loved adventuring and was an avid hunter/fisherman, surfer, motorcyclist, leader, and friend to many. He touched countless lives and will be remembered as a man of conviction and passion.[4]

Perhaps one of the most controversial issues surrounding the Hoka Hey is its founder, Jim Red Cloud. I considered Jim a friend and mentor, but others saw him as a cheat, a liar, and a fraud. Jim emerged as the face of the Hoka Hey. He traversed the country attending motorcycle events to promote the challenge and appeared in advertisements for various products and services associated with the ride. He was a symbol of the challenge and its participants. Because Jim Red Cloud was steeped in controversy, the Hoka Hey brand suffered during its early days and still does, according to many former participants. Throughout my research phase, women turned down the opportunity to share their stories because they did not want to be associated with Jim and the ride. While the sour opinions were rare and I found more women who spoke enthusiastically and sentimentally about their experiences, it is important to note the opposing view.

Some of the controversy and speculation from challengers regarding Jim included: he was not a "real" Native American, he was banned from the Pine Ridge Indian Reservation, and he was caught up in a mineral land rights money-making scheme that jeopardized the reservation. I find the accusation that Jim was not a "real" Native American to be an example of the ignorance of the cultural construction of race. Who exactly decides if someone is a Native American? Is there a percentage of that heritage you need to embody? Is it about cultural ties rather than biological ties? When you take on an understanding of race as a characteristic created by humans, it is easy to see that this point of controversy should not matter. For me, Jim's biological heritage means little to his passion for increasing awareness of conditions on reservations in the West. However, this angered many white participants who felt deeply that Jim was a fraud because of his claim to Native American heritage. Coupled with Western concepts of family in contrast to indigenous concepts of family, cultural misunderstandings created ill will and unnecessary division among challengers. Further, challengers speculated that the community at Pine Ridge banned Jim from the reservation. While I cannot find documents suggesting Jim's banishment from the reservation, there is clear evidence pointing to the reason Jim may have been asked to leave the reservation–his involvement in a zeolite mining issue via an organization called the Dakota Land Trust. Controversy about who gave access to the land embroiled a larger discussion about how to bring economic prosperity to the reservation. Was Jim's intent to make money for himself or to assist the tribe by bringing jobs to the area? This may never be known as Jim is now deceased; however, it does add to the perception of Jim as a controversial figure.

In 1996, Jim co-authored a book entitled *Sacred Buffalo: The Lakota Way for a New Beginning*. This text chronicles Jim's experience constructing an artistic work called the Sacred Buffalo, a buffalo skeleton with scrimshaw images of Lakota history and culture. His book offers an interesting glimpse into Jim's thought processes and gives context to some of his strong views regarding indigenous cultures. Throughout, Jim paints himself as a deeply spiritual and passionate man. He speaks to his challenges living in cities and touches upon his identity as a veteran of the Vietnam War. In my personal interactions with Jim, I found him to be sometimes distant and often cryptic. Standing alone, his behavior could make his intentions seem questionable and unclear. I do not think Jim saw it as his job to educate the challengers of the Hoka Hey to create a deeper cultural understanding of indigenous cultures. He would certainly answer questions if asked but he did not go out of his way to explain anything about his culture. This left space for white challengers who were uncomfortable (or reluctant) asking questions to see Jim as someone who stood in opposition to them. To be clear, I do not think this is Jim's fault; I do not expect Jim to have spoken for all indigenous cultures or think it was his duty to explain the nuances of cultural differences to his white participants. Rather, I think it simply put everyone involved in the awkward position to assume things about indigenous people. For as many people who saw him as a distrustful man, just as many saw him as a leader and an advocate. Regardless of how challengers perceived Jim, he was a symbol of the Hoka Hey and an important piece of this story.

2010 Hoka Hey Motorcycle Challenge

A simple Google search of the Hoka Hey Motorcycle Challenge reveals blogs, articles, and chat sites painting the ride as one shrouded in controversy. Much debate surrounded the Hoka Hey after the inaugural run in 2010. The challenge went from Key West, Florida, to Homer, Alaska, and drew in hundreds of riders based on the projected $250,000 prize. Naturally, that purse subsequently drew added controversy after the challenge ended. Jeri O'Barr, wife of a 2010 challenger, filed a suit against HHMC creators Jim and Beth Durham with the Florida attorney general alleging fraudulent promises and other issues about the challenge (Brown). According to an article from the *Rapid City Journal*, the way organizers treated participants created anger and distrust.

> "He is a self-proclaimed liar," O'Barr said.
> Other people at the meeting in Key West thought that Red Cloud was extremely rude to everyone.
> "My thought at the meeting was that Red Cloud had just intimidated everyone in this audience, and now, people were scared to ask questions," Schultz said. "I really didn't appreciate his swearing and the foul language and absolute disrespect he showed us in Key West."
> "He treated us like garbage and it absolutely blew me away," Schultz said. "He said to us 'I used you (the riders) to get money because my people (on the reservation) needed water.'"
> Schultz said that all of these riders paid thousands of dollars to participate, and she thought they deserved to be treated with more respect.
> To hear him come right out and admit that he had used them to get money "was shocking," Schultz said. "He was very abrasive."

Each participant has a right to their own opinions and feelings about the challenge and its founders, and these claims may be factual. If seen through a cultural studies lens, this dispute reveals interesting cross-cultural exchange. Here we have white participants challenging the intentions and integrity of indigenous operators. One explanation for the level of distrust felt by the challengers could stem from a simple misunderstanding of cultural norms and intentions. The idea of white participants demanding increased respect because they paid money to participate suggests a connection between Western concepts of money and respect. However, the challenge operators may not feel that same connection because of their own socially constructed concepts of respect and money. For example, in his book *Sacred Buffalo*, Jim gives a glimpse of his understanding of money. Jim describes prayer and intention used when praying with the *chanunpa*, a sacred pipe. He states, "You should never pray for unworthy things. You should never pray for money; what a huge misuse of that gift that would be" (33). A clear deviation between some challengers' view of money and the founders' view of money emerges. Had each group taken time to understand the other perhaps there would not have been such anger. The article further cites participants' anger at challenge operators, including the involvement of their religion and spirituality as part of the ride.

That Red Cloud said the riders would be warriors as part of the vision he had upset some riders. The vision claimed that 1,000 warriors would travel to seven of the sites of the biggest massacres of Native Americans in the

United States and collect their dead souls. Again, the *Rapid City Journal* reported,

> "I think he's entitled to his religion, but he has no right to turn this challenge into a religious agenda," O'Barr said. "He never spoke of anything but his vision of collecting the dead souls of warriors. It's unacceptable; … that is not what we paid for; we paid for a motorcycle race."

You will see throughout this book that some participants welcomed this thought and embraced this nuance of the challenge. Viewed through a cultural studies lens, this seems like another cultural misunderstanding. Here, O'Barr shows a distrust for and lack of knowledge of a non-white, non–Christian understanding of spirituality. Entering a motorcycle challenge with a very clear connection to Native American culture (as exemplified most directly by its name) without expecting some type of indigenous culture to be infused shows the myopic lens of the white motorcycling community.

After the 2010 ride, challenge operators struggled to find participants for the challenge. A significant decrease in participants in the subsequent 2011 and 2012 rides stems not only from the change in winning structure but also from the controversy of the 2010 ride. Fewer participants created a smaller winning purse and led to even fewer participants. While new challengers did join (myself included), the group has a base of 50–100 consistent challengers. These motorcyclists tend to look past the controversy and ride for the innate challenge alone. While there are grey areas and questions surrounding any sporting event, they are not important to me or to this book because they do not change the experience of the riders. They may create conversational fodder for riders at gas stops, but in the end are meaningless to the larger picture and experience.

Clearly, there are issues surrounding the Hoka Hey and this study— questions about methodology, roots in masculinity and whiteness, cultural appropriation, and an event steeped in controversy. For all its problems, this challenge does make people question themselves and their privileged positions in society. I have watched my own dad take a strikingly different position on Native American culture and American history as taught to him. While it may seem superficial, he does look at films portraying Native Americans through a critical lens. He teaches his grandchildren that it is not OK to culturally appropriate Native American culture by wearing construction paper feathers at Thanksgiving. Prior to participating in the Hoka Hey, he did not bother himself with these issues. He saw Jim Red Cloud as a friend and feels deeply about the death of Jim and Jim's grandfather. Simply put, he has grown, and he cannot be the only one. It is not only with respect to Native American cultures that the Hoka Hey changes riders' worldviews. After women participate in the Hoka Hey, their male riding counterparts view them differently. While women riders should not have to prove themselves to be accepted, their participation in the challenge forces male riders to see them as equals. Women of the Hoka Hey create cultural transgression by their presence and their riding ability.

The point of this book is not to show how flawed the Hoka Hey or motorcyclists are—I lay these issues out here so we can move on from them. They are an integral part of the story, but they're not the only story. This is a story of creating change, but also a story of female athletes and their shared experiences. I want to honor their grit and passion. With that, let us move on and focus on the fascinating women who rode the Hoka Hey.

3

An American Girl
The Women of America's Toughest Motorcycle Challenge

She looks like a badass on her bike. Hair blowing in the wind, a smirk plastered on her sun-soaked face; she is the epitome of confidence and strength. When you see her you can almost hear the soundtrack playing in the background. The Tom Petty anthem blares.... *Well she was an American girl, raised on promises. She couldn't help thinking there was a little more to life somewhere else. After all it was a great big world, with lots of places to run to.* She kicks up the throttle and continues chasing the American dream, riding across the country. She is a warrior. She is Hoka Hey. Riding makes her feel alive.

In this chapter, you will meet the women of the Hoka Hey. They are all different, driven by their own motives and passions; but in some ways they are all the same. They are all the same badass rider, confident (or crazy) enough to woman up and take on the challenge. In many ways each woman rider blows down the road with Tom Petty playing in her head, compelling her to get out and live life on her terms.

The women I interviewed are not necessarily representative of every single woman who rode the Hoka Hey, nor are they representative of all women riders. Some women who chose not to participate in the interviews may disagree with some points of our stories. In fact, I would argue that Hoka Hey women are a bit of a different breed, just like all Hoka Hey riders are different than the general populous of motorcycle riders, just like ultra-marathoners are different than the people who finish a 5K run. While these women speak for themselves, at times throughout this book I will combine us into one composite rider. Our comments mesh and blend together to form a work of composite narrative non-fiction. Here I intend to pay homage to the women who took time to participate in an interview. They all have a different story to tell, and deserve to be highlighted in a way that enables you to meet each of them.

As much as possible in this chapter I attempt to give you large sections of each woman's voice. As part of my methodology, I transcribed each interview, sometimes painstakingly, to capture the emphasis of certain words, of voice inflections, of emotions, and of accents. These quotes come straight from these amazing women. I chose to keep them intact because they are so incredibly interesting in themselves. Here you will experience what I experienced when I met them all. They are both similar and divergent—women who sacrifice time, money, and even health to challenge themselves and the motorcycling community. These women prove they can handle big bikes and difficult terrain while negotiating the unspoken challenges of competing with tough men in a masculine space.

I include below a chart of the demographics, which reflects each woman at the time of the research. You will see similarities within the chart—all women are white, many are similarly aged, and share blue-collar or motorcycle-related positions. These basic identifiers can supplement your idea of each woman but by no means tells her entire story.

Name	HHMC Year	Ethnicity	Gender	Age	Occupation
Junie Rose	2010–2013	Caucasian	F	52	Assembly plant operator
Tristica (T)	2010	Caucasian	F	33	Motorcycle test rider (HD)
Sheila	2010	Caucasian	F	54	Construction worker
Carla	2011, 2013	Caucasian	F	53	Motor clothes Retail (HD)
Jersey Pearl	2010	Caucasian	F	42	Self-employed (motorcycle shop)
Bryana	2010	Caucasian	F	28	Student (Ultrasound)
Kelly Quinn	2012	Caucasian	F	36	Self-employed (Throttle Girl)
Debra	2011	Caucasian	F	57	Maintenance
Wendy	2011–2012	Caucasian	F	45	Home Cleaning Service
Jane	2011–2013	Caucasian	F	50	Self-employed (real-estate manager)
Schatzi	2011–2013	Caucasian	F	56	Self-Employed (excavating)
Debby	2011	Caucasian	F	46	Self-Employed (HD Dealer)
Eden	2010–2011	Caucasian	F	50	Nurse
Sherie	2010	Caucasian	F	52	Drug and Alcohol Counselor
Abby	2012–2013	Caucasian	F	30	Higher Ed Administrator

Prior to the Hoka Hey, the longest distance I traveled on a motorcycle in a single trip was 2,330 miles from Laramie, Wyoming, to Daytona Beach,

Florida, while conducting research for my master's thesis. Compared to other participants in my research, I have done significantly fewer long-distance trips. Prior to the Hoka Hey, I considered myself a "fair weather" rider, one who only sets out on a ride in perfect or near perfect conditions. The Hoka Hey changed this for me. After having participated in the challenge, I am more willing to ride in the rain, cold, and other inclement weather conditions; however, I still do not believe that I ride at the same level as my fellow Hoka Hey challengers. One woman talked about how "we" rode and said,

> I think there are girls out there, like I said, that they get their bike out and they can't, because you put them in a compromising situation and they can't handle it. You know, it starts raining and we've got to sit here until it stops raining because I don't ride in rain. You know, that kind of a rider is just a pretty face. And you know, we all, every sport needs 'em. We love our pretty girls too. You know but I mean as far as a real rider, a real woman rider, those are the ones that uh, if the makeup tends to slide across your face then it's no big deal you're out there for the ride. And you'll keep comin' back for more.

Oh shit, I don't know where I fit in this, I think as she speaks. I feel like a fraud. I think I might be a pretty girl; but she thinks we're the same. I don't like to ride in the rain. I don't like to WALK in the rain let alone have it pelt me in the face at 75 miles an hour while semis whiz past me spraying their gross road crud all over me. I wear makeup. Mascara in fact, during the pre-challenge days in Vegas. Maybe finishing the challenge makes her think we were the same? WE are REAL women riders. WE are different. WE completed the Hoka Hey. I hope she doesn't find me out.

The process of reflexivity enables me to understand that I enter this research as a part of the motorcycle culture, which could arguably inhibit my objectivity. While I believe scholars can never be wholly objective, I have taken measures to ensure that my work is as unbiased as possible. My use of multiple sources of data creates triangulation by creating a dialogue between data sources; each source refers back to the other. For example, the participant observations and the informal interviews are in conversation. By seeing the work through multiple vantage points, I gain the ability to compare and fully examine the women riders' perspectives.

Eula "Junie" Rose

She wears these shin guards that make her look like she's sporting knee-high boots, road-worn with evidence of a bug massacre. Pan up to her jeans tucked into the black leather guards. Then her cut—the black leather vest that defines her as a rider. Emblazoned with the Hoka Hey logo and a semicircular rocker patch for each year she's ridden. Three when I first met her, many more now. She is a Pro Long Rider, as her patch reads. A consummate smile plastered on her face, she is gentle and yet ready to transform into a warrior at any moment.

She survived breast cancer twice and the Hoka Hey four times—Eula (Junie) Rose's stamina and determination to live life parallels none. At age 52, Junie worked a lifetime for the U.S. Postal Service and raised four children as a single parent. She is gracious, caring, and compassionate. She finished mopping her floor just prior to our interview and stopped to greet her son as he bellowed lyrically, "I'm a workin' man," walking through the door from work. A strong emphasis on Christianity and her personal sense of accomplishment drive Junie to do the right thing and reward herself with her passions—motorcycling and her family.

Junie is one of many lifetime riders. Starting on a friend's 75cc Harley and smaller bikes during her childhood, she became an "unintentional" Harley owner when she surprised herself with a seemingly spontaneous decision to buy a new bike.

Junie Rose (left) and Abby Van Vlerah (right) pose before the 2012 HHMC. Junie is a great source of support and encouragement for new women riders. Her kindness and wisdom make her an invaluable resource. (Author photo.)

When I saw the bike, it was just like I had already paid off my truck and I told myself. If I can get the bike payment within the amount of the truck payment then I'll just, it'll be just like havin' car payments again. And it was $4 difference! So I left there with a motorcycle. And I was out Christmas shoppin'. That's actually how I you know stumbled across it. I was just going to get a pair of boots for Christmas. And uh, I left there with a motorcycle.[1]

She felt guilty riding for some time; she questioned her dedication to her family when she made the purchase that would turn her into a warrior. After all, a motorcycle isn't exactly a family vehicle.

But the kids embraced it. It was kind of funny. All of a sudden it was like, "Cool! My mom rides a motorcycle." But you know, I started takin' 'em on trips and it allowed me to have one on one time with each one of 'em. Instead of tryin' to have a vacation with three kids or with four kids. Now I had a vacation with one kid and they had my undivided attention and uh you know, and it ended up workin' out really well and my family loves my motorcycle.[2]

Motorcycling truly has become part of her and her family's identity. By purchasing a vehicle designed for singular travel, she capitalizes on spending individual time with each of her children. Here she embraces the roles of both mother and rider—using a literal vehicle as a vehicle of love.

Junie has participated in every single Hoka Hey challenge. She is the only female rider to do so. She has acquired the moniker "Wrong Way Junie" yet somehow finishes the challenge every time (with the exception of 2010). She is the unofficial mother of the Hoka Hey, embracing new riders, giving pointers, and making sure to take a picture with each one. I admire her as a rider and as a woman who is unashamed to be who she is. Junie is the best kind of Christian woman. She is kind and lives up to the values of her faith through service and generosity. She is genuine and real. The Christian morality Junie embodies leads her to serve the Lakota in many ways. While there is a difficult history of Christians imposing "help" upon Native American communities, Junie shows the ways in which a culture of camaraderie, such as motorcycling, can break down barriers between divergent faith groups.

Junie Rose does not simply ride the Hoka Hey and go home. She carries its message with her every day. She does not think of the Hoka Hey as a fun ride, rather she does her best to raise awareness for the Lakota and keep the sentiment alive when she is not on the road. Junie single handedly began a blanket drive for the Pine Ridge reservation. Each year she collects money and blankets which have grown into substantial donations. She speaks of the donation she made in 2012:

> They were elated to have those blankets. Because I didn't just give 'em to Pine Ridge last year. Because they were at that Treaty Council Meeting, all those tribes left with blankets. So there's 32 different tribes out there who have now received blankets from the Hoka Hey Motorcycle Challengers.[3] So I think that in itself was just like initiating good will and saying, let's let the past be the past and let's work on today.[4]

Uniting the Hoka Hey challengers to continue to give and remember the Lakota after the ride is one of Junie's most impressive accomplishments. She makes people care. She has big dreams of really helping the Lakota and really ending the systemic poverty of the people. It's a lofty (and likely unattainable) goal, but one she strongly believes in. It is important to mention here that Junie is a white woman, which might make some critique her efforts as part of the larger white survivor or "great white hope" narrative. Lakota may view any "help" originating from white people as suspect because of the historical systemic colonization of Native Americans. It may bring up wounds of the many times that "help" came with strings that destroyed their culture. I think Junie's own grit and selflessness separates her from this narrative. Despite the problematic use of Christianity to assimilate cultures, Junie's faith motivates her and she possesses no motivation to proselytize. Her intention is not to swoop onto the reservation and receive acclaim or use a colonizing message. She just wants to be kind and help people. The intentionality of her generosity supersedes her race.

Junie certainly took me under her wing. We rode together for parts of the 2013 Hoka Hey. She was the first person I interviewed. I felt guilty for not being able to help her more with her blanket drive. Perhaps this makes me blind to her racial positioning—this is a product of my methodology. I acknowledge my subjective presence as a researcher and the difficulty to remain objective. Critiques of racial constructs appear later in this work. Now I would like to honor Junie because I, like many, am grateful for her.

Tristica Kendall

Her maroon beanie comes into focus through the computer, hiding any trace of hair. Her pale skin and bulbous nose seem stark in the glow of her screen. She is young—only a year or so older than me. She introduces herself just as "T." The shorthand makes her seem tough and (perhaps intentionally) erases any notion of gender identification. Seeing one of my favorite Old Crow Medicine Show lyrics under her Skype contact picture connects us. T does not own a car, only a motorcycle; in Arizona this means she often rides through the snow and makes her way to the grocery store with her tiny Sportster. *That's rough*, I think, aligning myself more with the fair-weather riders she disparages than her. "I am a motorcycle test rider, mechanic, and parts specialist. For Haley Davidson at their Proving Ground Facility."[5] Shit. She has to be tough.

For T, the Harley Proving Ground Facility where she works is far more than a place to test ride motorcycles. Here the test riders prove the ability of the motorcycles to be re-tinkered and sold. More than motorcycles, her colleagues test her. Daily she proves *motorcycles'* capabilities, but also repeatedly proves *herself* to many of the men with whom she works. The coincidental wordplay here is inescapable. As the only woman rider, she represents all women who ever dared to ride a motorcycle. The masculine undertones of the motorcycling community force her to do better because she is the token woman. Her actions form the opinions of women riders in the minds of men.

> I'm the only woman who works out at the Proving Ground Facility. I'm the only female test rider out there right now. They've had a couple in the past but they've … only lasted for like a couple of months. So for me it's like one of those things like hey,

you know. You can ride; don't let anybody tell you you can't. So it's.... I don't know. It's just personal for me.[6]

Certainly the barrage of you-can't-do-its and sneers have hardened her. With every course she completes she also grows in confidence and in her desire to help others find their passions. Being a woman motorcyclist means everything to her. She is never not a woman motorcyclist; riding is not an activity or even a job—it is her identity.

Under her seemingly harsh exterior she is caring and gentle, providing for her family, raising money for charity, and inspiring others to ride.

> Yesterday we did a Charity event for our work, for the United Way Foundation. And there were so many little girls who were like standing around looking at the motorcycle and I was like, "Hey, get on it. Climb on it. Touch it. Feel it. Do whatever you want." And their eyes just light up and she's like "REALLY, I can do that?" And I'm like, "Heck yah, and when you get older you can come be a test rider like me. Don't ever let anybody tell you—you can't do those things." And just to see that excitement in people and to give other women confidence.

Tristica ("T") Kendell on her Sportster. As a rider at the Harley Davidson proving ground, T is an extremely experienced rider yet still faces the challenges of being a woman in a masculine space. (Courtesy Tristica Kendall.)

In her voice you can hear the experience of someone continually told they couldn't barreling through. She not only overcame the "girls can't" attitude; she threw it to the ground, stomped on it, and rode over it with her motorcycle. She is a badass.

T fulfills many aspects of my sketch of a woman motorcyclist. Being a woman rider, not just a motorcycle rider, is something she embraces rather than tries to escape. Riding is part of her identity and shapes her sense of female-ness. The motorcycle adds to her gender presentation and helps her exude female masculinity. She puts up a rough and tumble exterior to fit in the heavily masculinized world in which she works and plays, but finds great enjoyment from inspiring other women to ride. Her lifestyle is a carefully negotiated balance of being approachable to women or girls and standing up, when necessary, to people who doubt her. The Hoka Hey, and riding at the

Proving Ground, brought her to new levels of self-confidence. This confidence stems directly from breaking stereotypes of women riders as weak or inexperienced. These experiences boost her ability to continue the dance of gender nonconformity in a conformist's world.

Sheila Hoehn (and Trixie)

Picture it—you're riding down the road, the familiar rumble of a Harley approaches from behind. Its engine blurts out *potato-potato-potato*. You glance over and see a woman on a silver Harley-Davidson Ultra Classic and a dog perched behind her, goggles on, tongue flapping in the wind, loving every second. It is a sight that attracts a great deal of attention, according to Sheila; her dog Trixie is a real "rock star." The small Jack Russell Terrier rides in a sheep-skin-lined basket on the back.

> She brings a lot of joy to people. You'll be going down the road and you'll, you know, someone is right beside you. Pacing themselves, and you know what's going on. You

Sheila Hoehn (and her dog Trixie) ride down the highway. Sheila and Trixie are the subjects of regular photos from passersby enthralled with the idea of a dog (and a woman) on a motorcycle. (Courtesy Sheila Hoehn.)

look over and you already know. They're taking pictures of that dog on the motorsickle. She's like a rock star. You know, everybody wants a picture of her on the motorsickle. I feel like sometimes my job is just like driving Miss Trixie.[7]

Sheila made her first long distance motorcycle trip the year after I was born. She is a true road warrior. A construction worker by trade and a solo rider by choice, Sheila has the ability to take off for long periods of time and put herself in the wind. While she has ridden with boyfriends and others, she prefers the flexibility of riding with Trixie. They stop where they want to stop, make new friends along the way, and rejuvenate their souls. She loves the smells of riding, the exposure to nature, and the sheer freedom of riding. For Sheila, riding is a passion.

She taught herself how to ride at the same time she started learning to drive. She watched more and more women adopt the pastime as she seasoned herself on the road. She speaks eloquently in the lingo of the community, her southern accent drips with feeling. Sheila, like many long-time riders, experienced a change in the community.

> Back then, there was more of a brotherhood between Harley riders. If I was on a trip and say I just pulled over on the side of the road and just stopped for a little while, to smoke a cigarette, people would stop and make sure you were OK. You know. And you'll go down the road and people would put their fists up in the air, you know, Brotherhood. And you know, today um. It's not that way.[8]

There is a tinge of sadness in her voice as she laments all things past; but the loss of community amongst motorcyclists seems to hit Sheila particularly hard.

Sheila loves the ability to travel long distances and feel free to see sights, meet people along the way, and travel at her own will. Perhaps because she felt like she couldn't go at her own pace during the challenge, Sheila only participated in the first Hoka Hey. She is stoic and thoughtful about her participation and her experience. Sheila embodies the will to live life. She is grateful for her experiences, her abilities, and her zest for adventure. Sheila also throws down the gauntlet for anyone, as so many riders do, to take a chance. "My motto to anybody is, the only thing that's holdin' you back in life is thin air. So just go for it. If you can dream it, dare to do it."[9] Sheila certainly enjoys life, with Trixie in tow.

Carla Dubois

"When I'm not motorcycling my heart bleeds."[10]

Carla is *the* Hoka Hey warrior woman. Her enormous red Harley-Davidson Street Glide is plastered with the Hoka Hey logo. She carries pamphlets about the ride and the Lakota in her tour pack. She is kind, compassionate, sympathetic, and spiritual. Her passion for motorcycling shows in all she does. Motorcycling is her life. She works as the motor-clothes manager for a Harley-Davidson dealer in her home state of New Mexico. She and her husband ride regularly together, making motorcycling a family affair. The Hoka Hey is not the only distance challenge in which Carla has participated; she has also completed an Iron Butt challenge—riding 1,000 miles in twenty-four hours.

> [Riding] is such a deep passion for me, that when I'm not motorcycling my heart bleeds. Um. I'm just, I don't hear anything else goin' on. My mind is clear when I'm riding, it's just such a remedy for me. And uh, nothing else truly matters. You know, the normal day of stresses are gone. It's just the road and enjoying the beautiful scenery that we have been given by our good Lord.[11]

Of the two Hoka Hey challenges (2011 and 2013) she attempted, she never finished, but she keeps coming back for more. That indomitable spirit is what Hoka Hey riders must exude. Carla *is* the Hoka Hey; in some ways, all of her Hoka Heys combine into one massive ride. She keeps riding as if the challenge is continuous, as if the spaces between each year are mere checkpoints on her ride of a lifetime. She plugs along and comes back every year, despite the challenges she faces on the road. Moreover, Carla faces the challenge many of us would not be able to conquer—returning, and with her head high.

Hoka Hey Warrior woman Carla Dubois on her bike. Carla's custom paint job enables her to advertise for the HHMC even when she is not on a challenge. This helps raise continued awareness for Pine Ridge. (Courtesy Carla Dubois.)

Carla's warrior spirit includes more than her ability to ride. When I met Carla, her healing scar from open-heart surgery peeked from the top of her Hoka Hey cut. It made her look tough and elicited otherwise un-askable questions. She and my dad stood in the parking garage at our Las Vegas hotel comparing scars. Carla's was not yet healed well enough to sustain the Hoka Hey. She was there checking in bikes and volunteering before the ride. Her story is unbelievable, a tribute to her spirit. In the midst of her first Hoka Hey, Carla became ill and had to return home. Her legs swelled, presumably from the combination of heat, fatigue, and extreme riding. Upon her return, she continued having problems. The blockage doctors thought she had was actually a life-threatening defect. "I was the one in the million."[12] Her sentiment looms with faith and strength, another illustration of her perseverance and warrior spirit.

Carla is one of the most genuine and caring people you will ever meet. Her positive attitude and willingness to help at every challenge makes her a beloved Hoka Hey figure and true lover of the cause. Once again, her Hoka Hey story certainly will continue well after the ride is over.

Kristin "Jersey Pearl" McKelvey

Her nickname precedes her. Jersey Pearl. She hails from the Garden State; her enormous east coast take-charge personality clashes with her small stature and sincerity. Her generosity manifests as family and friends pass through her kitchen while we Skype—refugees from Hurricane Sandy. She serves as the International President of Women in the Wind and a small business owner. Like the steel and chrome she rides, she is a dichotomy of strength and grace. Jersey Pearl stands on her own. She owns her own motorcycle clothing and accessory company—Fat Bottomed Girlz—a concept that shows the strength and creativity of women riders. In her words, "When you're riding down the road. And you see women riding. Most of us ride bigger bikes than the guys. So that's our fat bottom. They ride these skinny little things from bar to bar. And we RIDE. So that's what a fat bottom girl is to me."[13] The very name empowers women riders and professes a positive body image.

Like many Hoka Hey women, motorcycling is Jersey Pearl's life. It has become her source of income, her pastime, and her social circle. Since she began riding in 1998, the number of women riders has increased. As a member of a motorcycle club, she bands together with other riders. As with the increase in women riders, Jersey Pearl also has watched club life change. While the stereotypical underpinnings of clubs are rooted in destruction and crime, the experience of being in Women in the Wind far differs from the clubs of old. The old-school idea of respect still echoes in today's club life.

> Not everybody is necessarily in a hard-core biker group anymore either. So I've watched that change too. So you know, the ideals on that are different. I've also learned a lot more about that. 'Cause my husband's in a club too. So that mentality has changed too. You always think of the big bad ass Hell's Angels kind of guy. And they are. But you know they're really just normal people like you and me at the same

time. And you really just learn respect for one another which carries over into your whole life, your work life, your regular social life. You just earn a whole new respect for everything. For the road. For your surroundings. For other people.[14]

Jersey Pearl felt respect through the club and through the Hoka Hey. She cried as she discussed the connections and camaraderie she felt on the ride, connections that have lasted even after the challenge was over.

Jersey Pearl shows the gender dualism in many women riders—our gender presentations an amalgam of masculine and feminine. We ride big bikes and preach about respect but also open our homes generously to friends and care for family with feminine and maternal nature. Female masculinity is in part about a woman exuding masculine characteristics; however, the other side of that coin shows our femininity intact. We vacillate between the pull of gender expectations and alternative models of gender expression. We yearn for understanding, pushing ourselves to fit into prescribed boxes yet rip out of those boxes because we are who we are.

Bryana Mason

She is the closest to my age so far at just 28, and me 30. We are both students—her working and taking classes at night toward her medical degree (ultrasound technology, to be exact), me finishing my Ph.D. Despite our similarities she seems so far from where I am. She already has a son; she is a single mom who works during the day, taking class at night for the chance at a better life. She has one break in her day while her son naps and she chooses to fill it with an interview for my work. I feel selfish for asking such a price. I think the Hoka Hey was the hardest thing I have ever done, but it seems like a walk in the park compared to Bryana's everyday life. Sitting comfortably alone in my room typing away, I admire the arduousness of her life.

Bryana classically describes her Hoka Hey journey. Early morning rides though the mountain fog listening to music as she contemplates the meaning of her life, riding her ride, passing the boys, making friends, and overcoming obstacles. It is everything you expect from a romanticized cross-country ride. She remembers it fondly as both difficult and rewarding. She not only dedicated her Hoka Hey ride to a friend recently diagnosed with cancer but also raised money for her fight. The passing years between her ride and our interview dull the memories of extreme fatigue and difficult directions. She remembers the challenges now as pushing her to do more. Something I find myself doing as well, although not with the same sense of gratitude Bryana expresses here:

> That's where that strength that you don't realize you have comes in and you keep pushing yourself and enjoying every minute of it. And going even though this is

shitty and it's raining and it's pouring and I'm freezing to death and I can't feel my toes and I want to cry. But I'm not going to cry, because I'm never going to be able to experience this again. And I'm going to be able to say I got through it is what makes it worth it. And that's where the strength develops from. 'Cause you're able to push through what could be someone's stopping point. And go, I'm going to accept this. And I'm going to run with it.[15]

She laughs at this memory, a marker of her success and strength.

Like Jersey Pearl and many others, motherhood partially marks Bryana's femininity. Like mine, her motorcycling experience comes from her family. She rides with her parents and encouraged her mother to take up riding again after she purchased her first motorcycle. Bryana still rides, but questions doing the Hoka Hey again. When I asked her about participating in a second challenge she said, "I think the only reason that hinders me at all, honestly, is that I have a sixteen-month-old son. And I would be, you know I'd I would be worried that something would happen to me now. When I did it before I had nothing to lose. Nothing to lose."[16] Being new to motherhood has changed Bryana's priorities and perceptions of the danger of riding. This contrasts to the way Junie, and Bryana's family, embrace riding as a group activity. Perhaps time will allow Bryana to bring her son into the culture as a family.

Bryana is strikingly aware of gender expectations. She knows she must care for her child above all else. She knows riding a motorcycle may label her as a lesbian simply for riding a motorcycle. She knows people doubt she is a good rider simply because she is a woman. Simultaneously, she, in part, plays into this gender expectation by giving up the Hoka Hey for her motherly duty. While she loves that her own mother rides, she also believes for the sake of her young son she cannot endanger herself—a perfectly natural feeling. But where do we draw the line between when it is and is not okay to ride? When does her son become old enough for her to take up this opportunity again? When is it okay for mothers to ride and, in doing so, encourage their children to ride? These are questions women riders grapple with regularly and add to the complexity of being a woman on a motorcycle.

Kelly Quinn a.k.a. Throttle Girl

Kelly's life is amazing. Born in Alaska, she worked on commercial fishing boats, was a competitive racer, big mountain skier, and the youngest female heli-ski proprietor in the world after starting a helicopter ski business in Alaska with her father and brother in 1999. Kelly also worked as an athletic trainer with professional athletes in the NFL, NHL, and various action sports. After realizing she had gone as far as both her skill and gender would allow, she began her own company and brand—Throttle Girl—where she inspires many with her charity work.[17] Not to mention she's beautiful. The kind of model beautiful that can't possibly be real, but it is. We rode the same Hoka Hey, both of our first times. You needed a mop to soak up the drool the men left in her wake. So naturally my own gender baggage of feeling inadequate made me hate her at first sight, but she eventually won me over with her kindness, sincerity, and generosity. Because of course she's also sweet.

Kelly is uniquely aware of her place as a woman in a man's world. She has always been in this position—commercial fishing, the NFL, and motorcycling aren't exactly places where you'll find the *Ladies Home Journal* laying around. Because of this she became the outsider within as Patricia Hill-Collins describes. She knows both sides of the coin and while the boys' club may never fully accept her, she at least knows the secret handshake. Because of her position within the community, Kelly views her sexuality as an asset. She consciously uses her sexuality as a tool to grow her own company and promote various charitable causes. When I asked if she used her sexuality as a tool she replied:

> I don't want to feed that [image] too much, but it would be really negligent for me to say that quite frankly what I do as Throttle Girl, I have to capture the attention. It's not like I can be like, "Hey Abby, do you want to go down to the corner to the coffee shop and talk cancer?" You know, so it's utilizing the gift of being feminine and being female and tying it to this serious adventurous, adrenaline, you know, bike culture that's quite complex. But really the simplicity. I don't want to come off as that vixen on the back or feeding it in a negative way, it's using it for its beauty and grace is the ultimate meaning of it if that makes sense.[18]

Kelly Quinn a.k.a. Throttle Girl poses for a photo on the 2012 HHMC. Exquisite scenery and back roads marked the trip. (Courtesy Kelly Quinn.)

Although she may not identify directly as a feminist, Kelly's views of her sexuality mirror the girl power, sex positive attitudes of third wave feminism. A trend of empowerment weaves throughout these theories, and Kelly's attitude.

Kelly uses the empowerment she feels from riding a motorcycle to benefit others—continuing the cyclical nature of gender expectations and expression. She not only rides to raise money for herself, she rides to raise money for charities. Utilizing her sexuality is a part of her game. Kelly cunningly turns the vixen on the back stereotype into something to benefit a cause. But does it work? Some would say that Kelly is successful in her endeavors to better the world through motorcycling. Others may say she is not reaching a wide enough audience to make change. As Audre Lorde reminds us, the master's tools may not dismantle the master's house. The use of sexuality in this context may temporarily win the battle but it is yet to be seen if it can win the war. The fact remains, however, that Kelly feels she makes a difference and she uses the concepts and images of hegemonic femininity to do so. No one can take that away from her.

Debra Langley

Debra greets me with a delightful southern drawl. "I think it's exciting!" she exclaims after I thank her for taking time to be interviewed.[19] Her excitement exudes from her soul. She rapid fire talks for what seems like an endless amount of time, sometimes answering my questions, but more often reminiscing about her journeys and professing her passion for motorcycling. She rarely stops to breathe in the two hours. Debra is beyond sweet and kind. She works for the Lee County Board of Education in the maintenance department, mainly doing odd jobs or "whatever they ask me to do." She is proud of being a woman and perhaps even more proud of being a self-professed tomboy, having ridden motorcycles since she was young.

At the time of my interviews, she was the only woman who rode the Hoka Hey with her significant other. Stan had completed the challenge once already and Debra joined him in 2011 as they rode from their home in Alabama to Phoenix to start the route and then on through all 48 states and into Canada. That they survived the trip is a testament to their relationship. Debra describes their dynamic,

> You know, we were like partners. We would tell each other like when one or another was dozin' off we could tell how they drove or how they were weavin'. And we'd pull, or I'd pull up to him and say pull over. You know. I could tell he was sleepin'… a couple times we lost each other and that was scary.[20]

Their relationship endures. The two married shortly after the Hoka Hey.

Before the Hoka Hey, Debra's forays into the country extended only to a small handful of trips into Florida from her home in Alabama. For Debra the Hoka Hey is not only about raising awareness for the Lakota or about spending time with her partner or riding her bike. It is about seeing the country. It is a way out of Alabama, even for a brief period. Exuberant and laughing, Debra describes her awe with the grandeur of the trip like many would describe a relaxing vacation,

> We drove across the Golden Gate Bridge in San Francisco. And I just, you know, I just patted my Heritage and I said, "We're goin' across the Golden Gate Bridge! We're far far away from home." And the Pacific to me, was just awesome. The Ocean, the Pacific Ocean.... And it's just something that you'll never forget. You know, tell your grandkids, "Your grandmother rode her Harley in all 48 states!"[21]

The Hoka Hey Motorcycle Challenge is about seeing the country. Debra captures these intentions. Imagine seeing the country for the first time as an adult; your whole life spent in a small town, seeing those scenic vistas on television or in books. The motorcycle and the challenge are ways to escape. Because of the Hoka Hey, she finds herself living the fantasy of hitting the open road. This is Debra's experience—certainly one to remember. Beyond seeing the beauty of North America, the challenge asks us to respect and appreciate the country. We ride not only through picturesque mountains and national parks but also by landfills and through areas of extreme poverty. Beyond even that the challenge reminds us that the land is not ours. We ride though countless reservations and down historically murderous corridors where whites forced Native Americans from their homes. While riding your motorcycle across the lower 48 states is something of which to be proud, as Debra indicates, the challenge should also remind us that this land is not wholly ours. After all, the purpose of the Hoka Hey is to bring attention to the plight of the Native Americans on reservations in South Dakota, and from a larger perspective across the country.

Wendy Battles

I first met Wendy in Las Vegas before the 2012 ride. There was a shining purple Harley Davidson two car-lengths in front of my dad and I at the intersection of Flamingo and Mountain Vista. The reflecting light from the sparkly bedazzles on a helmet cover caught my eye and, as intended, drew attention from bike to rider. Curly dusty blonde hair, feathers, and earrings stuck out under the purple bedazzled helmet. Hair fell delicately down her back as it blew in the warm Las Vegas wind. She was wearing a Hoka Hey vest. We had been in town for a day but she was the first woman rider I had seen at the challenge. Overly excited and filled with the enthusiasm of meeting more than a potential participant but a fellow woman rider, challenger, and perhaps new friend, I charged forward, recklessly passing the cars that separated us, halted my bike next to hers and introduced myself. Meeting Wendy on the road signaled the start of my "real" research; and, unbeknownst to me, that moment would actually be the start of our friendship. In the years since that first meeting, Wendy has become one of the most beloved members of my

Wendy Battles poses for a promotional photo at Gowanda Harley Davidson before the 2013 HHMC. The photo lists Wendy's hometown and rider number. Unique numbers distinguish each individual on the GPS tracker and become a marker of identity within the community. Lower numbers mean early establishment with the HHMC. (Courtesy Wendy Battles.)

Hoka Hey family. She and her partner Bill rode the 2013 ride with my dad and I and they graciously took my dad into their group for 2014. She's picked my bike up, dried my tears, and celebrated with me at the finish.

Wendy encapsulates so many parts of my analysis of women riders of the Hoka Hey. Her story is a little unbelievable, but in her words, when she heard about the Hoka Hey she said,

> That's the vacation I want to do. That's something I need to do. It was something I wanted to do. And it brought back up being ten years old and watching all the people go off for the ride. So I had to do it. I didn't have the money, I didn't have a bike, I didn't have the experience. I didn't have nothing. But I had to go do it. I found a way. I got the bike, got my license, and within six weeks, I was on the Hoka Hey [with only] a thousand miles of experience with riding big bikes. If you want to do it, you'll find a way to do it.[22]

Yes, you read the passage correctly: She had only ridden a Harley for six weeks before she took off on the 2011 Hoka Hey. That intense desire to do the Hoka Hey resonates with many women who chose to take on the challenge. Wendy felt compelled to ride for inexplicable reasons. Yet unlike so many others, Wendy did not come with a lifetime of riding experience. While her dad rode motorcycles for most of his life, and she attributes her desire to start riding to him, she herself did not ride. Although nothing can really prepare you for the challenge, she had 1,000 miles in before she started on the HHMC, whereas most women had been riding their entire lives. She is amazing.

It's that find-a-way-to-do-it mentality and grit that not only keeps women in the Hoka Hey but also makes it feel so good when we finish. In the realm of overcoming riding obstacles, Wendy has done it all. She's ridden alone and with groups, been ostracized because of her gender, and found empowerment and herself along the way. Despite her incredible story, Wendy also shows traditionally feminine qualities by downplaying her own abilities and experiences. She is the first to tell *you* how amazing *you* are because of how *you've* ridden and throws in an "I couldn't have done that" each time. Regardless of what she says or how she humbles herself among other riders, Wendy is a badass. She's amazing and serves as an inspiration for women riders, and for her children and grandchildren who show her endless love and support.

Jane Bixby and Schatzi Brown

Jane and Schatzi are Thelma and Louise, except for that part where they actually ride over the cliff. Each woman leads her own life as an individual rider but they come together for the Hoka Hey and cannot be separated. Both are friends outside of the challenge and have become better friends as a result of the ride. Their husbands ride but not in the Hoka Hey. Jane and Schatzi are independent women who own businesses and command respect because of their strength, and they are the only group of women who ride the Hoka Hey together. They found themselves at first ostracized because of their gender. However, they have created a reputation for themselves as hard-core, badass women riders who refuse to put up with tail draggers.[23] The two women outride most men in the challenge. I cannot even begin to fathom keeping up with them. They are always the first women to finish.

The sense of empowerment found through riding is evident with Jane and Schatzi. Having ridden most of their lives, they each remember a time when they were the only women on the road or in the group, a place they had to earn. Jane describes her feelings this way: "It's not like it's a big feat. I think women can do anything men can do. I think the rest of the world sees it more than I, than we do, as black and white and women versus men. In my

Jane Bixby and Schatzi Brown pose before the start of the 2013 HHMC in upstate New York. (Courtesy Jane Bixby.)

eyes, we're just motorcyclists."[24] Yet despite their internal perceptions, they notice they draw attention when riding; this recognition produces feelings of empowerment. "It always makes you feel good when you're a woman rider and you're out there and people do a double take and say, 'Oh my God, that's two women!' It does makes you smile from within."[25]

In addition to feeling empowered by their gender, they feel empowered by what they have survived on the road. Jane had to fight for her place in the challenge, as initially her husband did not want her to participate. To be fair, the road can be a dangerous place for women. Many of the women interviewed for this project spoke of wanting to ride with a man or being afraid of possible danger from others. Jane and Schatzi experienced a robbery on their first Hoka Hey challenge. The expectation of danger from others impedes some women's ability to participate fully in the motorcycle culture. Jane and Schatzi's fight to participate in a riding community has not changed a lot in the forty plus years they each have ridden. Schatzi describes needing tools and a tough attitude to hang with the boys in her early days.

> It was a big thing back then, like "Oh my God, she's riding with us!" as I rode my little 500 Yamaha with a bunch of big guys all riding Harleys. We were riding to an AM Jam event and one of the bikes broke down. We all stopped to help and I knew I was

> accepted when they had to use my tools to get the bike fixed. No one else had thought of bringing any tools and I always carried them just in case I broke down, which, fortunately, I never did...[26]

In the challenge, both women had to earn her place alongside the men as an equal rider.

Men ride with men without having their validity or experience as a rider questioned. Men assume that a man can keep up with other men regardless of his actual abilities. The patriarchal nature of the motorcycling community forces Jane and Schatzi, like all other women riders, to prove their abilities prior to acceptance. When I met the two they had already won this acceptance. In fact, their male riding partner, Tim, even stuck up for all women riders. I vividly remember thinking Tim was crazy when he asked about the legality of using catheters during the challenge as it gave an unfair advantage to male riders. While none of us had any intention of catheterizing ourselves to win a challenge, one could say Tim was arguing as much for Jane and Schatzi as he was for himself riding with them; the mere thought of a woman being an equal competitor in the challenge was paramount. Schatzi describes their initial meeting:

> We kept meeting Tim at checkpoints and it was like, well, we were busting his chops a bit, "We keep bumping into you, if you want to ride with us, you can. We're going to go and get gas and if you can handle riding with us, it's fine. We know you like to ride by yourself...." I think he felt really bad that we had previously gotten robbed as he met us at the gas station and rode with us.[27]

Tim's surprise at enjoying the ride with women partners shows the challenge women riders face simply because they are women. After other men discovered Tim riding with Jane and Schatzi, his own manhood came into question.

While it may be incredibly misogynistic to assume that women cannot ride, defying this expectation leads to a greater feeling of accomplishment. Empowerment through sport exists in part because of these unfounded assumptions. Jane and Schatzi found empowerment through riding before they entered the Hoka Hey. Their sense of accomplishment compounded when this elite group of riders fully accepted them—now outsiders within. They are not only defying gender expectations but also excelling in an arena where few riders (regardless of sex) even dare to compete.

Debby Pearson

Debby is one of the most interesting people I've ever had the good fortune to meet. Her life reads like a choose-your-own-adventure book filled

Debby Pearson stops to pose for a photo in Yellowstone National Park during the 2010 HHMC. (Courtesy Debby Pearson.)

with epic hikes, dirt bike riding through Patagonia, a camping honeymoon on Enduros through Belize, cross-country motorcycle trips, and her own business. Simply put, she is fascinating. Like many others, she began riding at a young age, brought into the culture by her family. She cites her dad as the biggest reason she rides.

Debby is also incredibly self-aware. She speaks most directly about her gender nonconformity and recognizes its benefits and its setbacks. Debby identifies as "genderless" and describes herself as her "father's only son."[28] Her relationship with her father led to her passion for motorcycling and likely her adventurous spirit. "He didn't treat me like a girl. He liked doing these things, motorcycles and cars, and he just shared them with me whether I wanted to participate or not."[29] The idea of treating her like a person rather than like a woman simultaneously eliminates and reinforces gender expectations. While Debby may not have grown up in a home that followed prescribed gender roles, it is impossible to avoid culturally constructed attitudes about gender presentations. Debby knows she "intimidates men" when she rides.[30] Her gender presentation as a woman is inescapable. Rather than an androgynous gender presentation, Debby is petite with delicate features and long blonde hair.

Debby's upbringing in the motorcycling community is much like my own, and presumably like many other women riders'. However, our subset of motorcycle culture—women who have ridden all our lives—is an underrepresented image of motorcycling. Debby describes her identification and presentation as a rider below.

> It's hard to define myself without riding because I've always ridden. It's such a part of me. It's like trying to describe yourself as being a woman. You've always been a female. So I don't see it as different. I really don't. It surprises me that people are surprised. Say like last night someone said, "Oh, you don't look like a motorcycle rider. You don't look like a biker chick." And uh, I don't feel different. But yet people will stare and you wonder why. David will remind me, "'Cause you're odd. You're riding a bike and you're a girl. And you're by yourself."[31]

As exemplified by the quote above, Debby's identity as both a woman and a motorcyclist supersedes her adherence to gender roles. However, that her husband reminds her she is "odd" grounds her in the reality of a community entrenched in hegemonic gender expectations.

In many ways, motorcycling profits from the maintenance of gender barriers, which make women like Debby feel like outsiders, or "special" as she prefers. For example, motorcycle clothing, specifically branded by Harley-Davidson, plays on gender binaries. Men's shirts laden with images of semi-clothed women, fire-breathing dragons, or a lone wolf are in stark contrast to women's shirts emblazoned with lace and roses. Supporting the "tough guy" mentality sells motorcycles to many men. These images and stereotypes do not include women like Debby and make her feel odd. That said, Harley-Davidson has, as Debby notes, "been working hard to inspire and entice women into their fold."[32] She points to some of the new women's clothing lines, including "less pink" and more "edgy, sexy" options.[33] While these recent efforts are commendable, the lace (while seen less often) and "sexiness" of the clothing still reflects a traditional feminine standard.

Eden Mailloux

My first introduction to Eden was through the short Hoka Hey video clip on the website. Then almost every woman with whom I spoke talked about Eden. They claimed I *had* to interview Eden. She was infamous. In my eyes she was the one interview I needed to pull this project all together. And I couldn't get her to talk to me. She was nervous, or busy, or maybe just wanted to keep to herself. And then one day, she agreed to the interview.

Eden Mailloux lives up to her hype. A nurse from Arizona, she is petite and full of spunk. Hers is the greatest story of overcoming obstacles—borderline unbelievable—such is the case with any legend. It took Eden 10 hours to travel thirty-six miles, repeatedly dropping her bike, picking it up, and trudging on, all on the wrong road. Most people couldn't walk thirty-six miles in less than ten hours. She never gave up. Her tenacity and grit earned her the respect and admiration of women, riders, Hoka Hey challengers, and the general public.

Like Jane and Schatzi, throughout the ride, she is aware of the admiration from other women. She takes this role model status to heart and lives up to the expectations many have of her as a great leader. She describes her poignant finish line experience:

> I guess the biggest thing that I learned about myself that participating in the Hoka Hey the women were perceived by other women as heroes. I was even called that by several women in Tennessee. And there was one gal in Kansas City that I was the first female to cross the finish line there, I mean to get into that checkpoint. And there was one gal while others kinda took pictures and such ... I mean, I felt so much like a rock star at that time.[34]

She admonishes men who try to quit after hearing the challenge has already been won. She recognizes her ability to influence other women riders. She understands her story, her attitude, and her behavior could make or break someone else's desire to ride. She describes a brief moment when she contemplated leaving the route this way: "Some who have even called me their hero and here I am failing on them because gee, I don't get to participate in a party? What kind of hero is that?"[35] For Eden, the experience is also humbling. Like so many women leaders, she does not feel like a leader. She does not understand why she is important and downplays the idea that she might have the ability to impact others. Yet the ability remains. Eden impacted my own subsequent rides in many ways. Like the other women of the Hoka Hey, we downplay our own experiences in relation to the other women we see riding. For me, Eden's determination goes far beyond motivating me to ride. It motivates me to finish any seemingly insurmountable obstacle.

Sherie Newell

Sherie describes herself as being born in the wrong century. She lives in Alaska with her family and works as an assistant counselor for the Salvation Army. When she and her husband were married for ten years and their children were young, the family lived off the grid. They were off the road system in a cabin on the Yentna River. Their house ran on generators and they used outhouses. While it may not have been her children's favorite experience, she thinks it made them better people. This sense of adventure took Sherie on the Hoka Hey and made her complete the challenge by herself.

She primarily rides with her husband, but he was uninterested in the Hoka Hey. With her husband's support, Sherie chose to go alone.

> I started out by myself but I rode with a group of guys through parts of Florida, Georgia, and Alabama. I left that group and I rode by myself until I met another guy riding alone in Oklahoma, riding with him was just really companionable and nice. We rode together until Arizona. If I wanted to ride with somebody and be companionable and nice, I wanted it to be with my husband—that was not why I was riding in the Hoka Hey. I told him that I needed to ride by myself because I wanted the experience of only relying on myself and I had come to the conclusion that when you ride in a group you can hide your weaknesses, you can take the strengths of other people and not do the things that you're not the best at. But when you ride by yourself you have to count on yourself and you kind of have to rise above the things you're not sure of or the things you can't do.[36]

Riding alone reinforces Sherie's sense of independence and freedom. She takes pride in being the first solo woman to cross the finish line in 2010. While others may have crossed before her, they rode with groups or their husbands. She was on her own and proud of it.

Sherie's experience also highlights the issue of safety women face when we ride alone. She has unbelievable stories, including having a man pull a gun on her and worrying about where to sleep at night. She cites finding a place to sleep as one of the hardest things on the Hoka Hey. She says, "I went too many hours without sleep because I didn't feel safe just sleeping somewhere by myself." For Sherie, making it through the unsafe, difficult situations by herself made the ride all the more rewarding. Her gender (even with its perceived limitations) enabled her to find fulfillment and empowerment from riding.

Abby Van Vlerah

Figuring out what to say about myself in this chapter was the most difficult part of writing this book. Do I tell you about my riding history, my job and education, my identity as a feminist? I don't know; it all seems important and also completely unimportant at the same time. I suppose this is the kerfuffle that is the complexity of identity.

My family has been a part of the motorcycle community almost as long as I can remember. My mom purchased a Harley-Davidson 1200 Sportster for my dad as a Father's Day present in 1988. At first, my dad took my mom, my sister, and I each on separate rides, all to the same destination—the Dairy Queen. He went to Bike Week in Daytona Beach with his buddies occasionally; but as I recall we were less than weekend warriors then. Weekend warriors are riders who hit the road on the weekends and allow their bikes to collect dust the rest of the week. In retrospect, we were somehow less than that. We did not even go out every weekend. He rode on the occasional Saturday; however, my dad has always put our family first and since we all couldn't hop on the back of his tiny bike, he simply didn't go. He (shockingly) grew tired of eating three hot fudge sundaes in one day and soon enough convinced my mom to learn to ride—two bikes would allow the entire family of four to enjoy the activity together. I rode with my mom and my sister rode with my dad. I soon tired of being on the back. I wanted to be in control. I wanted to feel the wind pressing against my body as I barreled down the highway atop this beautiful machine. I began riding my own motorcycle when I was 16 years old. I had a strong woman figure showing me how to ride. My mom led the way for me to understand that women could handle our own bikes and my dad never allowed me to think I couldn't do something just because I was a girl. For me, motorcycling has always been a family affair. After all, a family who rides together stays together.

My dad and I became riding buddies shortly after I started riding on my own. He never left me out of a trip and always told me I could ride whatever kind of bike I wanted, no matter how big. In the summer I learned to ride, I hopped on his 1991 Springer and we took off to Sturgis, South Dakota, for the Black Hills Rally and Races. The cross-country trip to that iconic bike week made me a confident (albeit stupid) rider. I was so young. Fearless. And with the bravado of any teenager, I had my first accident, took a shot of tequila to calm my nerves, and got back on the bike the next day. I was tough. I drank. I swore. I had fun being around the adults and the men. I was a spectacle and also completely oblivious to everything around me. On that trip, we rode some of the most difficult roads in America. I took on Iron Mountain Road and recall being scared out of my mind but doing it anyway. My dad never allowed me to think

Abby Van Vlerah (age 7) on Jim Van Vlerah's Sportster. Many women interviewed began motorcycling as a family affair with fathers and brothers. A majority of the women of the HHMC starting riding at a young age, either as passengers or on dirt bikes. Long family histories with motorcycling make women more likely to participate in the culture. (Author photo.)

of myself as a little girl. He told me if I was scared of my bike, or the ride, that I would wreck. Don't look down, he would say, you always go where you look. He was right.

I grew up in my dad's garage, always around cars and motorcycles, always among a conglomeration of half-finished or not-yet-started projects. We got dirty and worked hard for our well-earned Pepsi breaks. When I was in high school, and probably beyond, I was thrilled to emasculate the boys around me with my knowledge and appreciation of cars and ability to ride motorcycles. I made my dad proud when I talked about bikes or pointed out what manufacturer made a certain car by the position of its distributor in the engine. I took on a role that his sons would traditionally fill; but he had no sons. I was it. While I never defined myself as a tomboy, in retrospect I certainly was one. I rarely showered. In fact, my parents had to force me to bathe every few days, something for which I begrudged them. I hated to wear dresses. I did not care about fashion, or getting married, or having babies. I hated pink. I had no interest in traditional sports but the attention I received from my dad when I was in his garage turned me into a gear head. What I know now, from years of studying feminist thought, is that I was (and still am) gender nonconforming.

Abby Van Vlerah poses next to her Dyna Wide Glide in Rocky Mountain National Park on the 2012 HHMC. (Author photo.)

Despite my gender nonconformity and occasional bravado, traditional gender roles confined me and I knew somewhere inside my brain what I did was not "normal." This insecurity coupled with what I assumed was the public's negative interpretation of motorcyclists lead me to only express my true nonconforming gender identity around my family and close friends. On the bike, I swear, wear jeans, get dirty, and stand with my legs apart. Not on the bike, I act the part of a lady, dress in feminine attire, and try to blend in in my everyday work life. As a result, I surprise new friends, teachers, mentors, and now colleagues with my ability to ride motorcycles. I do not present as a motorcyclist on a daily basis. I never have. Clad in a pencil skirt and peep-toed flats at the university, my motorcycle identity is invisible. When I feel comfortable enough to disclose my motorcycling identity, people commonly express surprise with my participation and affiliation with this culture. Despite beliefs of people outside my private life, motorcyclists are my people. I am more myself around the subculture of cyclists than I am in an academic environment, where I often feel like a fraud.

As I spend more and more time at work and less and less time on my research and on my bike, I feel an impending sunset on my female masculinity. While I still swear regularly (yes, even at work) and relish in the emasculation of men, I use this more as a novelty than as my real identity. In my new world, gender nonconformity is sensational rather than natural. Many motorcyclists must face this kind of dual identity; I am certainly not alone. I conducted this research partially because of my love of motorcycling and partially because I think motorcyclists tend to get a bad rap. The cultural constructions of motorcyclists, in part from popular media representations, limit the perceptions of the diversity of the motorcycling community and potentially hinder participation by groups other than white males. I am not naïve enough to believe that my words will significantly change the cultural constructions of motorcyclists or that people will take up riding after reading my work. I am, however, hopeful that at least one person reconsiders his or her negative interpretation of cycling, or on a larger scale, considers taking risks.

The Hoka Hey, and motorcycling in general, is about taking risks and acting outside of our comfort zones. My desire to conform to traditional gender and societal roles encapsulates my inability to claim motorcycling outwardly as a part of my public identity. My lack of confidence as a rider fuels this desire to remain hidden. Despite finishing the Hoka Hey, I do not typically feel like a legitimate rider. However, I know when I ride I have to answer to no one and can be fully my authentic self. I am (or should be) ultimately confident. Each turn of the Hoka Hey reinforced my ability to believe I could do anything. Completing this challenge enabled me to see my life in a different way. Now, years after the ride, I occasionally forget that sense of pride, gratitude, and success (likely why many return to the ride year after year).

All of these things—the fact that I ride with my family, have been operating a motorcycle since I was 16, have a Ph.D. in cultural studies, and do not present as a biker in my normal life—add up to equal a facade of self-confidence glazing over insecurity and instability. In some ways, I think this epitomizes women riders. Perhaps I seek the openness of the road and exhilaration of riding because it makes me feel confident and in control.

Abby riding into a sand storm on the 2012 HHMC. Encountering and managing weather events and natural elements are a key part of the challenge. This sand storm created a zero-visibility situation. The author could barely keep her bike upright due to the strong winds and was forced to pull off on the side of the road. (Author photo.)

I feel different from many of the women I interviewed because I do not feel like an accomplished rider. I constantly thought that I could not do what they did or did not have the riding ability to hang with them. However, that is what all the women thought about one another. We all downplay our own abilities in comparison to the experiences of others. When I step back, I realize I got through some crazy things—a sandstorm seems to top the list. I felt confident after my first Hoka Hey. I felt like I could do anything. This challenge is empowering. As a woman, I felt triumphant for completing it. I defied my gender role. I kicked ass.

The feeling of triumph post–Hoka Hey is something with which women challengers need to reconnect. The daily grind of living in a patriarchal capitalist society tell us we are less than. Women are confronted with glass ceilings and making the choice between work and family. We have to look good and be pretty to get ahead. We have to conform. The Hoka Hey brought me out of that sphere. It opened doors to my own untapped self-confidence and also spun me into fantastic things I never would have imagined, including this book. While it doesn't seem like a huge triumph to me now, it should. We should all relish in our accomplishments and celebrate our epic adventures as women. Similarly epic adventures happen all the time, every day, in the challenges we face living in a man's world. Each day we wake up and take on the challenge again—ready to smash boundaries and, as Kelly Quinn would say, "rev our internal throttle."

Conclusions

The women of the Hoka Hey are different yet similar. Throughout this chapter, I used the individual tale of each woman to describe a different theme of my overall analysis. The truth is that many of these women could highlight multiple themes. I suppose that is the purpose of reaching a point of saturation in your research—it verifies your findings. The women have a collective voice that rings true to their womanhood and the sport. I hope you return to this chapter many times to reconnect with each woman as you read.

The themes in this book illustrate the lived experiences of each woman. Their identities as mothers, riders, and women intersect. Their roles as women, and at times their religion, drive them toward the moral imperative to help others. They have overcome adversity, challenges, and stereotypes to feel empowered by what they do. Their passion drives them to ride despite the socially constructed ideas of gender normativity. They use the tools of femininity yet remain unshackled by the hegemonic masculinity that pervades their sport. They support their biological and motorcycling families. They are true role models for one another and all women riders. They are truly extraordinary. They are what make the Hoka Hey unique.

4

Feminist Ethics of Care and Intrinsic Motivation

I just returned from the journey of a lifetime. No, it was an adventure. A true adventure. I crossed the country; I've always just been in Alabama. I've never really gone anywhere other than Florida. And just to go across all these ... each state. It was just awesome.[1] *The Hoka Hey was my opportunity to get out, do something, and see the country. I had no clue what I was in for. I mean I really don't know why. 'Cause surely I hadn't done anything like this before and I didn't even really know why I tried this 'cause it just seemed like I was out of my mind.*[2] *I mean, who in their right mind signs up to ride across the country on a motorcycle for a month, sleeping outside the entire time, and risking everything? But, this was something I felt I had to do and I didn't want to regret not doing it.*[3] *I suppose I should back up a bit—you're probably wondering how I even found this challenge or what drove me to do it. I can tell you the story, but you might not understand. It's personal.*

It all started a few months ago, although it seems like much longer now. I was going through some health issues with cancer; I like to say the Hoka Hey found me. And it was just, I don't know, it consumed my every thought. I had to do it. I just had to go try it.[4] *I was in the doctor's office for what seemed like the thousandth time. I had been through a barrage of chemo treatments, trying to battle this life-sucking disease. There's not much to do while you're sitting around waiting for your chemo treatments, so I always took a magazine or two along. That's when I saw the ad. I found out about the Hoka Hey reading a Harley magazine, a HOG Magazine, in the chemo room. I was diagnosed with cancer in 2009. So I put the Hoka Hey on the bucket list. When you're diagnosed with cancer for a second time you really start thinking about that stuff.*[5] *I thought about how I could live my life, what I had already done, and what I wanted to do, and if I could make a difference. I read about the independence and the spirit and sleepin' on the side of the road and how grueling and tough it was and the adventure and that totally spoke to me.*[6] *I wanted to feel alive, and at* that point I thought nothing would make me feel more alive and test my spirit more than this challenge.

So I asked my doctor when he came in what he thought and if he thought I would be strong enough to do it. This was three months from when the ride started. I mean that was March and we were riding in June. And he said, "Go live your life. Yeah, you'll probably be strong enough by then, don't let this slow you down." And he gave me a hundred bucks to go ride the ride. So I either had to give the hundred dollars back or I had to go ride the ride.[7] I saw the opportunity and it just rang in my soul. I had to do it.[8] So I said, I'm just gonna start saving money for the fee and then all my friends, once they finally realized I was serious about it, they threw me fundraisers.[9] And that was it. Reading that magazine and talking with that doctor started a whirlwind of an adventure, planning, and encouragement. I still can't believe how quickly it all happened and how much I've changed since then. I feel like a different person.

As the planning went on, I decided I didn't just want to ride for myself. I wanted to ride for others, too. There were so many people who came out to support me at events, who wanted to help, and who put their confidence in me that it seemed selfish to do it just for me. I wanted a connection to a larger cause. Cancer would be my cause. I knew so many people affected by the disease; not all of them could get out and ride the Hoka Hey or even get on a motorcycle, but I could. I would ride for all of us. In January of that year, of 2010, my good friend was diagnosed with stage four breast cancer. She was 27 years old. And I thought, what better for her? 'Cause here she was bouncing off of being an avid drug user to turning her life around, a complete one-eighty. Going to school. Wanting to be a social worker and wanting to work with women survivors of domestic violence. Completely just turned her life around. She was just inspirational in that. I knew I had to do something inspirational for her. So I called her up and told her I wanted to do the Hoka Hey. And I wanted to do it for her.[10] She was excited and touched by the sentiment. She had been on motorcycles before with previous boyfriends and really liked the culture but never got an opportunity to learn to ride. I think it gave her something to take her mind off the cancer, just like it did for me.

When I started talking to the other women who were riding I found out that they were riding for causes, too. They were all passionate about finding sponsorships, raising awareness, or just being a part of something. One woman passed out pink woven bracelets for us ladies to wear on the ride symbolizing her friend with cancer. It was like she was riding with us, she said, a great idea. There was also the Northern Nevada Children's Cancer Foundation[11] and Pine Ridge. I had never really been a part of those charity rides that happen so often in the motorcycling community, but it's really cool, and I never would have known this, but there's something really cool about riding in a group for a cause. All the people and the support and being part of that group and it's a visual thing. I never would have known how cool that is.¹² The Hoka Hey reminded me that we could put our passions into action and really make a difference either for ourselves or for others. Before, during, and after the ride I remembered why I was out there. It was for me, but something else was pushing me on. Motorcyclists are pretty amazing like that; we're the second largest philanthropic group in the country behind corporations. If that doesn't say something then I don't know what does.¹³ Sure, there was a prize waiting for the winner, but my motive for riding the Hoka Hey was not because I wanted to win the money. I wanted to ride for me and for my cause.

We did a ton of fundraisers. We had to, it was expensive. I think minus the entry fee, it cost, I think it was like four or five grand. Or something like that. So it was almost six grand to do it. Just with gas and crap and all that other stuff. It was insane.¹⁴ I wasn't just raising money though; I was gaining supporters and raising awareness for my friend's cancer struggles at each turn. We tried to think of everything to make a buck. I had a Harley dealership sponsor me. I had donation boxes at the local Harley dealership; my friends and family threw me bar parties.¹⁵ I sold muffins to ride the Hoka Hey.¹⁶ But somehow it all came together and after all the support, I had the time and the finances to be able to do it. So you know, I took my money and I went and I did it.¹⁷ And it paid off—we were able to raise money so that my friend and her family would be able to fly out there, too, to Alaska, and hang out at the finish. And we were able to donate some money to the Susan Komen Foundation, the breast cancer foundation. We were able to give her and her family a nice little vacation up to Alaska for two weeks. That was ultimately what pushed me to want to do the Hoka Hey before I even knew what I was getting myself into.¹⁸ It felt so good to be able to do it. I was proud of myself (for raising the money and actually completing the ride and everything) and I think other people were really proud of me, too.

It was so much more to me than money. For me it wasn't about getting there to win the money. It was about, "Hey, can I ride from Key West to Alaska? Let's go find out."¹⁹ But so many people were so pressed. And they just thought, "Oh my gosh, I'm gonna win this money and I'm gonna do great on this and all this." And you know, it was just sad. There were people that literally died.²⁰ Of course, everybody wants to make it in time and win money. But for me, it was more; it was personal.²¹ I couldn't believe it when people would drop out of the ride. I was riding with a guy and as soon as he heard that somebody made it to Alaska first, he went home. He just gave up and went home.²² But I didn't care about the money. That's not why I was in this.

My family turned out to be a great source of support. At first I wasn't really sure about how they would feel. It's dangerous, after all, and I would be gone for quite a while. I felt like it was kind of a selfish thing because I was going to be gettin' on this bike and takin' off and going places on it, and you know, you can't be doin' it with three kids.²³ But the kids embraced it. I had a whole team of cheerleaders. Especially my family, my dad was my head cheerleader.²⁴ And my husband said "Yeah, sure," and wow, I had support from him? And he didn't care to come?²⁵ He was there at the finish line, but he's not the biker in the family.²⁶ It was amazing to see everyone get on board with this. I was really surprised. But I suppose not everyone thought I could do it at first. My uncles, when I told them they were like, "You can't do that. You can't ride your Sportster to Alaska." And I was like, "Well, I'm gonna do it. So either you support me or you know, whatever." And like I got back and they all called me and they were like, "We're SO proud of you! We didn't think you could do it. But you did it." And they watched me and after it was over they said, "We'll never doubt you again when you tell us you're going to go do some crazy thing."²⁷ Even if it was after the ride that they turned around, the support from my family and friends felt wonderful.

And then I had this whole little cheering section from the dealership. They were like following me on a computer and all this other stuff. And like every time I'd get to a checkpoint they'd call me on my phone and be like, "AAHH, keep going, keep going!"²⁸ There were so many people cheering me on; it was like they were out there with me. I was riding for them. I couldn't believe how many people were following my ride. They watched me on the GPS (it told them where I was in the country and if my engine was on or off—kind of weird but cool). At times, it felt like a lot of pressure, like I didn't want to mess up because they were all watching. But the support outweighed that. One time a friend texted me to ask why my engine was off in the middle of the day; it was monsooning and we were waiting to see if it would pass. I had people following me online. Someone would post it on Facebook and I would try to post pictures here and there. Someone took a satellite picture of the exact time I stopped; it was like four in the afternoon. There were definitely some groupies watching. And to this day, I still have people walk in the shop; I have no idea who they are, and they're like, "We totally followed you and that was so cool!" It's weird to have people say things like that. I'm not famous. I don't feel like I did anything really *special*. But I guess it kinda is impressive. Even now that it's over people still come up to me and say, "Oh I read that in the newspaper" or "Oh, I read your blog" or "Oh you know so and so told me about this" or "Tell me this story again." My husband gets a little annoyed by it; but I guess at the same time, I guess it's impressive. Because the normal person doesn't get to do what I did.²⁹

I'm a spectacle when I ride, like an impressive sideshow attraction ... cue the circus music.... "Step right up, Ladies and Gentlemen, Boys and Girls! Come see the amazing Hoka Hey Rider with a vagina!" It's not bad, just funny. On a motorcycle, it's like you're approachable. Because you can pull up to a gas station to get fuel and if you're in a vehicle, nine times out of ten nobody's going to talk to you. But for some reason when you're on a motorcycle, you're like approachable.[30] Especially when my dog's with me. She brings a lot of joy to people. You'll be going down the road and you'll see someone is right beside you, pacing themselves; and you know what's going on. You look over and you already know. They're taking pictures of that dog on the motorcycle. She's like a rock star. You know, everybody wants a picture of her on the motorcycle. I feel like sometimes my job is just like driving Miss Trixie.[31] Even without the dog, I seem to be greeted with open arms everywhere I go. People are actually fascinated by the fact that I ride a motorcycle. When looking at me you wouldn't assume it per se; but I guess here's the break in stereotype.[32] We'll be at gas stations and little old ladies will ask us how to pump gas or to help them with something. And my husband and I just laugh and say, "Well I guess we don't look very tough."[33] But people assume you want to talk to everybody. You're in a hurry and especially on the Hoka Hey that was a little hard. You want to be friendly.[34] You want to give a good impression of motorcyclists, to change the perceptions.

When I notice people watching me ride, sometimes I feel like a role model. I remember a little girl; I pulled up to a gas station and a little girl rolled up her window. She was scared. And when I took off my helmet and she saw that I was a girl, she looked over at her mom and she said, "It's a girl, it's a girl! A girl on a bike!" And she wasn't scared no more. And that was amazing to me. Because people judge people by what they look like and I was on like day seven of the Hoka Hey. So no shower, no nothing, my hair was a mess. And I think I inspired her.[35] [36]I hope to inspire. I really don't see myself as different than other people.[37]

I've been seeing more women riders over the years. There are still few women in the Hoka Hey but there are so many more women riders out there now, in all facets of motorcycling. I felt like I was out there for each one of them. I think that just by having a small group of women who are actually out there and doing these things that women didn't generally think they could do before has allowed more women to feel comfortable doing it themselves and to get out there. I think the number of women riders is starting to rise and I think eventually you're going to find a lot of women who are winning endurance challenge races all over the world. And doing BMX type stuff and off-road stuff, which has always been a male dominated sport.[38] I'm helping that perception. When I started talking about the Hoka Hey, people started telling me how great they thought it was. I didn't really know why so many people were interested in supporting me. I mean, no one really cares when I go out to Sturgis for the rally. But this was different, it was a competition and I was a part of something bigger. But now, I'm out there riding and doing this stuff and people are noticing. And now everybody rides. So now it's even more empowering 'cause I was there at the beginning and I was able to watch it grow.[39] It's always amazing to me when I notice women noticing me. It's usually women who don't ride motorcycles.

Sometimes I'll get the thumbs up and the women are like, "That's awesome, I wish I could do that. Like I wish I was brave enough to do that."[40] But they are brave enough, or they could be. If I can do it, I'm pretty sure anyone can as long as they wanted to. You do have to want it. And when it all comes together, women can do anything! We can make such a huge difference in other people's lives just by doing something like the Hoka Hey. I mean whether it's a guy or it's another female out there. Or they're actually riding it, or it's just some guy you meet at a gas station who thinks it's so cool to see some female not being afraid, or limiting themselves by the standards and the society that we live in.[41] I feel like I am inspiring people. I can tell they watch me ride; they talk to me. They tell me that they think what I'm doing is cool, that doing the Hoka Hey was impressive.

When I arrived at the start of the challenge, I realized it wasn't just my family and friends who were watching me back home. The other challengers had their eyes on me as well. When we were at the party beforehand, Friday night before the challenge started on Sunday, a lot of the guys were like, "It's cool that you're here, but I really hope that you *can* make it to Alaska on that bike," and "Do you know what you're in for?"[42] Of course I didn't know what I was in for, but I didn't want them to know it. Hell, they didn't know what they were in for either. None of us could have anticipated it. But somehow the others knew about me, or at least pretended like they did. Maybe it was just easier to remember the women riders; after all there were less of us. Even after the ride started, the other riders wanted to know if you needed help. I remember getting into the second checkpoint and Beth tellin' me, "Oh yeah, people keep askin' where you girls are." Everyone had this caring attitude. You really weren't in it alone. And nobody was going to get to Alaska without you.[43] The caring attitudes on the road were amazing. I can't exactly explain how or why we all bonded on the ride. I'm not sure if it was the shared experience or getting to know one another before and after the ride, but somehow the sharing meals and miles made us a cohesive group. A system of support. A family.

In the end, some of the other riders were surprised that we made it into the finish and voiced this opinion. Jim Red Cloud seemed astonished but also proud. "I didn't think you'd make it. We tracked you pretty close just in case." I didn't know how I felt about this. Clearly Jim didn't know how stubborn I was. Regardless of how surprised they were, people were there for me. There were so many people at the finish cheering me on. It was amazing that there were people involved that were willing to stay up that late to welcome a rider in. There were people there that if they had the time off they were there to say who's coming in next? I mean there were some really awesome people. Even non-motorcyclists came by to say what's going on and were impressed.[44] And I just remember at the very end meeting up with my friend who had the breast cancer and her whole family and everyone crossing the finish line. And I remember getting there and going like, "Is it over? Can I turn around and do that again? I'm not done. I'm so full of energy. I'm ready to go again." That was the most awesome experience of my life, and just seeing the excitement that all of that was done for her.[45] I was really proud to have done that for her, and to exceed the expectations.

So I wasn't just riding this ride for my own benefit. Sure my integrity was on the line but all of those people were relying on me. I was their role model, their hero. I know a lot of the folks that cheered me on may not have felt the hero part or just did it because, but I'm one of those folks that doesn't like disappointing people. It was really tearing me up inside that I even thought that I would disappoint the gal that called me a hero.[46] I didn't want to let anyone down; like my boss, the owner of the dealership, has been extremely good to me and my husband. I couldn't do that to him. He was my sponsor.[47] They were counting on me. That little girl, my sponsors, my family were actually counting on me. I needed to finish for all of us.

As I rode through the country and realized even more that I was being watched, I knew I didn't want to let anyone down. I focused on riding the ride right. I had to follow the rules. I try and live as honestly as possible. I'm not gonna go and run like 150 miles an hour and tell them that I was doing the speed limit the whole time. That's just not how I work.[48] I ran into people who were usin' a GPS. And I was like, "Wait a minute. You know you're not supposed to do that." And they would be like, "I'm doin' it. I'm winnin' the money. And I'm doin' it." You would just shake your head and go, "Where's your integrity as a person? Gotta have big brother watchin' ya to make sure you're playin' by the rules?"[49] I just wanted to play by their rules.[50] There was one time when I needed to deviate from the rules and one of the Harley dealers wouldn't let us sleep outside. They got us a hotel. But we felt guilty. We felt like we were not only cheating ourselves, but everybody else. There is when we felt we lost our integrity. But it was forced; we had no choice. That was the challenge; it was to be OK with that, with those decisions that we made.[51] I guess I just want to be true to the challenge. To know that I did the challenge the way it was supposed to be done. And I did that. And I'll never forget that.[52]

So many people were cheating. I mean these guys who have someone talkin' in their ear and tellin' 'em turn by turn what to do, that isn't the Hoka Hey. Those front-runners, those people that give a copy of the directions we received to somebody and somebody tells 'em what to do, they might as well put on a blindfold, too.[53] It was frustrating to see so many people before me at the finish who I felt had cheated. I didn't really get to gel with a whole lot of people at the finish 'cause I did the whole route. Not everybody did the whole route that year we did it. Which was a little frustrating. 'Cause you're like, "Aren't I doing well? I'm not sleeping a lot. I'm making ground." And people were like, "No, there's tons of people ahead of you." 'Cause people were cutting off stuff. And they didn't do the whole thing. And it made you feel disappointed.[54] I came in around 100th place but how many of those people who came in ahead of me didn't do it the right way? That was one of the frustrations.[55] But I upheld my integrity. I followed the speed limit the whole time. I wasn't racin', I wasn't ridin' like a crazy person. You know, I was just doin' my thing and I was doin' it the way that they explained it needed to be done. You know, to the best of my abilities.[56]

I picked up with groups and left them as we continued on the road. A few times I even had to help the guys I was riding with. I helped people with directions, sometimes people followed me. I found that group of fifteen guys that didn't know where they were at or where they were going. And so they followed me in. That first checkpoint was when they followed me in. And it seemed like every time after that I had at least one guy following me. 'Cause he didn't know where he was going.[57] Then there were some scary times that I thought people were going to lose it. There was another guy in front of me and he almost went off the road in Yosemite. And I was so tired I couldn't wake him up and you know again, you feel like you have to take care of these people. Anyone who's around you're going to try to help him.[58]

It's all over now and I've had some time to think about the experience. For me it was a personal challenge. I didn't need to cheat. I had my own goals. I wanted to finish.[59] I needed to finish for myself. It's only fun, I think, to challenge yourself a little bit. Set that bar up a little higher, stretch yourself out a little bit further, because at the end of the day, you're going to pat yourself on the back and you're gonna say, "Wow, look what I did."[60] With the endurance rides, it's a competition. And it's a competition not only with myself because I want to see what I can do. It's a competition against other riders and saying, "OK, I've passed that person a couple of times and we're leap-frogging. I've got to figure out something different so that I don't see that person again." Except maybe they cross the finish line and I'm on the sideline waving them in. A little bit of competition. But I focused on the relaxation, enjoying the ride, enjoying the experience instead of on winning. I'm going to do my absolute best.[61] Ride your own ride. I guess that sums it all up. Don't feel pressured to do anything when you're not willing to push yourself. Don't let anyone push you into anything. That's when it gets scary, and people get hurt, and things like that. I think it's important that you ride your own ride.[62] There was no trying to prove anything. It was just something I wanted to do. And it was one of my top five best experiences.[63]

I was very determined to not quit.[64] While I knew I was out of the challenge for the money, I needed to be in it for everybody else. I needed to not give up. So I did what I had to do.[65] Even when it was tough, I kept going. I don't know if it's just all the experiences you go through. You know, being scared and tired and then on your last limb. And wanting to quit, but you can't quit. But you just push on. You have to finish.[66]

Feminist scholar Carol Gilligan describes the ethic of care as influencing women's decisions and actions whereas men in her study indicated a more self-fulfilling decision and action strategy. An ethic of care is when one considers others while making decisions and taking action. No longer seeing yourself in isolation, care-based feminism encourages women to think about their choices in context.[67] Women with an ethic of care were raised to be less selfish and think of others first. Promoting the ethic of care and creating a connected web through and because of the Hoka Hey, women challengers see themselves not as athletes in isolation, but as taking on a challenge which is gendered, personal, and always in relation to those around them. For example, women who consider participating in the Hoka Hey ask themselves how their participation will affect their families, friends, and supporters. The ethic of care extends through women's internal struggles to justify participation in the Hoka Hey, as well as their motivations to participate and their external desires to perform well. Further, gender roles and social conditioning, as exemplified through an ethics of care, transcend their performance in the challenge and push women toward empowerment. As the composite narrative above shows, women riders use intrinsic motivation to perform an ethic of care through riding for a cause, incorporating spectators and family into their rides, and enacting caregiving on the road.

The women interviewed for this project describe the Hoka Hey as an intensely personal experience. We had the support of family, friends, and other riders, which drove us to aim high and take on this massive challenge. We competed at various levels but all strove to do our best because people paid attention to our ride, and consequently, to us. We felt compelled and obligated to do our best. It felt as if our families, our friends, our sponsors, and the people we were riding for were relying on us to achieve something great. This sense of intrinsic motivation—motivation extending from within rather than externally—transformed the challenge from something to win into something to accomplish in order to improve ourselves. Other female athletes rely on similar forms of motivation when fueling their desire to perform.

A recounting of a swim early on in Lynne Cox's career exemplifies this mindset and motivation. In her 2004 autobiography *Swimming to Antarctica: Tales of a Long-Distance Swimmer*, Lynne Cox details her life of outdoor distance swimming, her motivations for success, and her tribulations in achieving her goals. In one particularly affecting passage, Cox details a group swim in her early career. Swimming with a group of two boys and another girl, Cox's words show a sense of inner turmoil tearing her between finishing first and finishing together as a team:

> For nearly thirty minutes, I treaded water, staring at the California coastline. I wished they were faster. I wished we could break the record together... "Let's just finish now,"

Andy urged. "Look, she's not that far back. She will be here in only a few minutes. Remember, we wanted to do this as a team," I said. "I can't wait any longer," Andy said, and Dennis joined him. I waited for Stacey and swam with her to shore. (54–55)

While Cox could have easily continued to swim ahead and win the channel swim, she chose to say behind with her teammate. This source of intrinsic motivation—her desire to finish as a team and honor her word—triumphed over any desire to perform well individually. This episode reveals the different social conditioning of girls and boys as Cox's male counterparts swam ahead without thinking about their teammate lagging behind.

Like Lynne Cox, the women interviewed discussed a level of personal connection they view as different from men's experiences. Specifically, many women describe their motives differently than men's motives. They believe many men enter the competition only for the money; a number of women cite men who quit the challenge after they learned someone else finished and won. Although some men may enter the challenge with the intent of winning money, not all enter with this objective. While "everyone rides for their own reason" is a common sentiment in the Hoka Hey family, meaning all reasons for riding are equally valid, the women interviewed see their motivations for riding in relation to others. In rider meetings, it is clear that some riders participate in the Hoka Hey for Pine Ridge, because they love to ride, for bragging rights, or for the money.

A heightened level of self-esteem comes in part from the way the women view the competition. All of the women interviewed discussed the event as a personal competition rather than a competition against the other riders. Here, a non–Western competition style allows "winning" to be viewed not as the singular person(s) who win prize money but rather as what each individual achieves. Entering the challenge with a different competitive mindset enables women to truly ride their own rides and not worry about others on the course. Rather than focusing on winning, challengers focus on finishing the route. Measuring success on finishing rather than winning mimics sport literature regarding ultramarathons. Maylon Hanold's essay, "Beyond the Marathon: (De)Construction of Female Ultrarunning Bodies," shows women who compete in endurance sport focus on completing the course rather than coming in first. As Hanold suggests, this "creates a distinct category of distance running," much like the Hoka Hey emerges as a distinct type of motorsport, emphasizing an alternative competition model (173). While this competition structure affects all challengers, women challengers internalize their success as relational to their supporters. Although some women did mention traditional competition, they later mimicked the personal achievement statement in part because of their follower's support.

It is not easy to separate yourself from others while participating in any competition. Like any foot race or other event, Hoka Hey riders constantly compare themselves to others (both male and female) while on the ride; however, when reflecting after the event (such as when I conducted these interviews) it is easier to say you took your own pace. Had I conducted the interviews with each participant during the challenge, their comments about the competition may have varied. Eden's comments about leap-frogging with other competitors exemplify this sentiment. Although Eden's final words were that of a personal competition, the idea of competing against others is present. Likely, this feeling existed with other female challengers as well. Embodied femininity and socialization can lead to a competitive, yet supportive, sport environment. Specific examples from endurance sport suggest this sense of socialization toward communal competition. In endurance and lifestyle sport, some women assist one another in creating communities based on their marginalization (because of their disavowal of Western conceptions of competition which praises only one winner). For example, in the 2009 New York City Marathon, winner Deratu Tulu constantly encouraged world record holder Paula Radcliffe to complete the competition after Radcliffe sustained an injury. While Tulu ran past Radcliffe at the finish, Radcliffe's ability to stay with the lead pack came directly from Tulu's encouragement and support. Similarly, women runners encouraged one another during the difficult conditions of the 2018 Boston Marathon. Battling cold temperatures, rain, and wind, Desiree Linden became the first American woman to win the competition since 1985. However, throughout the race she encouraged and stayed with fellow American runner Shalane Flanagan because she know how important the race was for Flannagan. While Desiree pulled ahead in the last five miles, the women encouraged one another to perform their best like teammates rather than the individual competitors they were. These examples show collaborative competition and women's collaborative spirit in endurance sport.

None of the women interviewed indicated they were in search of a long-distance motorcycle challenge when they chose to participate in the Hoka Hey. Although each individual story varied, many discussed how seeing some small advertisement drew them to the Hoka Hey. They describe their initial experience with learning about the Hoka Hey as destiny. While you can explain these experiences as happenstance or productive marketing strategies on the part of the challenge operators, the women did not describe them as such; rather they attributed their entrance in the challenge to a series of connected events. The level of personal connectivity with the event increased because none of the women felt they sought out the challenge.

Many of the women challengers describe how the Hoka Hey "found them," further exemplifying the ethics of care through disassociating themselves with a specific decision. Rather than seeking a challenge that would affect those around them, they explain their participation as something out of their control. This sentiment rang clear throughout the interviews and stands in stark contrast to other riders who were drawn to the large winnings purse in the 2010 ride. Seeing themselves in contrast to men explains a gendered perspective to their desire to participate. Although most riders share common goals and passions, a division exists between those who are in it for the money and those who are not. Because women extended their web of connectivity to those outside the ride, they found more value in staying in the ride.

Starting with their initial decision to participate, many women made the challenge personal. The personal connection to entering the Hoka Hey builds on Roster's work regarding motorcycling as a leisure activity. Roster explains women often enter motorcycling after a major life-changing event. She states "feelings of self-renewal and confidence associated with riding seemed to fortify these women's inner strength and helped them to regain control over their lives following a significant self-altering experience" (451). While Roster discusses women who began riding for the first time, this project looks at women who have ridden motorcycles and have now entered a challenge. For some women, such as Junie or Wendy (who entered the Hoka Hey after experiencing cancer and becoming an empty nester, respectively), the change from leisure activity to competition/challenge reifies this sense of empowerment and motivation to participate.

Supporting the personalized nature of the challenge, women often enter competitions for different reasons than men. Constantly told that women are lesser competitors than men, some women have been socialized to transform their desire to enter competitions from winning to personal improvement. This is evident in Joanne Kay and Suzanne Laberge's discussion of lifestyle sport. Kay and Laberge discuss this alternative sense of competition as relevant to the lifestyle sport of Adventure Racing. In their discussion of women's views of success, Kay and Laberge note that

> ... the majority of women indicate that although the teams, which achieve high competitive ranking, occupy more powerful positions in the field, a "successful" race—for them—is one in which their team worked together. Women, accordingly, demonstrate a relative privileging of teaming over toughness by valuing participation over competition (162).

Here it is clear that some women value community and personal success over competition and winning (intrinsic over extrinsic motivation). Perhaps this focus on personal success allows for the level of stress associated with the competition to naturally decrease, thus allowing for increased focus on personal performance. The simple change in competitive mind frame from "I want to win" to "I want to improve myself" is significant and can have a large impact on an athlete's, or rider's, experience.

Hegemonic masculinity and femininity coupled with sport discourse reifies women's inferiority and contributes to the socialization process through which women are conditioned. "Gendered Social Dynamics in Sport," Vikki Krane's work applying social identity perspective to sport, suggests group identity can reinforce the masculine center of sport or more positive team environments. In other words, the group itself determines the positive or negative dynamic. The use of social identity perspective in relation to gendered experiences in sport shows that social conditioning influences group dynamics. The way we are treated as men, women, athletes, or motorcyclists influences the way we participate in a collective. By applying this model to other sport literature, we see that women are socialized to participate in sport differently than men, resulting in alternative models of participation and competition. Through this process, women are socially conditioned to participate on teams and compete with notions of traditional femininity in mind, encouraging nurturing environments and downplaying one's individual achievements for the good of the group or team. Notions of traditional femininity condition women to form inclusive conceptions of competition, whereas individual competitive nature evokes masculinity and is valued more within the sporting world. That is, as women we are socialized to understand our achievements communally—being attributable to the team—while men are conditioned to believe that their athletic successes are based on individual accomplishment.

While women are socialized to be less competitive than men, this form of hegemony is not always internalized. Competition does not rely solely on gender; this socialization can be used as a technique to marginalize women within sport. Krane suggests that group identities form in part through the identification of marginalized groups, such as female athletes. Positive group dynamics and unity can come from mutual experiences of exclusion or marginalization by creating positive environments in response to negative experiences elsewhere. For example, female motorcycle riders may choose to create a positive atmosphere of support in women's riding groups if the larger motorcycling community treated them poorly or ostracized them. Women on the Hoka Hey commonly cite using positive experiences and depending on sources of intrinsic motivation to succeed.

Women challengers spoke of the Hoka Hey as an experience that was both multilayered and relational. They see their participation in the Hoka Hey not only as personally important (i.e., they were intrinsically motivated) but important to various social circles, including their family and friends, communities of other women and riders, and the larger causes for which they ride. These layers of connection weave through their motivation to ride, their desire to perform, and their resulting empowerment and awareness. Women's social conditioning to perform an ethic of care constantly informs these layers of connection. While some feminist scholars argue an ethic of care reinforces women's traditional gender roles as caregivers and can be oppressive, I understand such care-based feminism to be a strength which should be promoted for both men and women.

Each woman found a personal connection to the challenge. However, women's motivations to participate in the Hoka Hey differ, ranging from riding for a specific cause to riding for others who chose not to or could not ride. The composite narrative earlier in this chapter highlights the differences and similarities in women's motivations. Each finds a source of intrinsic motivation that drives her to perform and complete the challenge without regard for winning. The one Hoka Hey woman warrior who emerges from the amalgamation of the women's voices speaks to the deep relationships women forge with fellow challengers, supporters, and themselves. The Hoka Hey was a personal experience for the women riders interviewed during this study. Overwhelmingly, they describe the ride as a personal challenge in which they seek to better themselves rather than to win money. Additionally, through their expressed ethic of care, they felt a sense of obligation to family, friends, other riders, and onlookers who took interest in their ride. Because women riders saw this challenge as a personal experience in relation to others, they felt as if they needed to participate in the challenge in a certain way. This sense of duty upheld their integrity and morals throughout the challenge. Further, the women who rode, regardless of their success in the challenge, felt a sense of personal interconnectivity with themselves, other riders, and sometimes a higher power. They described the challenge as changing, or greatly impacting their lives.

A translation of the feminist ethic of care, participants saw themselves as riding for a cause and thus extended their care to those they supported outside the ride. Here, the motivation to ride and connection to a cause came from within and was informed by the women's consciousness as women, spiritual beings, and survivors. Because the challenge started as personal, the women's connection to the event, its cause, and the people involved only grew. This aligns with research regarding cause-based marathon runners. Karin Jeffery and Ted Butryn's study, "The Motivations of Runners in a Cause-Based Marathon-Training Program," indicates runners' personal connection with a cause increased their motivation to train consistently (312). Likewise, women who rode for a cause in the Hoka Hey indicated the cause was a motivating factor of their success. Seeing themselves as part of something larger (both the cause for which they ride and the Hoka Hey itself) motivates women riders in their performance both before and during the challenge.

Riding for a cause illuminates the women challengers' ability and desire to promote social awareness and work toward social justice issues through their participation in the Hoka Hey. A feminist ethic of care weaves through this intention as women strive to create change and awareness for others through their actions. A study of young girls' leadership aspirations conducted by Emilie Zaslow and Judy Schoenberg contends helping others engage in leadership roles motivates girls and women more than boys and men (104). Further, the study shows that girls are more inclined to participate in volunteerism whereas boys are inclined toward political leadership roles (104). The emphasis on volunteerism shows a commitment of time as important to girls and women. This mirrors the women challengers' desires to volunteer their time, talent, and treasure to promote social justice through the Hoka Hey rather than their desire to create change through other avenues. While political leadership and the Hoka Hey both engender traditionally masculine qualities, the added social justice aspect and group mentality of the Hoka Hey position it as more feminine than political leadership. The women who rode the Hoka Hey for causes not only took time to complete the challenge, but also took additional time to engage in public service and fundraising activities for their causes. Media representations and social structures encourage women and girls to help others through their natural and learned abilities. Seen here as the ability to ride a motorcycle across the country in a nationally publicized event, women take action to support social justice issues. However, in order to participate in the challenge, they engage in more feminine learned skills and behaviors.

Additionally, riding for a cause highlights the women's class status. Their feminist ethics of care empowered them to make a difference by choosing a cause for which to ride. In turn, this reinforced their socioeconomic status; rather than simply giving money, these women had to give time and talent to raise funds for their cause. As discussed previously, many of the women involved in the Hoka Hey are not weekend warriors with disposable incomes to ride only for leisure or view their motorcycles as status symbols. Rather, many challengers ride motorcycles as a form of primary transportation or rode motorcycles for transportation in the past. While someone in a higher socioeconomic class may be able to afford the ride without fundraising, these women (along with many other riders) require assistance to participate and support their cause. They worked hard to raise enough funds to participate in the ride and to give back to their cause. The altruistic action of fundraising strengthens women's community connections and motivation through their ethic of care but also reinforces their class status.

Further, the women interviewed relied on traditionally feminine ways of raising funds and awareness. These women were not selling scrap metal to ride (as my dad does); rather they relied on their trained, gendered knowledge base to raise the money. As the composite narrative in this chapter shows, one woman made pink bracelets and another made and sold muffins to raise money. These traditionally feminine skills (making jewelry and baking) highlight the ways these women's gender performance transcends the male/female binary. They rely on their learned femininity in order to perform the masculine task of competing in a motorcycle challenge. Because they were women, their gender led them into kitchens to learn how to bake; however, their own personal interests brought them into the motorcycling world. They utilize their acculturated femininity to support their gender nonconforming interests. Again, this shows the fluid gender performances women riders and athletes engage in.

The women riders viewed themselves as completing the challenge for personal reasons—a cause, personal growth, etc.—rather than money. In part, this is due to the level of personal commitment and dedication women faced while overcoming the many difficulties on the ride. However, as the women spoke, it became clear that they also felt connected to the people with whom they came into contact through fundraising, the ride itself, or elsewhere. The women felt a sense of obligation to the family, friends, and supporters who followed and assisted them with their rides. This feeling began during the early phases of the Hoka Hey when the women raised funds and advertised their ride.

Interestingly, some women perceived their participation in the challenge as selfish. This happened most often with women who have children. Many of the riders who have children associate a sense of guilt with either riding a motorcycle or participating in the Hoka Hey. The societal pressure women feel to care for family permeates this selfishness. Because women are thought of as primary caregivers, they habitually give their time to others thus making the act of taking a long solo journey seem like a selfish endeavor. This is the explicit extension of an ethic of care. Seeing themselves strictly as mothers, understanding how their choices may affect those around them, and making choices based on those thoughts exemplifies the feminist notion of care-based ethics.

Not only does this feeling of selfishness arise because women must leave their families for an extended period of time, it also materializes because of the level of risk involved in the event. The thought of leaving behind children because of their "selfish" participation in a motorcycle challenge seems like negligence to some of the women. Women who had children or grandchildren at the time of their interviews but who did not have (grand)children when they participated in the event listed their (grand)children as a reason they would not participate in future challenges. The personal and social obligation of rearing children directly affects women's participation or feelings about participating in the Hoka Hey. Women overcome their guilt because their families support their endeavors. After hearing their children, parents, or partners support their desire to ride the Hoka Hey, they see the event as less selfish.

The sense of duty and obligation the women feel extends into their desire to perform well during the ride. The feeling that people are watching them profoundly affects their ride and begins during the planning stages of their experience. Many of the women feel as if people rely on them to ride and complete this challenge. While there are little to no consequences of how well any woman performs during the event and it is unlikely that supporters' perceptions of the women would change, the personal connection and social obligation women riders feel toward supporters makes them want to do their best and succeed. This desire to succeed and perform builds on the body of literature surrounding other gender nonconforming athletes. I point here to Ruth Chananie-Hill, Shelly McGrath, and Justin Stoll's work on female bodybuilders, "Deviant or Normal? Female Bodybuilders' Accounts of Social Reactions," which describes athletes' reactions to fans. As the scholars state, "admiration puts pressure on female bodybuilders to maintain a hard, lean, muscular body year-round, in much the same manner as men" (823). This desire to maintain a toned body even during off season is similar to women Hoka Hey challengers indicating a desire to perform to the best of their ability and with integrity. While it may seem contradictory to previously discussed notions of women seeing themselves as different than men who ride the Hoka Hey, this shows the subtleties of women's gender performances in that women's desire to perform at consistently high levels is informed not on their desire to perform for themselves but for and because of their fans. These pressures produce an athlete/fan connection that reminds athletes they do not compete in isolation, thus reinforcing their ethic of care.

Compounding this personal obligation is the small number of female Hoka Hey participants. Women feel the pressure to succeed increases because so few women ride. In a sense, the women riders feel as if they are riding under a microscope; there is no opportunity to become lost in the larger sea of challengers. The women interviewed feel like (and often describe themselves as) role models, not only to their supporters but also to all women riders. The added weight of being a role model for current and future women riders forces female challengers to alter or monitor their behavior. Again here, Chananie-Hill et al.'s work on female body builders applies; they show encouragement from fellow bodybuilders increases women's participation in the sport. Their findings indicate "without such subcultural encouragement and support, along with fan adoration and positive audience feedback, it is likely that fewer of the women would have chosen to enter the sport" (824). As these gender nonconforming athletes feel like role models and encourage others to participate in the sport, they subsequently feel a deeper sense of obligation to supporters, future athletes and riders, and other subcultural participants.

While swimming across the Cook Straight in New Zealand, endurance swimmer Lynne Cox used the young girls following her swim as motivation. In her work *Swimming to Antarctica*, Cox states,

When I started getting really discouraged, the paddler had me swim close to the lead boat so Keith Hancock could tell me what was happening. He was elated. "A Girl Scout just called in from Nelson. She said to tell you to keep going; she thinks you will make it. A farmer called in a minute ago from Christchurch; he said to send you his best wishes. So many people are calling, Lynne, to wish you their best. You've got the entire country of New Zealand pulling for you" (137).

Here we see Cox as a role model to the young Girl Scout. Being a role model in this sporting context pushed Cox to continue swimming.

Similarly, Zaslow and Schoenberg's study of girls' motivations to participate in civic engagement activities points to the gendered nature of this experience. The scholars point to studies in which seeing other women participate in civic engagement draws other women to such activities (105). Citing how much "exposure matters," the scholars note that it "is difficult for girls to be what they don't see" (105). To this end, women motorcyclists act as role models for young girls to try empowering activities such as civic engagement (riding for a cause) or motorcycle riding. The women's understanding of the impact of their actions speaks to their affirmation of exposing themselves for the good of others. Knowing they are role models for girls motivates these women to perform differently than they might otherwise. They are cognizant of their ability to create change and affect lives through their riding, which informs their gendered participation. Although the riders may not describe themselves as feminists, their actions speak to a feminist agenda to create change and work toward gender equality.

Despite feeling like role models, a position associated with prestige and power, some of the women riders downplay their own importance. This occurred when they stated they didn't see themselves as "different" and they thought anyone could do what they did. These comments seemed to be fleeting and were often inserted in an obligatory manner. For example, a woman would indicate that she was not special; however, upon further contemplation or after describing a particularly difficult portion of the course she would say that what she did was in fact impressive or that not all motorcycle riders could endure the extremities of the Hoka Hey. The initial urge to downplay one's achievements may be a result of women hearing repeatedly over time that they are inferior in some way. For example, women are less likely than men to promote their own achievements in the workplace; here we see this same tendency extended to their leisure activities. Alternatively, this points to women's social conditioning to perform femininity and thus not boast, as boasting is not ladylike or polite. However, the women did eventually admit that they were perhaps special, indicating an increase in self-esteem and empowerment after completing the challenge.

The social conditioning of women to feel a sense of obligation to friends and family drove women to challenge themselves on the ride. For example, one rider, who dedicated her ride to a friend battling breast cancer, vowed that she would not complain throughout the entire challenge as a tribute to her friend. She felt that complaining about being on a motorcycle, regardless of the conditions, would be disrespectful to her friend who battled cancer—presuming any Hoka Hey conditions pale in comparison to cancer. Devoting the ride and feeling a sense of obligation to her friend enabled this challenger to view the ride differently than other riders. While her friend or other riders may not have known that she was complaining about the ride, her personal dedication to her friend and the ride allowed her to overcome many of the mental roadblocks on the Hoka Hey. Often male riders told women riders that they were not likely to finish the course and in some cases even friends and family doubted the women's ability. When someone doubted the women, it often increased their desire to complete the challenge and subsequently increased their confidence by "proving" themselves or proving others wrong.

The women were surprised and humbled by how many people were watching their ride, following their social media outlets, and cheering for them. Some women associated the feeling of surprise with sentiments about their own unworthiness or lack of importance. For example, many women stated they could not believe anyone would pay attention to them. They downplayed their importance as a women riders and female athletes. The support from family, friends, the public, and other riders in addition to technological applications of the challenge made the women hyper-cognizant of their own actions. Because online GPS software tracks riders, there is a feeling of constant surveillance. The support they felt created a Panopticon-like effect on the women. The Panopticon is a power structure described by Foucault as a circular prison, which creates an illusion of constant surveillance and leads inmates to police themselves. In Foucault's Panopticon, the prisoners in the jail cannot see their captors but are relentlessly aware of their ability to be seen. In much the same way, while no one watched the women of the Hoka Hey at every minute, they felt pushed to do their best for and because of their growing fan bases watching from home.[68] The "I don't want to disappoint anyone" mantra rings clear throughout the interviews and supports the notion of normalization or performance through the perceived surveillance.

In part, women's sense of obligation to others drives them to participate in the challenge with the utmost integrity. They speak in detail about needing or wanting to follow the challenge rules while others violated the rules and state laws or simply cheated. Women are taught from a young age to behave themselves, act appropriately, and follow the rules. Many women internalize these messages, which transfer into decision making, work ethic, and leisure activities in their adult lives.[69] Women on the Hoka Hey made decisions about their participation with an air for morality and emphasis on how each decision would affect the people around them. The women describe how cheating would not only be cheating themselves but also cheating their supporters. This demonstrates how a feminist ethic of care and intrinsic motivation push the women toward success.

The issue of cheating is an almost constant topic of discussion among riders and followers of the Hoka Hey. The amount of cheating that took place on the ride disappointed the women interviewed, showing their emphasis toward morality and a feminist ethic of care. They scorned other riders who used the assistance of GPS or personal navigators, they scoffed at the idea of removing road signs, they bemoaned those who left the challenge after hearing someone else had won, and they largely were ashamed by the notion of needing to win so badly as to disgrace a personal reputation. When speaking of cheating, the women regarded some of their male counterparts as cheaters and never brought up the idea that women might cheat as well.[70] For these women riders following the rules was more important than winning. For them, the intimacy of the challenge drove them to be true to themselves, to the ride, and to their support networks rather than the solo mentality ascribed to men. The gendered experiences faced by women force them to disassociate with this typically male attitude and show the struggle women athletes face when executing their gender performances.

Despite the tendency to find solitude, riders also find a deep community in the Hoka Hey, as competitors do in other extreme sports. For many athletes, this juxtaposition between independence and community is part of the appeal of extreme sports. Those who rode with others described their relationships as being an important factor in their experience. For example, some indicated that their riding partners often challenged them but that these challenges led them to be better people or more connected with their partners. This speaks to a feminist ethic of care through understanding their ride in relation to their riding partners. On the road, women who rode together or with others did not view themselves in isolation. Rather than seeing themselves as an individual rider, they spoke of not wanting to abandon male riders or specifically providing care. Debby's experience riding through Yosemite in the composite narrative above speaks to this caregiving on the road. The women assisted with directions, kept riding partners awake, and assisted those in need. This specifically speaks to a care-based ethics promoting thought processes in context and in relation to others around them. Women's caregiving while riding a motorcycle and participating in an endurance challenge further complicates their gender identities. While women may not have wanted to assist other challengers, they felt a pull to do so. Women are not the only riders to practice aspects of caregiving on the challenge. Male riders also help one another, but the women specifically spoke about their duty to give care to the men and viewed this as a different experience than male riders.

Women's intrinsic motivation and ethic of care align with hegemonic femininity. We expect women to have emotional reasons to participate in any event. We expect women to help others. We expect women to put others first. However, because the women immerse themselves in the masculine environment of the Hoka Hey, they enact masculine traits. The women found retaining traditional notions of femininity important perhaps because of this masculine environment. Neither feminine nor masculine traits are better than the other. The women of the Hoka Hey show that blending gender expectations creates a holistic and positive sporting environment. Because they are able to perform in a traditionally male environment and retain aspects of their feminine identities shows the need for interpretations of gender that fit outside the male/female binary. These female athletes become more complete people and competitors because they can engage in fluid gender performances. This sense of wholeness in turn leads to the female athletes feeling empowered.

5

I Can Do Anything
*Finding Empowerment
Through the Hoka Hey*

We were real *women riders. We were different. We completed the Hoka Hey. And we were endurance riders. Not everyone was like us. Not all women riders were like us. We rode more like men. I think it takes a lot of endurance, to do it to the degree that we do it. I mean anybody can pull their bikes out of the garage on a sunny day and ride up to the next town and have dinner and then come home. Put it away and polish it. That's not really what I am.*[1] *Because not everybody can roll like that. And ride like that. Not everyone can ride like that, I'm sorry; we are special people. Not everyone can ride like that.*[2] *Yeah, I can't imagine Stubby, or even Larry, or most of the guys we know ever doing the Hoka Hey. Their riding technique is just so.... They'll go like fifty miles and like that's it, they have to stop. And I'm like, "Fifty miles, that's like nothing."*[3]

I came back from the Hoka Hey and did a trip to Ocala, Florida, for one of my nationals. It was like 1,100 miles with my husband. And we said, "Ah, let's Iron Butt it." And we got there in twenty-two hours. And then you know everybody was like, "Oh my god!" And then they took pictures when we got there. But it was nothing. It felt like nothing. You know, we would take motorcycle trips before and my parents lived, live in Tennessee. So we might do six hundred miles split that over two days. Now when we do a trip, we do no less than seven hundred and fifty miles in one day. And we're out for seventeen days at a time. Every ride has become an endurance ride.[4] *It averages three to four hundred miles a day if we do go out for a ride.*[5] *Last Saturday we went to Daytona for lunch. So 611 miles round trip for lunch is a typical ride.*[6] *For my 50th birthday, I'm going to be doing Highway 50 from Oakland, California, to Ocean City, Maryland.*[7]

Because we can't always find people to ride like we do we often ride alone. Solo riders. Just us and our bikes. "I'm a lone rider. Because pretty much no one rides like we do." Perhaps it's more of a longing for the Hoka Hey brothers and sisters and a sense of pride from being able to conquer the road alone? Eden, Jane, Schatzi, Kelly, Bryana, and Jersey Pearl all said the same. They were solo riders. As Eden put it, "[I ride] solo.... It's very rare that I ride with anybody." Tristica rode by herself, too, but said it was because "I don't necessarily like riding with a bunch of people." Maybe she would if they rode in her style. Some of us create and seek out (un)willing riding partners. Sheila comments, "[I ride with] myself. Now, I have a dog that rides with me, Trixie." I have my dad. Debra has Stan. Wendy has Bill. But those were Hoka Hey people. They can handle riding like we ride. I can't imagine riding alone. I don't ever like to be alone. Sheila lamented not having someone else with whom to share her ride, "And it's nice to have somebody to share it with; but it's hard to find somebody who's able to take off for that amount of time and all that." Maybe they didn't prefer to ride alone either, stuck between wanting to go the distance and not finding someone to share the miles with. Simultaneously lonely and never alone, tough and soft, both sides present.

We mark our riding by how long we've been on the road. How many years our butts have been in the saddle. A total of over 350 years of riding, many of us since before we could drive. The length of time alone speaks to our passion for the road. How could it not be part of our identities? It's all we've known. We also mark our riding by how hard we ride, how far. Riding is a celebration of our lives.

As we stood that night after the challenge in the parking lot of our hotel, shifting from side to side and stretching our road-worn butts, the tenderness in our muscles reminded us that not all of the challenges were external. Some battles happened within our bodies and our minds. We feared for our safety and grimaced with sickness along the route. Tristica emerged from her motel room freshly showered for the first time in days and joined our late-night conversation, "I got sick when I got into the Yukon. It was only like thirty degrees. I wasn't able to like hold any food down at all. I had to have my friend Jim help me actually put my kickstand down sometimes when we stopped. I was like really, really sick; I couldn't get warm."[8] Carla nodded her head in agreement, "I didn't anticipate having you know, the swellingness that I had. I'm used to riding in heat. And you know I consumed a lot of water and I was seeing a neurologist and a chiropractor prior to going on this and the one thing that they did forget, the biggest challenge was using up electrolytes when you're not moving."[9] Grateful for surviving the race, we stood from our chairs and hugged one another, offering support to those who faced the most physical challenges along the way.

We hadn't all been sick, but we all experienced physical strains and fatigue. Eden piped up from her seat, "Oh, the challenges! Sleep deprivation, that was a tough one."[10] Debby agreed, adding her perspective of how sleep affected her body: "When you're tired, you don't see real well. Like tiny, like especially a map. I had no idea that would happen. And I didn't know why everyone had these magnifying glasses. So I learned a lot about when I'm tired what happens to my body. I can't read. Which is frightening. Because you're like, 'Oh my God, I cannot read my map. And I've got to follow these directions.'"[11] Carla overwhelmingly agreed, "You know, the challenge I was experiencing there towards the end was keeping awake after day seven. Your body does some really strange things to try to put you to sleep when you don't want to.[12] And oftentimes I would just pull over and I would literally sleep with everything on. My helmet, my gloves, everything."[13] I didn't think it was possible to fall asleep while riding a bike. But it is. It was scary when you realized you were doing it. Jane chimed in with a tale about riding into the finish this year, "It was when we were coming in I was literally—and it's the first time it's ever happened to me—falling asleep and waking up. And I know I had to have been going like this—" She waved her hand in an S pattern indicating a large serve, "—and I'd have to slow down. I can't imagine what it was like for Schatzi to be behind me."[14]

The mood lightened again as someone broke the awe-induced silence to ask how many times everyone almost ran out of gas. Sheila discussed the benefits of her new Ultra Classic, her "big girl bike," over her previous ride, "Right. I mean, it's better to start out with a full tank than sixty miles down, yeah, sixty miles down you don't need it for another hundred. But now, I can go a hundred and sixty. So it was interesting. And you know, there were times where, I mean, I never ran out of fuel, but I was amazed at how far I could go, you know. 'Cause new bikes they don't have the reserve like the old ones; they just have the little light that lights up and you need fuel."[15] We could laugh about our gas scares now. But it wasn't so funny when we were on the road. Carla transitioned from discussing the bikes to one close call with gas, "I just reached deep inside of me and prayed. And several times on the Hoka Hey I prayed as I was riding my bike, and I said 'Give me an answer, help me out of this.' And before I knew it, there was the answer. I was up on a mountain path and I had been riding with my gaslight on forever. I know how much we can get off that bagger. And I was thinking, 'I'm gonna run out of gas out here. And it's gonna get cold.' And it was getting late, it was around four maybe five o'clock and the temperature was going to start dropping, it's going to start getting cold. That's the last place I want to be. And I come to a T in the road. And I go, 'Gosh, please give me a gas station,' and I look to the right—"[16]remnants of nervous laughter break her sentences"—Down the road not a quarter of a mile was a little gas station in the middle of nowhere. And I was like, 'Oh my God, I'm so happy! That gas station!'"[17] Tristica mimicked the excitement of finding a gas station. She threw her arms into the air as she articulated her near miss, "I was riding on fumes. I had to have been. There was nothing left in my tank. I put the nozzle in there and all I heard was just empty. You know, it was like echoing."[18] Knowing well that sound, Jane agreed, describing a fill up on the Pine Ridge reservation, "I had a five-gallon tank and I put 5.5 gallons in it. I had some guidance getting me there, too. I was sweating it. 'Cause there was no gas station for the longest ways."[19] We all had a story about siphoning gas, praying for gas, or just barely making it into a station.

We paid our bills and stumbled wearily out of the corner diner toward our bikes. Lighting them up one more time, the familiar roar of our iron steeds sounded like the voice of a comforting friend. We returned to the motel where most of us were staying before we left town. The star rating system failed to start low enough to accurately describe the accommodations; we sat outside in plastic lawn chairs provided by the establishment and continued recanting tales from the road. It seemed as if this conversation would never end; we didn't want it to end and we had enough stories to last a lifetime. The conversation moved on to the challenge of the directions. We commented that part of the difficulty was reading the directions from a piece of paper while riding a motorcycle. Junie, our most decorated woman warrior, described how she dealt with the directions on her first Hoka Hey, "I was havin' a lot of trouble readin' the directions. I didn't have anywhere to mount them on my bike. And that was a big struggle."[20] She went on to describe the plastic bag she kept the directions in and how she sat on them while riding and only pulled them out from under her when needed. Amazed at the proposition of not having a place to store the directions, Jane responded, "Yeah. No. They'd blow away! Yeah, I took mine the first year and put them in a zip lock, but folded them. And you know, taped them on my windshield. But I can't imagine. I'd lose them under my seat!"[21] We agreed in astonishment. Despite thinking that we were well prepared, none of us seemed to have anticipated what to do with the directions. Jane continued with the story of her first year, "I'm always the leader when we do rides, but I never have to read a map. 'Cause I know all the roads around where I live. So I can just do it. Or I can write something big. And we get out there, and I wear glasses, but I don't need them to ride so I never wear them when I ride, I just bring them and put them in my suitcase and we get the directions and I'm like, 'Schatzi…. I can't read these and ride.' I never thought about it. I was like, This is a problem.'"[22] But Jane figured out her problem with the glasses, just as Junie figured out her problem with the directions.

Debby reiterated the challenge of not knowing how the directions would be written, "I didn't actually anticipate the directions the way they were. That threw me. I'd never done anything like that, I'd never done a turn-by-turn rally ride or whatever they call those. So I freaked out a little bit the first day. I sandbagged in a sense. I just hung back to the very back. And I'd just follow people 'cause I had all my maps all confused. 'Cause it was tiny little roads and you had to read directions while you're riding with all these people around you. And they were just going crazy. And that threw me. So for the first day I just kind of followed people."[23] Bryana agreed that the directions were difficult at first, "After the first day I was able to sit down and go 'Oh my gosh, this is what

I need to do.' And, you know, I sat down with their turn-by-turn directions and I bought a state map of where I was at that had better interstates, and I was able to map it out ahead of time before even getting on my bike after getting the directions."[24] Most agreed that maps were an essential secret to attacking the directions; some of us had learned the trick faster than others.

Sheila pulled a chair into our circle and joined the discussion saying, "I thought the directions were really contorted and people had taken down road signs. I mean it was just kinda silly.... But you know, my sense of direction was good. So it was like, 'I can see, even though the road sign isn't there, there's a T in the road. I don't want to go south. I want to go north here. So, I'm just gonna go north and see if the next direction appears.'"[25] Voices rang out in agreement, Sherie's the most prominent, "Finding directions was difficult sometimes. I mean not all roads are marked and so you had to find new ways to figure out where you were and how to find the roads."[26] We nodded in agreement at the frivolity of removing signs from the course and applauded the commonsense approach to the race most women took.

If the directions were difficult, the roads were just as tough. As the night pressed on we discussed construction, road conditions, and the constant drain of riding through mountain after mountain. While riding the challenge in the summer brought more favorable weather, it also meant riding during construction season. Jane and Schatzi spoke about their first challenge, "Yeah, the first year we were riding on our pegs. Going through construction sites. In the dark. With cones, trying to figure out where the road was. 'Cause the bridge was out or something."[27] Schatzi agreed with her riding partner, "Yeah, the construction, oh my God, the construction sometimes we went through, thank God it was at nighttime 'cause I didn't want to see what I was going over. Then you had to go in some spots, you had to be there by 10:00pm or your opportunity was gone until the next morning."[28]

Jersey Pearl agreed that the roads were particularly challenging, "We were on roads that had no right to be called roads."[29] Bryana described a particularly difficult road condition and new-to-her phenomenon she discovered while riding through Canada, "Up there on the Alaskan highway when it snows the ground freezes and then when it defrosts the asphalt creates these heaves basically. So there's like a twelve-inch drop along the whole entire span of the highway for, you know, a quarter-mile, half a mile, twenty feet, like at random spurts. You don't know if they're in front of you. But if you go too slow you'll totally hit the wrong one and you'll fall over. It was intense. My bike took a beating. I have to redo the whole front end. I remember hitting those going, 'OK, I have to ride 'em like a dirt bike. I need to put my butt up on the back seat and just haul butt across 'em.' And you know, I remember catching air a couple times. The drop was just so intense."[30] The laughter and excitement in Bryana's eyes as she spoke made it clear that she was having fun despite the conditions. We compared which roads we thought were worst, their names monumentally infamous: the Moki Dugway, the Alcan, Arkansas County Road 22, California Route 4, the Tail of the Dragon, Iron Mountain Road. One woman summed it up well: "There were some back roads. I knew they were back roads. But my idea of back roads usually has some kind of town or something usually within like, fifty miles."[31] We all laughed as another contender for worst road emerged. Sherie said, "It's called the Moki Dugway. And it's like, you know those lovely high plateaus you see in Utah? It went up the side of one of those doing, you know, switchback turns. And it was like a gravel road almost with a little bit of pavement on it with gravel in the corners. There were no guardrails, no berm, no anything. It was just wide enough for two cars."[32] Debby agreed but added another contender, Iron Mountain Road, which we rode on when we went through South Dakota, "It's this big spiral and it kind of spirals up and it's like mountain, bridge, mountain, bridge, and I had never heard of this before. It's very famous but I had never heard of it. And then it goes through these really narrow windy roads, like almost single-track paved."[33] The thought that we had just ridden every difficult road in the country back to back amazed most of us. Most riders do one of these difficult roads as part of a larger ride; no one is crazy enough to do them all together except us.

Although our circle began to dwindle, several of us stayed outside the motel, building on one another's stories. This was the only time we would have a group of people who actually knew what we went through, knew what it was like. The Hoka Hey was so difficult to describe to other riders and even more difficult to describe to non-riders. If you weren't there you just didn't get it. It's so hard and so amazing at the same time. We savored the knowing laughs and recanted tales from the multiple days of technical riding. Junie shifted the conversation to the "twisties," those hairpin, figure 8-like switchback turns through the mountains that challenged us every day: "They were tough. I mean the second year when we did the 48 states we were in those twisties for 10 days. I never wanted to see another mountain again."[34] It seemed impossible that the course designers could ever find these roads let alone know how to connect them in a way that seemed artful, elegant, and inspired. Having ridden the same ride as Junie, Schatzi agreed, "We were doing all those turns, it was like, give me a straight away, please!"[35] Junie continued and exasperatedly rubbed her arms, "I mean my arms were so tired from the twisties. That I just…. I literally just … pulled up to a stop sign and my arms would be shaking. Because we were just constant … all day, all day, all day."[36] Schatzi's riding partner Jane confirmed the pain of that ride, "That was like a person with arthritis. It was crippling."[37] Crippling, yet they had all come back for more. This was not their first Hoka Hey. Though some of us were experiencing this unending pain for the first time, these veteran riders knew the pain would soon subside and in its place would form a yearning for the next ride.

One by one we gradually left the circle for the comfort of a bed. The soothing warmth of a hard motel mattress was coming to some of us for the first time since beginning the challenge. It didn't matter how horrible, hard, lumpy, or scratchy that motel bed was, we were about to enjoy the first night of actual sleep we had had in weeks. Those few days after the ride were the most bittersweet days we could fathom. Filled with laughing, storytelling, one-upping, and congratulating, they felt like a continual celebration of life and our recent accomplishments. As we staggered into our rooms, drunk off the high of the ride, we thought of more stories to tell tomorrow.

It wasn't just the difficulty of the ride itself that made the Hoka Hey such a challenge. Rather, it was riding at that same level of exertion day after day that made it seem almost insurmountable. Bryana described this as one of the differences between the Hoka Hey and other rides, "Just the fact of having to get up, took me twelve and a half days to get here, so twelve and a half days of making myself get up and ride and ride and ride as opposed to just getting up and just going for a quick put then coming back to reality. To actually live in that, and experience that for twelve days straight was a pretty awesome contrast from everyday riding."[38] The pace also made the ride different. This was no relaxed trip, and the time frame made the challenge more difficult. It is a challenge against yourself, after all. Junie's years of experience confirmed Bryana's sentiments, "It's not like a leisurely pace. You know you have to make some time to get these miles in. To get from point A to point B. I think that in itself creates a little tension, a little stress. You're riding a little bit more pressured than you are a leisurely weekend trip."[39] Debra agreed and mentioned the added pressure of having a riding partner, "I'd be wantin' to take it all in and just look. And he'd be sayin' 'Come on! Come on! We gotta go. This is a race, not a pleasure ride.' And I'd just be sayin,' 'I'm takin' it all in!' You know? I'd never seen this beauty."[40] Then we lamented the pictures we didn't take, the things we didn't stop to see, the things we only could have imagined we rode through in the darkness of night. The thought of the quick pace of the trip contrasted starkly with the heavy eyes we felt at the time. This time we didn't have to snap ourselves awake; there was no screaming, singing, or gum chewing to fight the fatigue. The pace of our conversation and our thoughts could slow down, but didn't. The excitement of the ride still pulsed through some of our veins, too alive to sleep but wanting to crash again at the same time.

But it did feel amazing to be at the finish line. Oh, that was awesome![41] People came out to see me. The other women were there and so were the people in charge of the challenge, and a few other riders and people who didn't even know me. And the attitude in Alaska was a lot different than the reception at the beginning of the race. I mean I did make it up to the finish. There were only 12 women that were in that race. 763 people. And I know that myself and Jersey Pearl and a couple of other girls were the only ones that actually got up to

Alaska. It was pretty cool.[42] *This one woman waited so patiently just to have her picture taken with me.*[43] *I could tell I was an inspiration to some. I think everybody needs to step out of their comfort shell on something. If I don't inspire them to ride a motorcycle I hope I'm inspiring them to follow a dream.*[44]

It makes you feel good.[45] *And it's an ego booster, handling a good-sized motorcycle.*[46] *But, finishing the Hoka Hey has really changed me; it makes me feel stronger as a woman. Exactly. Stronger. It makes me stronger as a woman.*[47] *You find out just how strong of a person you are and what you can endure. And to me it wasn't all that hard, other than just tryin' to stay awake.*[48] *It made me feel so good, but there's nothing special about me. The other women are amazing. Stories that I hear about Eden, and Junie, and Carla, that's amazing. What I did to me, is not, it's amazing for me.*[49] *And riding a motorcycle, it's something that I feel enables women to feel confident in themselves. Feel stronger.*[50] *Just thinking about all the things that I participated in and I accomplished them by myself was a really neat thing.*[51]

I did the Hoka Hey by myself.... And it was a really neat decision. 'Cause I just had a wonderful time doing it.[52] *I figured I'd always want to be with people the whole time. But it made it more clear that I like my independence.*[53] *I actually could get on a motorcycle and feel like I was accomplishing something. For me. Without anybody else interfering and saying, "Oh you need to do it this way. You need to do it that way."*[54] *The independence that I had to show in going through some of those areas, not giving up, the perseverance. I mean I could have given up at any time. But I was not going to do that. It was never an option. If I had managed to break something, like a leg, then yeah maybe I would have called help. But I found the independence, the perseverance, the strength of character, willingness to do more than what I had ever expected of myself.*[55] *You really start diggin' deep in your soul and um learning about yourself.*[56]

Junie Rose (left), Abby Van Vlerah (center), and Jim Van Vlerah (right) at the HHMC finish line in the Seneca Nation. Women riders waited at the finish line to cheer on other women riders. (Courtesy Wendy Battles.)

"I thought it was just awesome."[57] *"I had so much fun, man. I did. Yeah, I've got stories to last a lifetime."*[58] *It was an adventure. "And I was like, this is*

going to be outrageous! You know, heck of a great ride. The 48 states, and two provinces in Canada, and the roads we went on. Some of the roads I don't want to do again."[59] It proved to be outrageous. That first day was fun! *"That first day out you know you've got all that momentum. You're really well rested, you know. Because you've been sitting at the hotel for two days waitin' to ride. And you're ... you're ready. You're pumped."*[60] As we looked around the parking lot, we realized that not only had we had fun and found an adventure, but we met some amazing people.

I was a newbie on the Hoka Hey. Overcome with bravado, I thought I had it all figured out, I mean how hard could riding your bike for a few days really be? "Hard. Really fucking hard, you dumb ass," my voice, now wiser, rang in my head. That was before the ride. I quickly realized that I had a lot to learn and I had no clue what I had gotten myself into. After speaking with the women at the finish line, I understood that there were many things I still hadn't figured out on my own trip. It really was unbelievable, the whole thing. I heard Tristica's thoughtful voice in my head, *"I think there was over 600 that started and only just over 100 that made it all the way, so. You know, a lot of people did drop out. I felt really good when I made it up there. Made it the whole way, too, we never went off course or anything."*[61] I was proud too. Just as proud as Debra when she said, *"It's just something."*[62] Other people are proud of us, too. Sherie's husband always tells everybody "She was the first woman solo finisher in the Hoka Hey." Sherie was the first solo woman to finish,[63] and that's something to be proud of.

I'm proud that I got out and did something for once. *It's something you know you want to do in your lifetime I guess. Even though it has its challenge, and some of it is dangerous and scary, I still wanted to do it.*[64] *You get the rest of everything else, all the clutter, out of your mind because all you've got to do is ride and think and focus on what's on your mind. You know whatever happens to be on your mind at that time. Just to kinda clear yourself from all the hustle and bustle, all the stuff that's going on and just embrace life. Because at any minute it could be over. It could have ended for me on any one of those three rides at any given time.*[65] *So I got out and did something, otherwise you're gonna sit around and just spend your life dreamin'. I didn't wait to live my life.*[66] And I enjoyed it.

Once I came back, people asked me everything. What was it like? Had I learned anything? Would I do it again? Would I do it differently? Did I have any advice about the ride? Sometimes it was hard to put into words exactly what I meant or how I felt. Because for me, *it's the most amazing thing by far that I have done in my life.*[67] And I would do things differently. And I did learn things. And I would do it again. It gave me time to think. When you're on your bike for so long like that, your mind has time to work. And I think women are always thinking of four different things at once and multitasking in their heads.

And I think men can ride mindless. I think they just enjoy the moment. That's one of the things I've learned while motorcycling is to just enjoy the moment. And to leave everything behind. And so now when I ride it's just a really comfortable feeling and I'm just enjoying the moment and I'm not thinking about what I'm going to do next week or next month or anything like that, I'm just participating in a moment in time. And I think men tend to be able to do that easier than women. And I think I've learned how to do that being on a motorcycle.[68] It was just amazing to me now after doing the Hoka Hey—the new freedom. Less stress, just me and the bike. And I'm calmer. My kids say I'm calmer. I'm a high stress person. And it has calmed me down.[69] Looking back maybe it was all personal. I didn't do it for anything other than me. And that might be selfish that I needed it in my life. And, I found something. I can't tell you what it is. But I found it. 'Cause I'm happy. I'm at peace. I love my life. I want to wake up in the morning. I'm not grumpy and old and grouchy anymore.[70] And it's been a growth. It's allowed me to grow in ways that I hadn't planned.[71]

I didn't anticipate any of it to be as spiritual as it was.[72] I grew up Catholic and had to go to church and do that whole thing but that's not my realm of life anymore. And we had someone watching over us in more times than one. And I really felt that presence. And I felt blessed.[73] Sometimes at night we'd be zoomin' through a city or somewhere and I'd be prayin', "Lord, Lord, I need you now! I need you now. Just get me out of this."[74] I had a couple of spiritual awakenings on two mountain passes. I do have an open heart. I guess I don't know if you want to say it's to spiritual things. Someone once told me that you have to have an open heart to experience those. And I had three spiritual awakenings I guess is what you'd call them on this ride. I was up on Route 12 and just out of nowhere enjoying the ride and watching the sun come up and beat off the mountains and the next thing I know I'm in tears. Something reached inside and touched my heart and it was the most wonderful experience I've ever had in life. I can't explain whether it was a spirit or whether it was God or whether it was someone that I loved that passed on. But it happened and it happened three times. But I truly believe that you can have spiritual awakenings. Which is something that I didn't maybe buy into a hundred percent prior to the Hoka Hey.[75] Some of it felt weird, odd. I prayed more but I also felt spirits.

One night when I was really in a bind, I had run off the road. I couldn't get out of this ditch. Then the old ones came to me and they told me that there were watchers everywhere and that they were watching us. And that they were taking care of nature and they were keeping us all safe and everything. And they revealed themselves to me and there were two of them down in the ditch. And you know the way the leaves twitch or the ears of the deer or something, and nature protects animals by mimicking them. This is odd. Anyway, they came to me and they told me that they would protect me, and that I was on the right path, but that I had to choose the right path and stick with that path.

If I did that then I would be ok. And so it was all about committing to your path in life. And doing, being committed, and trying to not go back the way you came but choosing a path and going forward. And I realized that in order to get my bike out of the predicament I was in, I had to find a path and stick with it, basically. So I walked down into the ditch and I figured out where I could go and everything. It was kind of like a metaphor for life actually, like finding your path and being committed to it. I actually had to drive my bike down into the ditch and turn around and drive it back out in order to get out of the situation; because I couldn't back up and I couldn't go forward the way I wanted to. So I had to take the path that was best. And from then on in the ride, every time I saw any type of animal, they wouldn't run across the road in front of me. A big elk or a big dear would be just standing on the side of the road and it would stand and watch me. All through Montana, I would see animals and they would be right there and they would stop and watch me go by. And it was kind of odd. I've always felt since then that I've always been protected by the watchers. I don't know how that works but it was weird.[76]

We rode through places that were imbued with spirits—a Japanese internment camp, countless Native American sites and battlegrounds, the Trail of Tears. You don't really hear about those things a lot so to be able to go ride past some of those places, the energy from those places was amazing. Even though you weren't stopping and like taking a tour and like getting the history, you could feel a change in the energy even as you were riding by them.[77] *Every different place brought its own story and its own, you know, revelation of who I am and what I was doing there, and the true purpose of the Hoka Hey and what it was really meant to show people. And to prove to people. And to teach them. And how for granted a lot of it was being taken.*[78] *When we got into the rider's meeting in Florida and Jim Red Cloud started pouring his heart out to us and telling us about his people and I mean just. He was actually crying. And he said, "What did my people do to deserve to be treated like this?" The whole no water, the birth defects because of the contaminants on their land, and just the whole thing of how the Indians have been treated so badly and it was something that took my heart. It turned the focus of the ride to something so much different.*[79]

I think we take a lot for granted. I knew the Hoka Hey was for the Indian reservation, but I never really knew what existed at the reservation until I went to Pine Ridge. And that really opened my eyes. And how the Indians are living and how they're being treated. And the conditions they live under. I mean I kinda had an idea. I know, 'cause I know what's going on in the world. But it's out of my element and I don't really pay attention to it. And then when it was right in my face when we drove there, wow. That really woke me up.[80] *There we were on Pine Ridge, at the Chief's house. Meeting Chief Red Cloud was really an honor.*[81] *We went to the Chief's house and he lived in a trailer with I* don't know how many other people.[82] You think the chief of a nation is going to have a manicured home. It wasn't. Very humble.[83] But they're so poor, no one is really doing anything about it. And it's not easy in Pine Ridge. The weather in the Dakotas can be hot as heck in the summer time and cold in the winter. It's extreme. We get very spoiled.[84] They're part of us. They're not aliens. They're legal. They were born and raised here in the States. So why are we treating our own this way? Granted it's an Indian reservation but we put them where they are today. Our ancestors did this to these people. And it was wrong. I'm learning a lot about it as I go on. Each time I have some involvement with the Hoka Hey I learn something new.[85]

Entire books exist on women using motorcycles as vehicles of empowerment. Liz Jansen's work *Women, Motorcycles, and the Road to Empowerment* follows women riders and discusses their journeys toward self-actualization. Much as this work suggests, Jansen notes, "riding fulfills a psychic need for women and gives their masculine energy an outlet" (11). This duality she contends, leads women to feel empowered. Similarly, sports are an area in which women drive themselves to feel confident and strong. Vera Koo, champion target shooter, modestly describes her feelings of empowerment in her memoir *The Most Unlikely Champion*:

> Following my win, and after seeing my photos in the magazine, I actually felt pretty good. Sport shooting had built up my self-esteem and self-reliance. I'd achieved something that people said wasn't possible (98).

Koo's use of the word "actually" indicates an element of surprise at her feelings of achievement. Her sense of accomplishment extends from breaking gender expectations and thriving in the masculine world of sport (and more specifically, sport shooting, which men dominate). Similarly, Hoka Hey riders spoke to finding empowerment through riding alone, completing the challenge, overcoming physical challenges, connecting mind/body/spirit, and finding community.

After completing the Hoka Hey Motorcycle Challenge and reflecting on the obstacles they overcame, the women who participated in the Hoka Hey felt a deep sense of accomplishment and empowerment. This resulted from facing the many challenges of the Hoka Hey and successfully achieving their goals. The sense of accomplishment from completing the Hoka Hey follows them from the finish line into their daily lives. They feel pride in what they achieved and subsequently people around them feel proud. By taking on and overcoming the many challenges faced along the ride, women find an increased self-worth. The personal success felt through the Hoka Hey enables women to look fondly on their experience and return for more.

As Catherine Roster explains in her article "Girl Power," the empowerment women motorcycle riders find through riding comes from "developing new knowledge and skill sets" (456). My study confirms and builds upon Roster's analysis of female motorcyclists. Women who rode the Hoka Hey specifically found empowerment through developing their motorcycling skills. While Roster contends that these are new skills, this study suggests that women also find empowerment from perfecting or improving upon already established skills. Using their abilities at a heightened level affords women the same positive feeling of empowerment described by Roster.

The bodily effect of the Hoka Hey stays with a rider long after her finish. I recall speaking with Carla prior to my first ride as she discussed how she cried for days after she returned home, a bodily response to releasing the emotion and fatigue of the trip. I failed to appreciate fully the drain on the body she described until after I experienced it. Sport cultures equate pain with success; the adage "no pain, no gain" represents this phenomenon.[86] While riding the Hoka Hey, challengers normalized pain by continuing to ride through sickness and fatigue. Expressed by the descriptions of the pace of the trip, the desire to complete the ride in a given time frame taxes challengers mentally and physically. While challengers listened to their bodies by engaging all their senses (for example, smelling animals, the air, or even burning brakes or tires), they ignored signs of pain and fatigue to continue and complete the challenge during the given time frame. Again, we see a breakdown of oppositional forces with the normalization and overlooking of pain. No longer is the pain/pleasure binary solidly in place; rather, the challenge reminds participants that bodies are constantly in flux.

When initially hypothesizing about this work, I imagined that women's high tolerance for pain (as anecdotally indicated through their ability to endure childbirth) might contribute to their success in the Hoka Hey. Surmising that women may stay in the competition despite injury, soreness, and fatigue, it did not surprise me to hear the many stories of such things expressed during interviews. However, sport scholars link the normalization of pain with hegemonic masculinity, not femininity (here I point to Markula, Pringle, and Sabo). In particular, Don Sabo's work "Pigskin, Patriarchy, and Pain" describes how the "pain principle ... stifles men's awareness of their bodies and limits [their] emotional expression" (450). In the Hoka Hey, women's association with accepting and enduring pain pushes the boundaries of what we consider feminine. Women riders embody female masculinity by pushing through pain to become successful. However, as Carla's discovery of a congenital heart defect indicates, women will listen to their bodies after the challenge to recover effectively. This attunement to their bodies shows an emotional growth which Sabo places in opposition to sport masculinity. By first ignoring then listening to their bodies, women riders dissolve the masculine/feminine dichotomy. Because they embody both the traditionally feminine characteristic of listening to their bodies and emotions and the traditionally masculine experience of pushing through pain, the women challengers express both sides of the gendered experience. This dual role shows that a combination of masculine and feminine traits is welcome and necessary to succeed in this environment while also challenging the widely accepted notions of what is masculine and feminine.

In addition to the breakdown of the masculine/feminine binary, sport scholars point to bodily experiences as sources of empowerment. Physical activity leads women to feel good about themselves and engenders positive thoughts.[87] Because the Hoka Hey challenges women physically, it enables them to garner a greater sense of self-worth and to feel the direct impacts of their efforts by the strains on their bodies. By challenging their bodies to overcome fatigue and stress, women feel empowered.

For women on the Hoka Hey, the positive effect of the challenge is not limited to empowerment. Because of the elevated risk associated with the Hoka Hey challenge (including the length, distance, fatigue, and technical riding), challengers feel that they face death and emerge on the other side with a heightened appreciation for what they have. Sport scholars, such as Brymer and Oades, suggest that risk-taking is a major contributing factor to the possible positive transformations in extreme sport. In their article, "Extreme Sports: A Positive Transformation in Humility and Courage," the two describe the positive effects of risk, saying, "Participating at this level involves real fear and brings one in contact with nature at its most extreme. It is these points that act as frameworks for experiencing humility and courage" (124). Like other extreme sports, the Hoka Hey puts challengers in direct contact with fear and challenges them to connect with nature in a way that enables them to experience growth. For these challengers, the positive aspects gained—an appreciation for life, connections with their bike and fellow challengers, and accomplishment—outweigh the possibility for intensely negative consequences.

Linked to fear, expecting the unexpected became a common theme among women interviewed. The difficulties of directions, finding gas, and tough technical roads added to the overwhelmingly constant feeling of not knowing what will happen next. Challenge operators consciously construct difficult rides with long stretches between checkpoints and gas stations to test challengers' mental and emotional competencies. On the road, the women describe feeling vulnerable through being lost, sensing unease from contorted directions, and riding on unfamiliar back roads. Perhaps an (un)intended consequence of the challenge, the vulnerability felt by challengers links directly to the stripping of white privilege as well as other privileges such as economic and geographic.[88] While the challenge does not actually strip challengers of their whiteness during the ride, it removes them from comforting confines of the interstates, suburban landscapes, and GPS systems. The Hoka

Hey deliberately takes away power from white challengers and places it in the hands of Native American course designers. The frustrations felt by "confusing" directions (perhaps more accurately described as directions with which white challengers are not comfortable), difficult rides, and the solitariness of untraveled roads allows many challengers, not yet prepared to face their privilege, as an easy way to quit the challenge. Often, disgruntled challengers blame Native Americans' inability to write clear directions as prohibitive to their ability to complete the challenge. This form of racism stems directly from the systemic obliviousness to white privilege.

My personal struggle with privilege and power came a year after completing my first Hoka Hey, with the passing and funeral of Chief Oliver Red Cloud. The Chief died while we rode in the 2013 challenge and Jim invited Hoka Hey riders to participate in his grandfather's funeral. All riders received a mass invitation via text to "ride in the Chief's funeral." Not knowing what this invitation really meant, if Beth and Jim intended it for us, or if we were just part of an obligatory large group message, my family and I struggled greatly with how to respond to such an invitation. On one hand, I questioned my own whiteness as an outsider to Native American culture and wanted to make sure, if I attended, I was not just going to be a cultural voyeur or tourist. I felt horrible and riddled with white guilt as the "but it's a once in a lifetime opportunity" thought crept into and out of my head. Further, I questioned if I had enough time to take off work to ride to South Dakota and back for a funeral. I selfishly wondered if my time would be better spent writing. I questioned if it would be better for me to send money rather than show up. After all, funerals are expensive and certainly there were not stockpiles of cash on the reservation. I grappled with feeling like a failure, the "Great White Hope," and also wanting to support my Hoka Hey family. This was a deep internal and external struggle that seemed to last many days, though in reality only spanned about twenty-four hours.

A convergence of motorcycle and sport cultures in action, my desire to show up outweighed any other thought. Two separate events in 2013 demonstrated the desire for sport and motorcycle cultures to show support through presence. As displayed in marathons after the 2013 Boston bombing, runners showed support for those affected by the acts of terrorism by attending races and wearing symbolic bracelets. Similarly, in motorcycle culture, as exemplified by the 2 Million Bikers to DC event to support and remember those affected by the 9/11 terrorist attacks, presence is far more important than other supportive acts such as sending funds. Showing support and coming together is why and how we participate in races, rides, and rallies. In other words, athletes, like motorcyclists, show up. In the end, through my physical presence at the funeral, the experience of traveling to South Dakota deeply touched me. We were welcomed as family and invited to experience rich traditions and ceremonies. It was a transformative, spiritual, and meaningful experience.

This decision exemplifies the cultural exchange that happens so often between whites and Native Americans in the Hoka Hey. As a white woman, I entered the conversation thinking about what I could give back to the Native Americans when in reality I learned and gained a great deal from the Lakota on Pine Ridge. The invitation into the group ended up being far more beneficial to me than entering a culture as an outsider interested only in philanthropy. In this situation, our physical support meant far more than any monetary donation. On the day we grappled with going or sending money, we transformed from benefactors and apologists into people who seriously considered the wishes of the family and the tribe. Asking what they wanted, what is most respectful of their culture, rather than doing what we thought they needed, was a moment where our identities shifted in thought; doing the more difficult thing, traveling cross-country, was where we lived out that identity change. Here an ethic of care informed the decisions we made. We changed emphasis from doing what made us feel good and doing what was easy (sending money) to acting on the family's desires and on other cultural traditions (showing support in person). We thought relationally, eliminated the us/them binary, and extended our interrelated family.

As exemplified by my shift in identity, the choice to attend the funeral also illuminates the interconnected nature of motorcycle culture and the paradigm shift required to understand sport in a postmodern context. The interconnected web woven between members of the tribe, the Hoka Hey family, and the Chief's family were strong that day. Rather than thinking of how *we* could help *them*, we were part of an intentional assemblage and mixture of individuals coming together to heal and honor. Attending the funeral made us part of the larger collective. As theory in action, we embodied postmodernism, which emphasizes touch points of connection over linear hierarchies.

Emerging as a meaningful event, the Hoka Hey combines fear, pain, success, personal growth, and an examination of white privilege. The constant breakdown of binaries throughout the ride speaks to the transformative Hoka Hey experience. Be it pain/pleasure, masculinity/femininity, fear/safety, white/Native American, or natural/urban binaries, the women who participated in the Hoka Hey experienced a negotiation and reformation of self which reminds us that our worlds are messy, incongruent, and ever-changing. Regardless of their intention or realization, the changes and growths that occur during the Hoka Hey alter women's self-perceptions and awareness. These changes also lead to shifts in identities further reinforcing omnipresent change and fluctuation.

Perhaps most exemplary of the phenomenon of empowerment and ethics of care in the Hoka Hey is Nancy Theberge's exploration of women's empowerment through sport, "Sport and Women's Empowerment." Although only given a fleeting section in the larger article, Theberge describes how women's softball teams encounter empowerment through working as a team, altering their competition styles to match all competitors, and reconstructing their conceptualization of sport (391). The women she describes find empowerment by thinking of others, which I describe as an ethic of care. Thus, as in the Hoka Hey, women's empowerment in sport comes not only from a bodily expression of overcoming challenges or physical adaptation but also through an understanding of self in relation to others. Here teamwork stands in as a simple reference to empowerment. Because we work together and achieve a goal for the group, we feel better about ourselves.

Women riders often described their new Hoka Hey brothers and sisters positively; Debra felt welcomed and succinctly stated, "Everybody was really, really nice."[89] Junie also described the lasting effects of Hoka Hey relationships, "I hope that we can have some long friendships together. I think that's the best thing about Hoka Hey. It's all the people that I've met. I hope that the majority of them are friends for life. Because I think most of them are really cool people."[90] Another challenger, Jersey Pearl stated, "To actually grow to love these people. And there are many that I still talk with today. You know. Never had any idea that that was going to happen."[91] The connections we felt with one another ran deeper than waving to fellow motorcyclists. These connections were deep bonds of sisterhood felt only when you survive something so great and so difficult. This form of connection mirrors the connection felt by sports teams and leads to feelings of camaraderie and accomplishment.

Motorcycle scholars such as Catherine Roster and Liz Jansen point to the creation of community as a benefit of motorcycling as a leisure activity. As Jansen describes, when motorcyclists "find our clan ... we discover a common bond from which we not only derive strength as individuals but also gather that strength to increase the cohesiveness of the community as a whole" (10). The formation of a Hoka Hey family speaks to this group cohesiveness. Most women list this as a primary benefit of the Hoka Hey. Motorcycles themselves are reminders of the complicated interconnection between independence and group solidarity. While motorcycles often carry a single rider, they bring people together through the creation of communities. Many riders seek the independence and freedom felt by riding solo while yearning for the connected community of a family of riders. Motorcycle clubs, both outlaw and otherwise, have long built on this conflation. The motorcyclist, as an independent member of a family, symbolizes the inadequacy of the either/or option.

The small number of women challengers may increase the feelings of community among women riders because women find commonality as part of the minority group. While men and women both find community within the Hoka Hey family, the women group themselves as a community of riders within the larger community. For example, during pre- and post-challenge events, the women group together for photographs whereas the men do not ask for a gendered photo. Similarly, when I arrived at the finish of the 2012 challenge, Wendy and Junie met me with open arms. While there were also male challengers present at the finish, Junie and Wendy both noted a desire to come and support "one of the girls."

Similarly, social media and technology allow participants to remain in contact with one another after the challenge, allowing the benefit of camaraderie to remain in the forefront of challengers' minds. As technology often desensitizes us from human experience, motorcycling communities show a linkage of technology, community, and humanity as riders are not satisfied with online connections and remain rooted in older notions of connecting. For example, Junie describes the "befores and afters" as the most important parts of the Hoka Hey. These are the times in which community bonds form among riders while they spend time in person. Within this community, which leverages both social media use and in-person connections, the lines between impersonal and personal blur.

Although many of the women riders participated in organized sports or other endurance events prior to their participation in the Hoka Hey, they described this challenge as "different." The main difference between the Hoka Hey and other challenges was the endurance aspect of the event. Thus, the level of difficulty combined with the length of the event likely added to their increase in self-esteem. Additionally, the marketing of the challenge by organizers could add to the level of confidence felt by women. Operators market the challenge as "the toughest ride" for "the toughest riders on Earth" (Hoka Hey Motorcycle Challenge). Although self-appointed or an aspirational statement, this designation allows riders to feel they have achieved something other motorcyclists are not able to achieve. From a gendered perspective, this designation gives women an even greater sense of importance and empowerment. As mentioned by Tristica in the previous composite narrative, the small number of women riding spurs feelings of importance. Here, the othering of women creates a positive effect because few women ride motorcycles and very few women riders participate in the Hoka Hey. Difference is key to women's feelings of success and empowerment.

For these women riders, the Hoka Hey was an opportunity to push themselves and create independence. While many women rode with male or female riding partners, those who undertook the course alone spoke of the solo ride as accomplishing a separate challenge. These riders prided themselves on being able to complete the ride autonomously. Many women who did ride the majority of the challenge alone often rode in small groups at times. Further, they remained connected to other challengers and those watching at home through social media and at various stops. These women spoke of an independent spirit gained from finishing the challenge. As Ethan Rouen suggests in the article, "Taking It to the Limit," many challengers in extreme sports find "the actual moment of competition is a time of solitude" in which challengers are "competing mostly with self-doubt and fear" (55). While a large number of riders spoke of personal and inner obstacles throughout the ride, those who participated in the event alone felt impressed at the idea of finishing such a daunting obstacle alone. For some women riders, the Hoka Hey was their first trip alone, creating a greater feeling of accomplishment and growth.

Regardless of their riding partners, the women all spoke of learning more about themselves while on the Hoka Hey as they constantly battled self-doubt and fear on the road. The ride forced them to face their own shortcomings and celebrate their accomplishments. While being interviewed, some women volleyed between downplaying their experiences in comparison with other women riders and speaking highly of their own achievements. This comparison shows a need to remain humble and be proud but careful not to expose hubris. Again, a feminine gender performance keeps the women from being overly boastful while simultaneously feeling empowerment.

The ability to complete the challenge in the way they intended led the women to achieve a great sense of confidence and personal growth. While some women grew through seeing new parts of the country or leaving their comfort zones, others grew by increasing their self-esteem. Regardless of their individual motives, women left the challenge feeling better about their personal lives and their ability to achieve any goal. The most common response when asked "What did you learn about yourself on the ride?" was "That I can do anything." This exhibits a growing confidence and empowerment and mirrors the body of sport literature indicating women find empowerment from participation in sport. Theberge's 1991 article "Reflections on the Body in the Sociology of Sport" describes women's empowerment through sport as related to the physicality of a sport. However, the added relational connectivity though an ethics of care enabled women to feel empowered not only through their physical bodies but also through their emotional and spiritual connections to the ride. The interconnection of mind, body, and spirit present in the Hoka Hey shows women's holistic approach to sport. Women's participation in dragon boat racing explains the holistic nature of sporting activities for women. Diana C. Parry's article, "The Contribution of Dragon Boat Racing to Women's Health and Breast Cancer Survivorship," describes the interconnected physicality and spirituality of dragon boat racing as imperative to the success of women's health, survivorship, and participation in the leisure activity (231). In turn, this interconnection affects women's ability to feel empowered through their leisure activity.

Many of the women who participated in the Hoka Hey reached a higher level of spiritual fulfillment and personal growth from the challenge. This is not unlike the euphoria felt after participating in other endurance sports or the spiritual quests some who participate in lifestyle or extreme sport describe. Sports scholars such as Ethan Rouen and Duncan Simpson suggest that extreme athletes find a higher power or transcendence while competing in extreme sport in part from the solitude and physical challenge. While pushing their bodies and minds further, the women riders often found this higher calling.

The physical and mental taxation of the body and mind during the challenge mimics the transcendence of extreme sport. During the challenge, some riders feel as if spirits accompany them, that they see visions, or that a higher power leads them. This connection with a higher power, and seeing their experience in relation to another being, is an extension of their care-based ethic. Regardless of a spiritual encounter happening because of a gas scare, being lost, or being in an accident, riders prayed and sought council on the ride. Breast cancer survivors who participate in dragon boat racing similarly describe spirituality through sport. Again, Parry's article describes a connection between "dragon boat racing and spiritual awakening" as women "developed a new purpose in life through dragon boat racing and, consequently, a new commitment to life" (231). However, in regards to the Hoka Hey, it is unclear if this spiritual fulfillment lasted after the ride. Some women riders did experience visions; while they spoke of their visions in terms of spirituality, many also added that they were extremely tired or sleep deprived at the time. Attributing visions to fatigue rather than the presence of spirits indicates that not all women retained a higher level of spirituality. This could also be in part because of their discomfort or unfamiliarity with a different religion or sense of spirituality. Further, being in a state of isolation, as is typical on the Hoka Hey, could increase a person's inclination toward spirituality. Connecting with a higher power or visualizing beings is a common tactic to feel less alone.

The Hoka Hey was truly a transformative experience for the women interviewed. They not only grew personally by increasing their self-esteem, they also grew spiritually and faced their own privileged positions. The spiritual and personal growth achieved on the Hoka Hey by women riders is a direct result of their social conditioning and women's ability to create an authentic experience in which they were primarily concerned with remaining true to themselves and those who supported them. Although women may not express it as such, this desire for an authentic experience is informed by a care-based feminism. The women expressed an ethic of care because they saw the challenge and their participation as an extension of their larger networks of family, friends, supporters, and causes. Further, and because women already saw themselves always in relation to others, they felt a greater sense of empowerment.

The act of participation took women from being participants in a leisure activity to being challengers. Women's multilayered relational experiences informs their Hoka Hey transformation and extends from women's empowerment to become a part of the women's identity. As discussed in the next chapter, women's identity, spurred from empowerment, creates substantive changes in the Hoka Hey culture through both male and female participants.

For the women, who lean on each other during the HHMC, the challenge operates as a club. Roster notes that as women begin to join clubs or ride with others, they become part of the collective group of motorcyclists and create bonds and group identities (452). This same identity construction happens within various subcultures; speaking specifically to lifestyle sports, Wheaton investigates the relationship between collective identities, popular culture, and identity formation, stating, "Understanding how these social identities and forms of collective expression are constructed, performed, and contested, recognizes popular culture's significance as the basis of people's identities" (9). This mirrors Wheaton's work on windsurfers, in which she describes how "hard core" members of the culture "are extremely *committed* to one (or more) complementary activities, dedicating large amounts of time, money, and effort investing in a lifestyle and social identity" (9). As women become more ingrained in the Hoka Hey and motorcycle culture more generally, they assume this as a larger part of their social identity. As a lifestyle sport becomes part of a woman's identity, she becomes increasingly empowered through participation. A cyclical connection between empowerment and identity exist in which pride felt from accomplishment feeds the sense of identity and a deeper sense of identity further increases the desire for participation. In essence, if we do something that makes us feel good we want to keep doing it and identify with it. As such, these empowering experiences become markers of our identity.

Roster's 2007 work points to ways that riding motorcycles facilitates women's empowerment. One of her primary findings indicates women motorcyclists experience empowerment by entering the leisure activity after a major life-changing event. This can be seen in my research, with many of the women who participate in the Hoka Hey riding after cancer diagnoses, divorces, or becoming empty nesters. Junie's discussion of finding the Hoka Hey in the chemo room, discussed in chapter four, exemplifies this point. Likewise, Wendy connects her grown children leaving the house and her participation in the Hoka Hey. She states, "I was faced with the fact that, you know, [the] kids are gone, now what do I do? My kids think I was going through a midlife crisis" (174–175). For these women, the Hoka Hey served as a point of empowerment to reset their lives after traumatic or life changing events. The Hoka

Hey becomes an opportunity to (re)form or (re)claim parts of their identity. This builds on Roster's premise by showing that more intense or extreme riding can forge a deeper sense of passion, identity, and empowerment, leading to an increased sense of self-worth and appreciation for life. Women were more empowered to ride motorcycles, as Sheila says,

> I really have progressed as a rider and in my confidence and the Hoka Hey had a lot to do with that. Before I always followed my husband. We always rode how he rode. Rode at the speed he rode. I was parroting what he was doing to some extent. When I did the Hoka Hey I kind of learned how to find my own path and do things my own way. And it was really nice (98–103).

Later in the interview, Sheila expressed the empowerment she felt beyond motorcycling, saying, "I think I found out that I can rely on myself and I don't need other people to do things for me. That I can handle anything" (473–474). This independence resounds with warrior-like confidence. The ability for Sheila and other riders to extend empowerment beyond riding emphasizes the Hoka Hey as a meaningful and transformative experience, which in turn affects identity.

In part, the experience includes an identity transformation to becoming Hoka Hey warriors. Becoming warriors extends from excelling as a woman in a male-dominated environment. Women's success in a masculine space, such as the challenge, empowers them to take on the label of Hoka Hey warrior. A clear example of this can be seen in Carla and Wendy as they literally take on the warrior identity through their dress (Wendy wears a warrior patch on her Hoka Hey vest) and social media (Carla's social media page uses the name Hoka Hey Warrior Woman). Although not using the words warrior, all Hoka Hey riders use dress as part of our "becoming" rituals. In other words, as we become Hoka Hey Warrior Women, we literally change our clothes from nursing scrubs into our motorcycle garb. Here the motorcycle vests or cuts adorned with the Hoka Hey moniker embody masculinity in dress. As we transform into warrior women, that masculinity becomes normal or at least gender neutral. Beyond dress and gender presentation, the women interviewed state that the Hoka Hey itself can be a major life-changing event. From their comments, it is clear that confronting risk on the Hoka Hey gave them a deeper appreciation for their lives in a very literal way in which they appreciate their bodies but also as seen through identity reformation.

The composite narrative in this chapter not only shows these challengers as skilled motorcyclists, but also that they are confident enough to ride alone. Studies such as Roster's suggest riding alone is evidence of moving beyond traditional gender roles for women who ride motorcycles typically enter the culture through families or men. This sort of empowerment leads women to further their participation in the sport outside of social groups, families, or relationships. Because they have become skilled motorcyclists through rides like the Hoka Hey and spending considerable time on the road, they are comfortable riding alone and formulating an identity around being a motorcyclist. For example, Eden's desire to ride across the country for her birthday links her to motorcycling as an identity and shows her level of confidence with riding (stemming from empowerment). The relationship between empowerment and identity is cyclical. As Krane et al. describe, female athletes "feel empowered because of their strength and skill" and despite reminders that they were "not considered normal women, these athletes savored the benefits of their athletic participation" (325–326). As this sport research suggests, empowerment shaped identities as female athletes.

6

She's Got Bigger Balls Than Most Men, They're Just on Her Chest
Gender, Identity and Change

I walked into the rider party and fifty heads turned in my direction. Bearded faces hidden under dark sunglasses and scraggly greying locks. I felt their eyes drill into me and slip up and down the length of my body. The pushup bra layered under my tight white tank top made me feel confident, sexy, and powerful. I could hear them thinking, "There's nothing like a female riding on her bike." They think it's sexy. A woman on her own bike.[1] *Me on my bike. But I'm not like all the other women who don't ride. There are still so many women that are passengers and that are just like ornaments versus actually participants. There's just a big difference. Women are still kind of the pinup girl mentality. You don't see half-clothed guys at Sturgis, it's naked women.... It's still a man's thing.*[2] *That's why they're staring at me. Let them stare. They'll see when we're out there on the road. See that I'm different. That I ride like they do—a fast, nonstop, gun-it-on-the-straightaways, drag-my-bags, don't-stop-until-you-run-out-of-gas, Hoka Hey style—because I'm not just another pretty face. I sit down for the rider meeting, listening attentively to the instructions, all the while I can feel their eyes burning into the back of my head. I try to concentrate on what Beth is saying, but it's not working; thoughts from a lifetime of living in a man's world parade through my head.*

I have worked in maintenance departments, on construction sites, ran my own companies, and have been the only female in the game many times.[3] *The guys at work even know I'm more masculine than them. After all, I got my CDL license [commercial driver's license] and some of the guys don't have theirs. I think that's cool. Plus I have a Harley. And none of the guys at work have a Harley. And that intimidates 'em when I ride my Harley to work.*[4] *I'm not really any different than they are. I guess in a lot of ways I consider myself one of the boys. I've always put myself in fields with men; I've grown up with a group of guys.*[5] *When I think about being a woman riding a motorcycle, it really doesn't mean anything to me 'cause when I started, there weren't very many women riding motorcycles.*[6] *I've been doing this my whole life. I see myself as genderless. I'm my father's only son. So I guess I don't see myself as woman first. I see myself as a person.*[7] *Why do these guys think my gender matters? Why can't I just be a person?*

His massive arm, covered in tattooed, tanned, rough skin went confidently into the air. The older man with a white mustache and cap looked puzzled at the operators. His almost too unbuttoned shirt offered a glimpse of his strong pectoral muscles. He spoke with a thick east coast accent after Beth called on him. "Yeah. Uh. Is catheterizing allowed this year?" Chuckles and snickers arose from the crowd. *Seriously?! I thought as I shot a stunned, awkward look at my dad who wore a look of disbelief across his face. These people are fucking crazy.* He followed up his absurd question, "I know a lot of guys catheterized last year, and it is really an unfair advantage. Women can't catheterize themselves so the men shouldn't. It's not fair." *Holy shit, he's advocating for women's rights.* More chortles erupt from around the room. *Were those laughs really jeers because he stood up for the women or because the proposition of catheterizing yourself to ride farther sounded so crazy?* The two veteran women riders he sat next to spoke up, "We don't need to catheterize ourselves. We're cool." Beth chimed in at this point, offering a voice of reason, "If you think you need to jeopardize your health by catheterizing yourself then go for it." *The proposition seemed crazy but obviously had happened in the past.* After the meeting, I inquired about the catheterizing comment, choosing to ask the two women rather than their friend who posed the question. They explained the process to me. Men put a tube into a condom on their dicks, stick the tube down the leg of their pants, and pee as they're riding. *This actually happened! It wasn't a tall tale. They actually want to win badly enough that they pee into a condom, down their leg. I certainly wouldn't want to ride behind anyone who was going to pee on me. Gross.* More importantly, they explained that Tim, the man asking the question, rode with them for part of last year's ride and planned to ride with them again this year.

Jane started reminiscing about meeting up with Tim. She stared into the distance as if replaying a scene from a movie in her head, "So many times we'd meet up with him and say, 'You want to ride with us?' And he would say, 'No I was just riding with somebody and he was on my shirttail' and 'I had to do all the navigating. And they just followed. And so no, I'm not doing that anymore.' And then the next time 'Oh, I gotta stop and get a map' or the next time 'Oh, I'm stopping at a friend's house.' And we thought, 'OK, whatever, Tim.'" She threw her hands up in exasperation and continued, "So then the final time we were in Murfreesboro, and one time even when we got robbed we told him about that, 'cause we saw him in Ohio, in Columbus. And he felt bad, but he didn't ride with us that night. But then when we were in Tennessee we were all taking showers and he happened to be there. And we were getting ready to leave, and I said, 'We're leaving. You can ride with us. Join us if you want. If we go too slow, pass us, no hard feelings; but if you can't keep up, so long.' And then he never left our side." A roaring laughter sprang from her chest. "And then we got the name Thelma and Louise."[8] So that was it. They changed his mind about riding with women. Schatzi iterated my thoughts, "He rode with us. And he was like, 'Wow, you girls can ride! I actually don't mind riding with you.' And it was actually really enjoyable to have his company."[9]

When I asked if they thought they had changed his mind about women riders, Jane nodded her head and brought it all together answering, "We have a little bit. But I don't know if he puts that to every woman rider. He likes women riders. He has a few other women that he rides with. But I think before he rode with us and then he rode with us and he went back home and he talked to his friends, they couldn't believe he rode with two women. Could not believe it. I mean, he told us that several times." It wasn't just Tim, though. Jane noted others who they influenced, "Bubba, and Blackie, and Mickey. The three of them, we certainly changed, 'cause they came up on us one time in North Carolina. We were riding with Tim and they asked Tim at the stop light, 'Why are you riding with the girls?' And Tim said, 'Oh, 'cause they can ride.' 'And you let them lead?!' And Tim said, 'Yeah, we take turns. One will, and then the other one will, and then I will.' So then they go and we get to the next stoplight. 'Cause we were in a rush to get to North Carolina, Rocky Mountain, before they close. And the guys go, 'I know why you ride with them. They are the original Thelma and Louise.'" She boomed with laughter, the pride in the earned nickname roaring from her chest. After calming herself she continued, "So it changed their mind, too. 'Cause they were obviously thinking that women couldn't ride. Mickey was like, 'You girls ride better than the guys that I ride with back home.'" Their ability to ride had changed the minds of these large men. I knew Bubba and Blackie and Mickey. Nice guys. Salt of the earth. But I wouldn't exactly call them feminists. Maybe there's hope for them to be feminists yet!

As the rider meeting came to a close, a small crowd began forming. Photos taken. A picture of all the riders. Then a picture of just the women. The photo of the seven of us drew a large interest of novice photographers and cell phone cameras. There were far more than the anticipated seven flashes going off. We stood arm in arm, smiles plastered across our faces as more and more people came to see the women who ride the Hoka Hey. Girlfriends and wives of bashful male riders snapped quick shots and ran back to their beaus for approval. Everyone hoping they could sneak in a picture before we broke our stance. Zoo animals? Side-show freaks? Respected and venerated members of a motley family? It didn't matter; we were a spectacle. It's almost like they can't believe it. A woman could ride that far, that long distance. Eight hundred miles ... a thousand miles a day ... back roads. I think that really shocked a few people. And got them thinking. And I know they probably see it as 'A woman did that.' But we're riders here, we enjoy what we do.[10] The flashes finally stopped and we gave one another a final squeeze before heading our separate ways to make final preparations for the trip. One last hot meal, finishing touches on the bikes, making sure everything is packed as tightly and as efficiently as possible. Then sleep, one more night of sweet sleep (if we could actually quell the excitement building in our bodies) before the seven, eight, nine, or more nights of five-star parking lot and rest stop accommodations.

It's still early on the first day. We've been pushing hard and have almost completed the first page of the directions. It seemed like a monumental feat; but when you really added up the mileage we had only done about two hundred miles. It was a lot of short distances. We weren't covering much ground. It seems like this state will never end. As I stood at the gas station I pondered my own trip so far. I had done pretty well, considering I had only spent a few days combined on this new bike. Its weight still amazes me; it's so much heavier than my other bike. But that's probably all in my head. The guys I'm keeping up with haven't acknowledged me. Then again, we've mostly been on the bikes and haven't had a chance to really speak yet. Apparently I am "lucky" that they are riding with me at all, but it is early in the ride and groups were still pretty tight. It quickly went through the system that I was a newbie. And people didn't want me around 'cause I would slow them up.[11] But, I'm a very, very competitive rider. And they didn't want nothin' to do with me. Well, they didn't dump me at all because I wound it up and I hung with him through these twisties and everything else at 80–85 miles an hour.[12] These were some really aggressive riders. I felt really cool that I kept up with them on the mountain roads.[13]

Then I snapped back into reality as the gas filled in my tank. I turned my focus to the men I'd been riding with. I hadn't been listening to their conversation so far, just stuck in my own head. When I tuned in I couldn't believe my ears. They were veteran riders complaining about the directions being wrong. It didn't seem like they would be happy even if Beth rode on the back with them and pointed out all the turns. They were disappointed. They were frustrated. They were already tired. And nothin' tellin', I didn't have a problem. I pumped my gas and I turned around and I said, "You know what, wow, I've never heard more *pussies* in my whole entire life standing around a gas tank right now." I was like, "You signed up for this. You knew it was going to be an endurance challenge. You knew it was going to be a test. It wasn't going to be quick and easy and painless, they clearly stated everything. And you're going to stand here and bitch and complain about it. And we're only five hours into it. I'm glad I'm *not riding with you guys." And took off on my own.*[14] *I can't believe I just had to shame a bunch of grown ass bikers like they were children. Who's tough now? I climbed back on my bike, strapped on my helmet, and took off, watching them pick their jaws up off the concrete in my mirrors as I continued down the route. Maybe I didn't want to ride with those dildos after all. New friends to be found down the line.*

The small gas pump icon illuminated in orange on my speedometer. Shit. I'm in the middle of nowhere. Alone. Shit. Fuck. Shit. Should have stopped at that station even though I had just filled up sixty miles before. Dumb. My eyes scan the horizon for something, anything that might resemble a gas station, house with running water, or a store. Not seeing much I immediately lay off the throttle to conserve what little gas I had. Then, a clearing of trees down the lane, the soft lights of a kitchen window shrouded in old lace curtains offer hope and quicken my heart. Please Lord, let them have some gas, just a little to get me to whatever station is closest. I take the helmet off and just try to make myself a little smaller than I usually am. I slumped slightly and made sure I looked less intimidating than what I might appear at first—a nondescript leather-clad biker climbing off a Softtail Deluxe. I am short anyway, but I need to be less intimidating now. Less powerful. Less masculine. I can't believe I am walking up to a private residence; I don't want to be misunderstood. I'm not going to hurt them; I'm the vulnerable one. I don't want them feeling that. They probably will anyway. I knock on the door and am met with a confused stare from the woman who opened the door. As I begin to tell my story of the Hoka Hey, the Lakota, my empty tank, a small crowd emerges from different rooms of the house. The small girl looks up at me with bright eyes as her father moves to the garage to get me some gas. Thank God they were nice enough to help.[15]

Next day. Back with the guys. I pulled my bike onto the side of the road, following the large group of men. Jokes and comments about the heat immediately started to fly as I watched them unsaddle and stand with bravado, quickly whipping down their zippers. The sound hit my ears like a clap of thunder. I can feel my eyes growing wider, face stretching. I'm not at all alarmed at the thought of men relieving themselves in front of me. They don't have anything I haven't seen before. But as the rushing sound of urine hitting dirt blew into my ears, I could feel my bladder swell. Tightening in my stomach, feeling like it might explode out of my front rather than where it should come out. I have to pee. Now. Right now. I don't want to drop trou right here in front of these guys. I'll never hear the end of it. My eyes dart back and forth across the road and I see nothing but a vast horizon and low, scraggly grass. Come on; give me anything to hide behind, a bush, tree, a large rock. Nothing. Quick decision made, I dismount and cautiously walk behind my bike. I can use it as a shield. I squat low to the ground, feeling the intense pressure in my already tired thighs. I ease closer to the earth and my shield. SCORTCH! SIZZLE! OUCH! SHIT!

6. She's Got Bigger Balls Than Most Men

I jump, startled and scorned, into the air, smelling the pungent steaky smell of burned flesh. Any thought of needing to pee flies from my mind. Bit by my blazing hot muffler. Yeah, I burned my ass on the muffler trying to squat and pee so people couldn't see my fanny.[16] Lesson learned.

Another day. We pulled into the gas station thankful for the awning that alleviated some of the pouring rain. Despite the thundering sound of gallon-sized drops pelting the rooftop above my head, a wave of relief passed over me as I realized I was no longer drowning in a downpour. Soaking and saturated I slid off my bike, feeling more like a wet noodle than a human. Unlatched my full-face helmet, face exposed for the first time in hours. The narrow winding road we just emerged from in Vermont would have been a challenge in dry weather; but the rain seemingly came from the ground and the sky at the same time and made dodging boulders and oncoming cars on the tiny one-lane highway even more difficult. "You did pretty well back there, sis!" The southern twang-laden voice came from an adjacent pump. A short man I'd never met approached, his swaggering legs made farther apart by his saturated jeans. My head glanced over both shoulders; I looked around to see if there was another "sis" in sight. Confirmation, just me and my dad at the pump. Did he seriously just call me sis? That's a first. "Even my butthole was puckered in that rain," he says, continuing with his backhanded compliment, walking directly toward me and confirming my suspicion, that yes, he was calling me "sis." In my head, a mother's sickie-sweet voice echoed, "Be nice, Abby, graciously accept his compliment." The conglomeration of women's voices creating the mom in my conscience is correct; he honestly was surprised at (and affirming of) my riding ability. I eeked out a "Thanks" and looked back at the ground, not exactly knowing what else I could have said. I choked back the urge to sarcastically ramble on about how I knew it was surprising but my lady bits didn't actually get in the way of my riding. Yes, "thanks" was more appropriate than what I wanted to say after the sarcasm would have stopped—a blunt "Don't call me sis." But this time my sense of decorum overtook my feminist sensibilities. "You're a good rider." Again, surprise rang in his voice. Well, if I had to be called sis, at least I might have changed his mind about women riders, I thought as I climbed back onto my bike and into the rain. One step at a time.

It felt like a vast swath of time passed between then and now. We sat at the picnic table in the dark telling stories about the ride. Stories of triumph, wounded pride, and great escapes. "Did Joe Smith finish this year?" I asked about the big-talking, strong Southern man who I was surprised to find out had rode every challenge and not finished a single one. He did. An inexplicable pride swelled in me. Good for him. Wendy and Bill had ridden with him for part of the trip that year. Wendy started chuckling at my question. "He almost quit. He wanted to quit when he was riding with us. He asked me if I wanted to quit. I said, 'Yeah, sure I do. But I got kids, and what kind of message would that send to them if I quit?'" She described the quizzical look that flashed across his face that I can vividly picture even though I wasn't there. She continued, "Then he said, 'Well, I got kids.'" She said that he stood there for another minute and walked over to his bike. A smirk grew on Wendy's face as she said, "So I don't know if I had anything to do with it or not, but..." We all let out a knowing laugh, mine louder than anyone's.

I sat down for my first interview, nervous about how the conversation might go. Is this voice recorder going to work? Yes. You tested it on the phone a hundred times. It's going to work. Just calm down, you know the literature: Thompson says that women riders don't see motorcycling as part of their identities, it's just something they do. It's just something they do. Not who they are. They're here because of family connections. Like you. And Braidotti—identities are nomadic, fluid, and constantly changing. You know the questions. You've talked to Junie before. You like her. She's your mentor. Is that a problem? Do you like her too much? Shut up, Abby. I dial the phone and erase the thoughts from my head.

> ABBY: What does it mean for you to be a motorcyclist?
> JUNIE: I have been doing it for so long that it's ... you know ... it's kind of become part of me.
> TRISTICA: Exactly. But for me it's, it's more of.... I don't know, it's kind of like my lifestyle.
> SHEILA: I liked motorsickles from the time I was a kid. And I was never able to have one as a child. You know, my parents were just opposed to that. No mini bikes, no dirt bikes, nothin'. I knew that I would have a motorsickle. And from the time I got my driver's license, I've always had a motorsickle endorsement on my driver's license.
> JERSEY Pearl: It's become the only thing that I know. It's it. It's my entire life.
> DEBBY: It's hard to say, 'cause I've always been one. So it's hard to define myself without riding because I've always ridden. It's such a part of me. It's like trying to describe yourself as being a woman. You've always been a female.

After the first few interviews I am no longer surprised at the constant affirmation that motorcycling is a part of their identities. They are motorcyclists. Perhaps not every day, perhaps not every second, but today, in these interviews, speaking about their riding, they are riders. Warriors. Women. Just as they are mothers, daughters, grandmothers, wives, construction workers, and nurses, they are motorcyclists. Is it also becoming a greater part of my identity? I can't tell if it's the process of writing the dissertation that is bringing me closer to identifying as a motorcyclist or because I participated in the Hoka Hey for the second time. I used to shroud my identity as a rider; it was the last thing I would tell people about myself. You had to be in the circle to know. Ashamed? Now I find myself beginning to use it as a marker of my uniqueness—something I never would have done before. Being a female rider of the Hoka Hey did make me unique—there were so few of us, after all. And to deny it would be to deny these women and the thing that linked us together. To cast off their identities would be unfair, against my nature, anti-feminist.

The passion sprang from their voices. I heard them sifting through their memories of riding to find the perfect moment to describe how they felt about being on a bike. I have no clue how I would answer these questions myself. They speak with such strong voices. Maybe I don't have this same passion? Maybe I do? I find it hard to describe why I ride or how I feel when I do ride. Jay asks me about it frequently. Rather than finding words as passionate as these women, I stammer and fail to come up with an adequate sentiment to describe how I feel when I ride, why I like it, what drew me in. I say I just didn't want to be on the back. Wendy said that, too. She laughed while she reminisced about her dad's '78 Gold Wing and said, "I remember being a passenger on the back of that. Again, I was not a passenger."[17] I felt drawn to her laughter at the absurdity of wanting to ride on the back. I, too, wanted to be in control. But it's so much more than that. I think it's indescribable, like trying to describe how you feel when you're in love or agonizing over the loss of a friend. I should just tell Jay what these women said. They get it. They get me.

Carla knows how hard it can be to explain, "I haven't found the exact words that I'm happy with at this point other than, it's such a deep passion for me, that when I'm not motorcycling my heart bleeds."[18] Her heart bleeds. Debra mimicked the same sentiment, "I just I want to stay on the road and ride for the rest of my life. I didn't want to come home."[19] The feeling of being on her bike pulls her. Bryana and Kelly described how we're all in it for "the love of two wheels."[20] I'd never before heard this statement, but now it resonates. We are linked by our passion. Eden paid homage to the ex-husband who put her on her first bike, "Little did he know that he instilled this little bitty seed that turned into a massive love of motorcycles."[21] The love of two wheels extends beyond relationships with people to create a relationship with person and machine. Debby was succinct, saying motorcycles are "my thing. I love these things."[22] Being who we are and living our passions help us live our lives.

> JUNIE: I guess to encapsulate the whole thing what the Hoka Hey is ... (she pauses and I feel the anticipation). It's a ride that makes you really become like one with yourself, with the earth.

They all mimicked the same happiness, the same joy, and the same passionate feelings. The Hoka Hey had become part of their identities and shaped their lives. Each woman expresses it in a different way; each woman eloquently shows her love.

> CARLA: The Hoka Hey kind of put a great big old wrap, a great big old bow on the whole package and said, "You know, we don't know what tomorrow is going to bring."
>
> WENDY: It's just where I'm at in life but I love it. I smile. I'm happy. I found my happiness. Someone went on a ride and they did their once in a lifetime ride.

And they said they were looking for something. And I think that's what I did. I was looking for something. All I can tell you is I found it. But I can't tell you what it is. But I found it. And I'm running into a lot of people that know exactly what I mean. And they're the same way, "I can't tell you what it is." But they found it out there on the Hoka Hey.

SHEILA: Don't wait to live your life, don't put your life on hold and [say], "Oh, I'm gonna do that when I retire" or "I'm gonna do that when my kid gets old" or "I'm gonna do that when...." No, do that now. Because you're not guaranteed anything in the future. And there's a reason they call now the present. Because it is a gift. And you better enjoy it.

After the interviews I could see their passion clearly. They were living their lives through, for, and because of this ride. The Hoka Hey meant the world to them. Riding meant the world to them. It was part of their identities.

Being a woman in a traditionally male environment can create difficult, compromising, or perplexing situations. Because of the socially constructed masculine nature of both motorcycling and sport, women may feel restricted from full participation and acceptance. However, the women who participate in the HHMC feel deeply connected to both the event and its surrounding culture. Riding motorcycles and participating in this challenge are parts of our identities as women, as motorcyclists, and as challengers. In order to survive in this masculine space, women who participate often choose not to conform to standard notions of femininity. In some instances, this materializes in the form of their dress, shown by women wearing pants, boots, and large jackets. Nonconformity with standard femininity can also include the words women choose to use when participating in masculine cultures. For example, swearing is prominent in motorcycle culture and women often use words during the challenge they would not use if they were conforming to hegemonic femininity. This gender bending allows female challengers to become a more complete person but also find acceptance within the riding culture. In turn, they have the ability to work as agents of change, directly affecting their male counterparts' ideas about women riders.

Women who participate in the Hoka Hey often speak in conflicting ways regarding their gender identities. For example, one woman simultaneously indicates her gender is unimportant while also stating that she is cognizant of her intra- and intergender relationships. Likewise, other women describe how their gender matters in issues of safety (such as when they describe needing to find safe sleeping spaces on the road) and then associate with the machismo of the riding culture when they describe their tough riding style. They uphold gender expectations and find novelty in their deviation from these norms. What is clear from their words is a constant negotiation with their own femininity inside a masculine space—at times this culminates in bodily encounters and at others with interpersonal interactions. What emerges in the Hoka Hey is a carefully constructed nomadic gender dance in which identities become fluid markers of (self)worth.

In turn, the women riders of the Hoka Hey use their identities as female riders to create change. They alter their femininity to fit into the masculine culture but also retain markers of traditional femininity to show that they (women) can ride hard. The women utilize gender-bending performances to do this. For transgression within the culture to happen, the women need to embody both masculine and feminine qualities. Using a fluid gender presentation not only allows the women riders to become more whole or complete people but also shows their male counterparts that women should be equally valued as riders within motorcycle culture. In other words, they have to prove they can ride like a man but remind men (and themselves) that they are women.

Women who participated in this study indicated that motorcycling is a large part of their identity. Many, raised in the culture from a young age, felt that it was part of their social fabric. A majority of the women interviewed felt that motorcycling was actually part of their identity. They exhibited passion in their tone of voice and identified motorcycling as crucial to who they were as a person. This runs contrary to William Thompson's study, which indicates female motorcyclists see motorcycling as "what they do, not who they are" (58). Although Thompson does not offer a postmodern construction of individuality, he does indicate that women see motorcycling "as one of many statuses" although not the "master status" (69). Thompson's research indicates that women view their motorcycling identities as less important than their other socially constructed identities (race, age, social roles, or occupation). My findings indicate that the women who participated in the HHMC find motorcycling to be an equally important identity to their other social identities. In a postmodern world in which there are seemingly more questions than answers and nothing is stable, identities similarly fluctuate based on age, social class, mobility, and a myriad of other factors.[23] For example, a working mother might first describe herself as a mother at home but use an identity marker in line with her occupation while searching for a new job. In the postmodern age, we use our multiple identities to match our needs. Conditions no longer force us to choose between being mothers and lawyers; instead, we take on a number of different identities throughout our lives and on a daily basis. In other words, one identity is not necessarily more important than another is; rather, we assume different identities at different times. These asynchronous identities explain how some women in this study find riding to be a part of their identities while others do not. This act of becoming or transposing an identity is crucial to the ability to create change. When we align various portions of our multiple identities, we create an environment in which fluctuation is possible. By understanding who we are and adapting as we become woman/rider/warrior, we challenge dominant structures and emphasize a shift in our own perspectives. In other words, in order to become change agents, we need to be able to change ourselves.

In this vein, women riders constantly engage in a process of becoming women/riders/warriors through the Hoka Hey. In the postmodern world, which emphasizes our pluralities through deconstructed binaries, our identities constantly change. That is, instead of just being wholly either one thing or the other, we can be both or many at the same time. For the purposes of this study, we Hoka Hey women find ourselves embracing and employing various sides of both our femininities and our masculinities (consciously and unconsciously) at different times along the challenge.[24] These women constantly negotiate with their feminine identities within the masculine space of the Hoka Hey. Because of the gendered power dynamics within the challenge, the women must carefully work between being a woman and being a woman in a man's world. Similarly, Nancy Finley's article, "Skating Femininity: Gender Maneuvering in Women's Roller Derby," discusses the combination of gender maneuvering and intragender dynamics that speak to this dual role. Finley describes the ways in which women who participate in masculine environments "engineer the intergender dynamics in femininities that support or challenge intergender relations with masculinity" (363). Intragender dynamics can be labeling women with pariah status (e.g., slut, bitch) or positioning oneself as higher in status than other women (e.g., faster, stronger, harder riders, etc.). Like Finley's "Derby Girls" who dress like 1950s pinup girls and housewives while aggressively bashing into one another on the rink, women of the Hoka Hey carefully position themselves both as feminine and masculine. For example, Junie Rose, who made muffins (a conventionally feminine task) to raise money for the Hoka Hey, places herself in opposition to other non–Hoka Hey women riders, who she describes as "pretty girls."[25]

Although all women who participated in the study showed a passion for riding, not all women indicated that riding was a specific part of her identity. How much they rode generally spoke to how strong of a connection they felt to motorcycling. Scholars such as Wheaton, Roster, and Thompson confirm that participating in sport and leisure activities leads to the development of identity. Identity formation through leisure activities allows individuals to create both collective identities and self-identities. Two major factors contribute to identity formation surrounding sporting activity: frequency of participation and community involvement. Women who rode on a daily basis or those who grew up in a motorcycling community often felt stronger connections to the motorcyclist identity marker than did those who rode less often. The Hoka Hey combines both the community and the frequency (albeit, concentrated into one block of time) aspects to help create in most of these women the identity of rider/biker/warrior.

The women who ride the Hoka Hey separate themselves from other Hoka Hey challengers and other women riders. They make clear distinctions between the way *they* ride and how that is different from how other people ride. The Hoka Hey offers opportunities to ride long distances at excessive speeds and on incredibly difficult roads. This is different from the way they perceive most motorcyclists to ride. It is important to note that these women are also insiders in the culture; they formulate opinions of other riders based on their personal experiences, conversations, and pasts. Women of the Hoka Hey perceive other non–HHMC riders to be "weekend warriors" who do not put in the same mileage in the same amount of time as they do. Clearly, there are riders who do not participate in the Hoka Hey but who do ride in a similar fashion as these women. What is important, however, is the perception and posturing of the Hoka Hey women. The divide they place between themselves and other riders indicates a passion for the way they ride, a desire to be tough or at least different, and a need to legitimize their place in the culture. This is a subtler way of gender bending as women take on the competitive and condescending tone that typically reflect masculine tendencies.

For many women, inter- and intragender maneuvering happens not only in their riding lives but in their occupations as well. Intergender is a relationship or system between both men and women while intragender points to systems within one single group (here, women). The women's occupations ranged from traditionally feminine positions, such as nursing and cleaning, to more masculine jobs, such as working in construction or maintenance departments. Many women also held positions working with motorcycles (test rider) or in motorcycle-related industries (marketing or retail). Specifically showing intergender maneuvering, Sheila and Debra both described working in a construction-related field. While Sheila, who has worked in construction since 1976, indicated

2012 women riders and support staff pose in Las Vegas during the pre-ride meeting. Male riders gathered to take photos of the women riders, which, coupled with our small numbers, indicate our uniqueness within the group. Left to right: Schatzi Brown, Wendy Battles, Junie Rose, Beth Durham, Jane Bixby, Abby Van Vlerah, Kelly Quinn, Carla Dubois.) (Courtesy Jane Bixby.)

that being a woman "meant nothing," Debra was constantly aware of her status as a woman in a man's culture, stating how her ability to ride a motorcycle or win at arm wrestling competitions intimidates the men with whom she works. Upon further reflection, these seemingly oppositional viewpoints show how women must negotiate their own identities in masculine environments. In some situations, women embrace their status as woman/other, showing intragender maneuvering while at other times women employ intergender maneuvering to align themselves with men, resulting in a perceived erasure of gender lines.

With respect to the Hoka Hey, women challengers positioned themselves against other women riders who do not participate in the Hoka Hey. This intragender dynamic allows the women riders of the Hoka Hey to situate themselves in the layered masculine culture. Because men perceive women to be less skilled riders than they are, women who ride the Hoka Hey often downplay other women's associations with motorcycle culture in opposition of the difficult rides they endure and enjoy. A new sense of machismo emerges from these women as they one up other nonendurance riders. For example, Junie commented about "pretty girls" who do not want to ride in the rain and Wendy compared herself to other women in her riding group by saying, "I guess with the Hoka Hey I found that I do like it a little extreme" (495). By creating a division between themselves as women of the Hoka Hey and other women who ride and by affiliating themselves with masculine riders (that is, those who are hardcore/real/endurance riders) rather than other women riders, women challengers reinforce the patriarchy. Intragender dynamics are complicated to say the least. Intentionally or not, when women associate masculine traits with quality or performance, we perpetuate a cycle of feminine inferiority.

The association with a macho identity speaks to women's fluid identities and gender nonconformity. As their identities as riders develop, they more fully embrace the toughness associated with motorcycling culture. As Finely suggests of roller derby women, "skaters use interactions in derby to manipulate meanings of gender positions and meanings, to redefine statuses, and create contradictions in complementary gender relations" (371). In translation to the Hoka Hey, women use riding to change their own perceptions of self and redefine or reinforce their gender identities. Many women indicate the reason they feel a fluid gender identity is because they have ridden motorcycles for so long or have long since felt that their gender identities were not singular. Thus, through their participation in a heavily masculine culture, their gender bending feels like a natural part of their identities. In essence, they are becoming a more complete person, latching on to all versions of themselves. For example, as women identify with masculine attitudes, including boastful sentiments about completion of the course, we show an adoption of hegemonic misogyny prevalent in the larger subculture. When we turn our view from pro-woman to pro-exceptional woman, we reinforce traditionally masculine attitudes of success.

However, when comparing their own rides and experiences against those of other female Hoka Hey riders, they often downplay their own success, a display of ingrained feminine manners. Many women asserted some sort of sentiment ("I could never do that" or "Oh, that was so much harder than my ride") when discussing the stories of the other women. For example, when comparing her ride to mine, with my lack of windshield even during a dust storm, Wendy asserted, "That's amazing. 'Cause when I heard that I was like 'Oh no, I would have turned around and went home!'" (481–483). Likewise, Kelly Quinn downplayed her own experience as a rider by saying, "I'm just a baby compared to most. You know, I hear all these people sayin,' 'I been ridin' thirty years.' And I'm like, wow" (217–218). Despite hoping to be role models and inspire other women riders, they make a point to describe themselves as endurance riders, skilled riders, and just as good as the men. This shows a need to be tough (masculine) while retaining traditionally feminine characteristics of downplaying their own success. These women dance between needing to say, "I ride more than that (non–HHMC) woman" and "I couldn't ride like you (my HHMC sister)." This shows a strong display of nomadic identity and gender maneuvering. It is a confusing, complex, and difficult position to find oneself in; however, both indicate a desire to create community with their Hoka Hey sisters. Underwriting these conflicting sentiments is a connection to other Hoka Hey riders. Because the Hoka Hey is such a large part of the women's identities, they feel the need to associate with the ride and other riders.

Living and riding on the periphery and within the context of masculinity forces women to negotiate with their femininity through becoming gender nonconforming. Kay and Laberge argue that while women are marginalized, elite women competitors of adventure racing legitimize male domination through valuing traditional "male capital" (e.g., toughness and strength) over feminine attributes. While this notion may stretch toward essentializing masculinity and femininity—where all men are strong and all women weak—it shows the discourse of the sporting world perpetuating these binary oppositions. Binary opposition is based on only two opposite or alternative options (here, femininity and masculinity). Binary conceptions limit opportunities for fluid definitions of identity, gender, and self. Pflugfelder states that discourse in motorsport inherently genders women and, when in vehicles as "racers" or "drivers," expects them to undergo an erasure of their gendered body. As discussed previously, Danica Patrick must compete with men during the race while her gender vanishes, yet becomes gendered once again when she wins and her female body becomes a cause of her success (because she is smaller and thus faster than men are) or when her sexualized female body promotes a brand. These gendered experiences serve to highlight the marginalization of women's participation in male dominated sport. Joans agrees that women must assume some level of gender nonconformity within the hypermasculine motorcycling world. Joans contends, "All [biking] women have broken with stereotypical femininity. All these women have rejected, consciously or unconsciously, the written and unwritten rules of female behavior" (139). By joining a traditionally masculine leisure activity, often linked with aggression and power, women in the motorcycling community challenge gender norms and break with the notion that femininity must be demure and soft. Furthering this example, straddling a motorcycle suggests an aggressive form of sexuality, which does not align with dominant conceptions of femininity.

Leslie Heywood, in her chapter "A New Look at Female Athletes and Masculinity," describes an athletic process through which she "becomes" her male alter ego, Lester. Heywood describes a process though which she embraces the masculine qualities already inside her by pushing herself to the limits while power lifting. Through athletics and physicality, she unleashes the man inside her womanly body. She describes this not as a glorification of hypermasculinity, as some other scholars suggest, but rather as a process through which she becomes more complete. She writes, "Lester disproves stereotypes of female incompetence and weakness, and, more important, shows that men and women and the qualities associated with them can be broken into something other than polarized categories" (63). Through sport, Heywood challenges traditional norms of femininity and explores her whole self, embodying both masculine and feminine traits. The women of the Hoka Hey mirror this type of gender nonconformity when they ride their motorcycles. Both part of their identity and something they do not always carry with them, like Lester on the weight bench, their masculine traits expound when in competition on their motorcycles.

Much like Leslie/Lester, women of the Hoka Hey speak of themselves or others in relationship to women as men. During an interview with Jane and Schatzi, Jane promoted Schatzi's female masculinity.[26] The excerpted interview below indicates a formation of social identity and behavior consistent with group athletes.

> SCHATZI: ... motorcycling was my only transportation. And I remember being out there at like fifteen below.
> ABBY: Fifteen below?!
> SCHATZI: Yeah. That's cold.
> JANE: I used to think 74 was cold. I've really changed my standards. (All laughing).
> SCHATZI: Yeah. It's called a snowsuit. It's what you have to wear at that point....
> JANE: She has bigger balls than most men; they're just on her chest. (All laughing).

Jane not only promotes Schatzi's masculine qualities (here, riding in extreme conditions), but also makes a clear association between her female friend and a man. Describing Schatzi's breasts as engorged chest testicles shows the association with masculinity and links her female body to male anatomy. As Kauer and Krane's article "'Scary Dykes' and 'Feminine Queens': Stereotypes and Female College Athletes" suggests, "these athletes constantly negotiated their social identities as athletes in conjunction with social expectations. They were empowered through sport and developed valued qualities, yet these qualities also conflicted with hegemonic femininity" (54). Social identity perspective used by Kauer and Krane suggest that Jane and Schatzi develop social norms (presenting a nonconforming gender identity) consistent with their group (female riders of the Hoka Hey) that may not be accepted by those outside their circle. The quotes above as well as the previous stories of negotiating femininity show the women exude both machismo and socially constructed feminine characteristics. Through the fluidity of their identities, they are able to form a more complete whole, playing both with their typically male and female qualities. The fluidity of their identities, as well as group social constructions, allows them to bend, blur, and ignore traditional gender lines. Motorcycling is a part of who they are because they ride hard, ride long, and keep up. However, in order to maintain this sense of self they must constantly adapt their identity to fit within a given situation.

Many women riders of the Hoka Hey display a fluid gender identity. While they may not have explicitly stated that their gender identities were fluid, they discussed having a changing idea of their femininity. Debby described feeling "genderless" (238); Sheila and Schatzi spoke about how being a female motorcyclist "didn't mean anything" (Sheila 107; Schatzi 165). Rather than not finding value in their gender, I believe this means that they, like Debby, feel genderless or feel gender fluid. As Judith Butler suggests in *Gender Trouble*, their genders are not "natural"; rather, they are a "cultural performance" which the women alter at their will (xxxi).

Over time, these long-distance riders develop an inclination toward female masculinity. Many women described their childhood selves with some degree of a male identity marker—either as tomboys or "one of the boys" or a "father's only son" (June 248; Debra 511; Schatzi 184; Wendy 153; Kelly Quinn 259; Debby 239).[27] Their association with tomboyism makes clear the idea that these women challenge traditional gender norms. The female masculinity they felt as children extends now into their motorcycle riding. Many women who ride the Hoka Hey grew up in a motorcycling culture, with either their families motorcycling together or by owning and riding dirt bikes as young children. As such, the association with a masculine culture supersedes their femininity; or rather, their femininity includes a masculine edge. Because many of the women grew up in a masculine environment, they now feel an erasure of their culturally accepted female gender specifically when they ride their motorcycles. Some women even noted an attempt to physically alter their bodies to appear more masculine or feminine while riding.

As three-time rider and two-time cancer survivor Junie Rose stated, "And a lot of times you can't even tell [if] it's a girl on the bike. I try to, you know, stick my hair so you can't really tell I'm a girl. Easily anyway" (207–208). Likewise, Debby indicated that the gear she wears serves as a gender eraser, "I look like the Michelin man a lot of the time. I got a lot of layers on. I got my heated gear. You know. And I look very, I guess intimidating in a way" (252–254). Each of the instances in which the women discuss altering their appearance to be more masculine is in reference to safety. They feel safer looking like a man on a motorcycle than looking like a woman on a motorcycle; this points to the culturally constructed notion that women are less safe and more vulnerable than men. While sexual assault and violence are prevalent in the United States, this also suggests a learned understanding of vulnerability, directly linked to their gender (as discussed in previous chapters in regards to fear on the road). These women, like most women, have long been told they should not walk alone at night, not wear revealing clothing, or attract unwanted attention for fear that they may become victims. Victim blaming remains a prevalent way in which men exert power over women. In order to combat this learned feeling of vulnerability, these women assume masculine tendencies, appearances, and attitudes. This includes an alternation of their gender performance. While riding, these motorcyclists identify more with their masculine side; however, their traditional markers of femininity remain present as a part of their gender performance when they are not specifically riding their motorcycles.

Women who ride the Hoka Hey negotiate gender dynamics between both female riders and male riders, sidestepping boundaries of femininity and masculinity. As indicated in the narrative section of this chapter, some challengers grapple with their desire to remain feminine (here, by not wanting to urinate in front of men) and needing to exist within a masculine space (a tough road with no bathroom). Similarly, Tristica and Bryana told stories of stripping down to their underwear in front of men in order to dry wet, cold clothes. Tristica's comment, "I didn't have like one stupid ass remark or comment from anybody. It was kinda like everybody was in the same boat. Everybody was freezin' their ass off. And everybody was wet. And they just wanted to get dry,"[28] indicates her surprise at the fluidity of her own and the men's gender performances. While Tristica, Bryana, and Wendy all remained cognizant of protecting their bodies from men, they transgressed boundaries of traditional femininity by ignoring the prescribed gender performance. Also, the men in each situation, by treating each woman like one of the guys, erased the line between men and women. These stories indicate a shift in gender performance and gender identity. Because these identities are nomadic and constantly in flux, they are able to fulfill multiple needs at any given time.

Similarly, Annie Londonderry, the Victorian-era bicycle rider who was the first female to ride across the world, battled traditional femininity and had to negotiate her female body on the road. In regards to the feminine prescriptions of the day, Annie said,

> I firmly believe that if I had worn skirts I should not have been able to make the trip. It must not be thought that I lost the attention which is supposed to be associated with feminine apparel. I was everywhere treated with courtesy, and for the benefit of my sisters who hesitate about donning bloomers I will confess that I received no less than two hundred proposals of marriage (167).

What is interesting to note here is that Annie tries to show that she is still feminine—indicated by the number of marriage proposals she received—while also entering into a masculine space of sport, accentuated by wearing pants. Like Wendy, Annie's biographer describes how she "also had to become accustomed to relieving herself in creative ways and not always in pleasant places" (20). Here we see how we perceive women's bodies to be something that we need to overcome while in a masculine space. By expanding their comfort zones to include masculine bodily experiences, female athletes pushed themselves and found empowerment through blending their masculine and feminine attributes.

At times, the women describe harboring traditionally and hegemonically feminine qualities, such as needing to be clean or when discussing their sexuality; however, when they ride the Hoka Hey they overwhelmingly alter their feminine gender identities. In essence, they pick up and leave their female gender identity when necessary. Kelly Quinn, who works in the motorcycle industry, describes how she uses her sexuality as a tool in her job. She is cognizant of her feminine sexuality and uses that to promote her brand and philanthropic endeavors. Kelly states, "all of the promotional speaking and stuff that I do, I have to look sassy. I have to look the part. Well, you look the part in your jeans and your chaps sure; but I can't walk into a college campus or a women's seminar to give my spiel.... I wear [the clothing brand Bebe's] stuff, I buy their leather pants, I buy their studs, I buy their studded heels" (396–404). Here, while not actually riding her motorcycle, Kelly is able to perform her femininity through her sexualized clothing. This sexualization of the athlete for media and marketing purposes echoes the representations of other female athletes of masculine sports. For example, Sisjord and Kristiansen's 2008 work regarding female wrestlers notes that female athletes who conform to traditionally feminine standards of beauty are photographed by media more often than athletes with more muscular bodies. While some female wrestlers scoffed at the sexualized media portrayal, others noted any representation of a female wrestler did "a lot for the sport" (361).

Both situations represent a pull between the desire for any representation and remaining true to the gender identity of others in your sport.

Other women noted their female gender identities through their attention to hygiene on the ride. Although I did not ask a question specifically about showering or cleanliness on the ride, many women inserted comments regarding their hygiene into their descriptions of the Hoka Hey. For example, Wendy described her appearance saying, "So no shower, no nothing, my hair was a mess" (210). Here she makes note that while riding the Hoka Hey she pays no attention to feminine standards of beauty while also indicating her awareness of that expectation. Others described the first shower they took during the ride as an amazing feeling. Some even rented a hotel room just for the shower. Bryana notes, "They opened up the civic center down the street for all of us to go take showers and I did not expect to be able to take a shower. And I was like, 'Oh my God! A warm shower! I'm not coming out of here!'" (504–507). As Bryana and others note the need to shower and appear clean, they show that clean is what they "should" be under the standards of hegemonic femininity. They move between accepting and embracing their dirtiness and yearning for a shower. I took a picture of my dirty fingernails on the second day of the 2012 ride and posted it to my blog; here, the photo shows both the oddity of me being dirty and the desire for cleanliness. I felt terribly disgusting. I reminded my riding partners of this frequently. The men I rode with did not seem phased by their own personal hygiene.

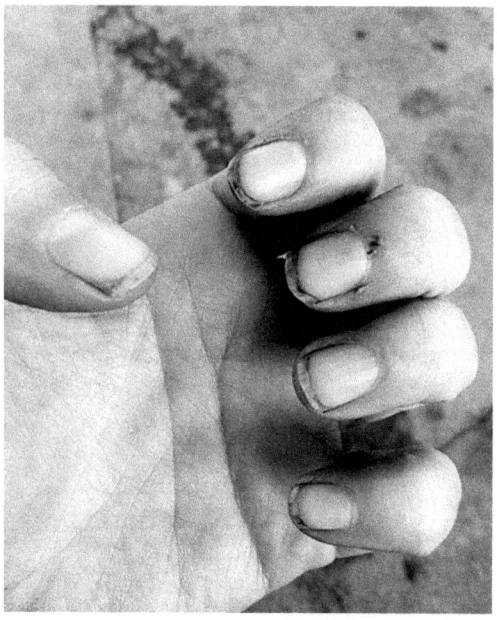

Abby's fingernails on day two of the 2012 HHMC. Many women interviewed spoke of how dirty they were from not showering during the challenge. This indicates a desire to maintain notions of traditional femininity while participating in a masculine environment. (Author photo.)

These descriptions mark their understanding of femininity but also serve to show the necessary machismo associated with the Hoka Hey. The ride is a time in which women must abandon their femininity and they laud themselves for not showering for days on end. Jane and Schatzi play with their traditionally ascribed gender performances when they say they "don't like to drive from like 2:00–5:00 in the morning, [they] like to get [their] beauty rest. And that's also when all the animals are out too" (990–991). This gender play both acknowledges their socially constructed idea of femininity and honors the masculine nature of their ride. Here, gender play highlights the limitations of the masculine/feminine opposition, which does not allow these women to explain fully their own gender identities. Further, the assumption of cleanliness shows the riders' position of privilege. Like sleeping outside, not bathing is an oddity for these riders. The fact that we can bathe on a regular basis, and have a place to do so, places us in opposition to those in lower socioeconomic positions. The lack of cleanliness serves as a point of realization of our own affluence.

Women who ride the Hoka Hey have an "outsider within" perspective of a masculine culture. In other words, they understand the culture from the standpoint of a marginalized woman while simultaneously being accepted into the male culture because of their riding abilities. They are both part of the dominant male culture and part of the marginalized group. This allows them to understand the nuances of motorcycling from a different vantage point than their male counterparts. By calling fellow male challengers "pussies" and keeping up with the men as they ride dangerously or at excessive speeds, they prove themselves to possess the rough and tumble (hegemonically) masculine qualities. This gender performance positions them as one of the boys. In a sense, they pass as men because of their ability to alter their gender performance while they are on this challenge. Because of this ability to move between gender boundaries, they are able to create their niche in a masculine culture. This in-betweenness creates a gender identity which does not fit neatly into a male/female box. It begs for new understandings of what it means to be a woman and what it means to be a man. Perhaps rather than being seen as masculine and feminine qualities we need to embrace these as human qualities, assuming that we all embody some degree of both. When we take on this assumption, we can view gender nonconformity as a way of becoming a more complete person. For the women of the Hoka Hey, femininity is marked not only by their ability to care for themselves but also by their ability to ride hard. As such, while women come into, and understand, motorcycling from a female perspective, they create fluid gender identities to help them gain acceptance to, and remain a part of, the masculine culture.

Steve Briscoe, Hoka Hey veteran and author of the book *Solitary—Without the Confinement: A Rider's Life-Changing Experience During the 2013 Hoka Hey Motorcycle Challenge*, illustrates the ability women riders have to affect change within motorcycle culture. Briscoe's 2015 work about his experiences on the 2013 HHMC spends some time addressing women who ride. He describes reasons men and women ride motorcycles and their abilities to do so. He attempts to address some of the frequent misconceptions that reinforce hegemonic femininity—such as the idea women's primary motivator for choosing a specific motorcycle is color. Rather than dispelling such misconceptions, he draws attention back to the men who ride by challenging them to "be honest and ask themselves what exactly they based their last purchase on" (110). This indicates that Briscoe feels many men also choose a motorcycle for its color. While Briscoe makes an effort to defend women as equally capable riders (he could have left us out entirely), he retains traditional markers of femininity to discuss women riders. For example, he cites the primary difference between men and women riders being women look and smell better than our male counterparts. Albeit flawed, the underlying notion of this interpretation is women and men are equal riders. If we only differ in our smell and looks our riding must be comparable. By limiting our differences to looks and hygiene, Briscoe erases the possibility that women are lesser riders than men. To Briscoe, our differences do not lie in our ability to ride at top speeds or negotiate difficult roads. Although still not entirely gender neutral, this opinion is a step in a positive direction from the larger subset of motorcycle culture, which continually relegates women to inferior positions as riders or accessories.

The possibility to affect change within a deeply rooted culture does not come easily; however, the brave few women who ride the Hoka Hey directly affect change in the Hoka Hey motorcycle culture. In turn, the riders with whom they interact on the challenge might slowly begin to change their motorcycle cultures at home. These women riders challenge gender stereotypes that hold women in inferior power positions. While the change may be slow, their presence in the culture and ability to excel at the Hoka Hey, a challenge reserved for only the toughest riders, affects male participants' perceptions of female motorcyclists. By simply entering this competition, women earn respect. The respect of one Hoka Hey rider to another surpasses gender boundaries, allowing female and male riders to be equal competitors. As feminist scholars such as Butler, Finely, Birrell, and Theberge suggest, women's presence in traditionally male environments can affect change and create transgression. While it may remain on an individual level, women who participate in the Hoka Hey certainly create change. Further, these individual instances of change have the ability to cause a ripple effect throughout the larger system of motorcycling networks as Hoka Hey riders interact with riders in their local communities.

This mirrors the experience of other athletes, as scholars suggest room in sport exists for the possibility of transgression, a state in which the dominant cultural perceptions change. While some scholars such as Kay and Laberge and Pflugfelder conclude that though some lifestyle sports could be sites for transforming gender regimes in sport, some actually reaffirm and legitimate masculine domination. Furthering this idea, Pflugfelder exposes the unstable assumption that motorsport is an arena in which men and women compete equally. Despite motorsport being one of the few sites in sport where men and women compete together (e.g., auto racing, BMX, rally racing), the discourse of motorsport creates a gendered experience for women by highlighting the differences in men's and women's bodies. Joans, however, contends that motorcycling is a sphere in which traditional ideas of femininity can be reshaped. As she indicates, most women who ride consider themselves to be feminine; she and they understand femininity not as based on actions but rather rooted in feelings. In this vein, Joans believes that "femininity has lost its restrictive and dependent component" (150). By understanding motorcycling and femininity on a continuum in which there is not one but many ways to be feminine or a motorcyclist, Joans contends that female bikers see themselves as feminine while actively challenging gender roles through their presence in the male-dominated culture. I agree with Joans's premise and argue that femininities in plural can alter previous misconceptions of women, their bodies, and their participation in sport. For example, by understanding that being strong is not only a masculine trait but also a component of femininity (or female masculinity), we can imagine a more egalitarian experience for athletes at all levels.

As each woman rides with various men throughout the challenge, she proves herself a worthy competitor. This can be seen most clearly in Jane and Schatzi's story, described above, as they made their mark as skilled riders and changed the mind of a life-long rider to accept women into his fold. The Hoka Hey allows for this form of change in part because men and women compete on the same course and ride for the same prize. There is no separation of riders by sex; instead, like other motorsports, men and women compete equally. Using the same rules, course, and competitive environment eliminates the possibility to say that women play an easier game. As Kane suggests, sport has the ability to transform culture when women perform alongside men and surpass men's athletic abilities. Changes, such as those Kane proposes, take place in endurance motorcycle challenges where men and women compete together and women succeed at high levels. In the Hoka Hey, ability supersedes sex.

Feminist scholarship suggests the empowerment of women can lead to the transgression of sporting contexts. Susan Birrell and Nancy Theberge's 1994 article "Feminist Resistance and Transformation in Sport" applies feminist perspectives to sport to uncover the world of sport as a site of cultural resistance. This work informs my definition of both resistance and transgression. The scholars maintain that we underestimate the cultural and political significance of sport and overlook it as a site of possible transgression. Birrell and Theberge define resistance as "the process by which disempowered groups or persons refuse to submit fully to their disempowerment" (363).

However, the two go on to state that resistance alone does not transgression, which is a shift in the ideological and power structures of an institution. Birrell and Theberge argue excellent competitors and performers in sport who are women and girls can challenge masculine superiority (365). The authors argue that some sports women challenge patriarchal practices. For example, girls and woman can (re)claim their own bodies. Sports have helped women's liberation. The historic legal changes of Title IX, which since 1972 has changed the face of our culture by allowing access to sports to women and girls in high school and college, cannot be underestimated. However, more masculine sports such as hockey, auto racing, and motorcycling, are small sites of transgression. The below quote from Bryana shows the theory Birrell and Theberge discuss in practice:

> And we can make such a huge difference in other people's lives just by doing something like this. And you know. I mean whether it's a guy or it's another female out there. Or they're actually riding it, or it's just some guy you meet at a gas station who thinks it's so cool to see some female not being afraid or limiting themselves by the standards and the society that we live in but…. Don't give up. That's always a big thing too. Not to give up.[29] But having done what I've done and the men that I do know that ride a lot tell me I've got more balls than most men they know. And I know a lot of women who ride the same way.[30]

By being a woman in a masculine culture, Bryana creates a site of resistance. By empowering herself to ride hard with men, she shows them she is an equal competitor. This is a form of transgression and change. Similarly, Kelly Quinn says,

> You know, I'm looked at as the girl who would typically be eye candy on the back of the bike. Or like, "You can't possibly ride that big bike." I'm looked at as that girl, and then when you ask me how many miles I typically ride, then it's like, "Wow, you ride more than I do."[31]

The emphasis of surprise when the male rider finds out how much Kelly rides shows the ability of women riders to alter perceptions.

Hoka Hey women riders feel as if they are creating change within their culture. They tell stories of men offering their surprised kudos after difficult rides. For example, Debby discusses the men she rode with, saying,

> They say they would love to do the ride, again together and things. And a lot of them complimented me on my riding, when I wasn't really tired. But so yeah, they realized that I could be an asset and helpful. And I'm good with directions. I'm a good navigator.[32]

Each compliment about their riding capabilities marks another mind altered because of their presence. Men often do not compliment one another on their ability to ride on a certain road. While male riders may reminisce about a difficult road, hard turn, or steep grade with one another, the thought that any man could not complete a ride does not come into question. When speaking with the women, however, men often offer comments such as "You kept up pretty well," or "You did a good job back there." The affirmation directed by men toward women indicates their previous disbelief in the woman's ability to perform. While these men may not directly admit women riders affect their thinking, the women feel as if they are making strides within the culture to change perceptions of male and female riders. This quote from Junie Rose shows her surprise when men see women as equal competitors:

> But you know, it's more about riding to me than uh, the show, and so then when you talk to these guys and they're telling their tall tales and I'm right in there, one-upping them with what I did. It's fun. To me it's competitive (pause) to some degree and it's a lot of fun. I mean, women just don't get into that circle, you know, even with sports.[33]

While it may be a stretch to assume that large-scale transgression—the entirety of motorcycle culture changing—takes place because of these actions, transgression within the Hoka Hey community exists. It is important to note that the Hoka Hey creates an incredibly tight-knit group of riders. They ride together, live together, and die together throughout the course of the challenge. This could lead to an increased acceptance toward the women riders. Tristica describes one male rider's comments at the end of the ride:

> And you know, at the end of the ride, her husband came up to me and said, "You know, you really changed my point of view on a lot of things. You know, I probably wouldn't have made it out of Florida if it wasn't for you."[34]

Because men and women become Hoka Hey brothers and sisters along the ride, it is likely that men begin the challenge with a greater tendency toward accepting women who share the challenge. However, this camaraderie is something felt only *after* riders complete the course. The wholesale acceptance of one another, especially women, does not take place at the outset. In essence, women must prove themselves to be worthy riders rather than enter the culture as deserving. Their perceptions of women riders may not extend outside the confines of the Hoka Hey and thus may not be considered (by some) to be actual sites of transgression. However, the fact that men's perceptions about any woman rider are malleable is noteworthy.

As sport and motorcycle literature suggests, women become empowered through riding motorcycles and participating in sport; it assists female athletes in constructing gender identities. Empowerment from riding the Hoka Hey informs women's identities as riders/women/warriors. A process develops. Passion creates the desire that inspires the action of riding. Riding creates the feeling of empowerment. The empowerment creates the confidence and forms the identity of motorcyclist. Because of their self-conception as motorcyclist, they feel like they can participate in the Hoka Hey, then the cycle continues—they always are becoming Hoka Hey warriors. Further, their identities as motorcyclists inform their gender identities. Participating in a masculine culture, while living in a larger society that values traditional (often sexualized) images of femininity, makes these women gender benders. Because they exist within the conflicting confines of both masculinity and femininity, they find ways to express their gender identities as fluid, transformational, and nonconforming. As non-gendered or masculine females, or as more complete people, they either bend or break the rigidity of the masculine/feminine binary. This form of gender bending becomes a tool in their chest used to work toward group acceptance.

Identity plays a crucial role in understanding the women of the Hoka Hey. They find riding to be a part of their identities and their gender identities are constantly in flux. These women are gender nomads who remain cognizant of their fluid identities and adapt to changing situations. Further, they use their riding and gender identities to affect change within the culture of the challenge. The ability to adapt and change not only affects greater change within the culture but also makes each woman a more complete person. Through their ability to ride, their determination to succeed, and their personalities, they transgress gender boundaries and challenge gender binaries. What is important to note with women in sport/motorcycling is their ability to blend feminine and masculine traits to become better competitors. By embracing their female masculinity, they easily adapt to the masculine culture of the Hoka Hey, which allows them to be successful, and consequently change the minds of their male riding partners. By eliminating the rigidity of hegemonic masculinity and femininity, they spur transgression and affect change. Women of the Hoka Hey carefully craft gendered identities as riders and as more complete people to earn respect and ultimately change men's minds about women.

7

I Cried All the Way Home
The Difficult Reality of Leaving the Road

The loop plays over and over in my mind. "Women finish at a higher percentage rate than men." "You have to stay in. You can't quit. You will ruin the statistics." I will finish. I will finish. And that's that. I've already told my boss. I will finish this.... I'm not comin' home until I do finish it.[1] *It would be really frustrating to start out and know that you can't finish it. You know people lose their jobs to stay out this long.*[2] *If I quit, I will let everyone down. I told so many people I was doing this. Humiliation. Seriously, I'm riding for my friend who has cancer. This is nowhere near as bad as that. If I can't do this, I'm nothing. I need to finish. I can't quit. If I do, everyone will know. How stupid will it look if I end this challenge before the finish? I can't imagine showing my face again. Can't quit. Won't quit. I continue riding and staring at the never-ending page of directions. Suppressing the thoughts. Keep on going. Determined not to quit.*[3]

Through interviewing women for this book, I heard stories of quitting—it was the hardest decision she ever made; she cried the entire way back across the country going home; she did not really have a choice in the matter. When I first started this project in 2012, I had successfully completed the Hoka Hey. I did not quite grasp what each woman said about her quitting experience. I did not really understand why it would be such a big deal to leave the road. I could not imagine even having to make the choice. I assumed if I did have to leave the road, it would be the road itself that took me out. I could not identify with these women. Then my dad and I made the decision to quit shortly after leaving the first checkpoint in 2013 and I understood every word each woman had uttered about her quitting experience. I am still bitter we left the road. Still bitter my dad blames me, even if it's not out loud. Still disappointed in myself for failing. Still disappointed in my dad for not believing in me. It was a rough ride home and rougher time after; but, our relationship now (mostly) repaired, I look back on the experience as further understanding of the Hoka Hey. I now can identify with the women who quit and feel why that decision is so hard.

A subtle difference exists between the word reason and the word excuse. The word excuse can carry a negative connotation associated with a sense of shame. Often made after the fact, we contrive excuses to lessen blame or justify actions. Conversely, reason connotes a legitimate cause and effect scenario not always in the rider's control. We can categorize accidents, animal encounters, and breakdowns as reasons to leave the road. These are all reactions to potential outside forces, physical determinants. These do not reflect poorly upon the rider because they are outside of the rider's control. They are *reasons* to leave the challenge. Determinants associated with emotional factors (such as feelings of guilt, lack of time, illness, or the desire to quit) make a rider seem inferior. These are *excuses* to leave the challenge. As excuses, they call into question a rider's ability, commitment, place within the community, and as a result, masculinity. Further, there is a dichotomy between emotional and physical characteristics of reasons for leaving the challenge. There is a preference of the physical over the emotional, brute strength over nurturing, masculinity over femininity. As such, riders long for a reason to leave the road rather than an excuse to quit.

Also important to note is that few riders with whom I spoke use the word quit. Instead, they chose to frame their departure as "leaving" the road/challenge. The heavily masculinized culture of the Hoka Hey promotes a necessity to exit. Like many extreme athletes, riders of the Hoka Hey do not give up. They take grit to an extreme and will themselves to perform through pain and any number of other emotions. Just as images of runners hobbling over a marathon finish line are common, many riders do all they can to remain in the challenge unless they are forced out. Grit is necessary among extreme athletes. Lynne Cox sums up this desire to push through difficult situations and not quit. She speaks of her motivation to continue swimming, saying, "In many ways, the effort to obtain permission and support for this swim reflected life and the essence of long-distance swimming: as long as you hang in there and keep going, you have a chance at succeeding. Once you give up, you're done" (195). Cox's grit-filled words mimic the notions of the Hoka Hey women. However, while riders may strive for a reason beyond their power to leave the road, many do leave the challenge because of other scenarios.

I would be surprised to find out that anyone who sets out on a challenge like the Hoka Hey intends to quit. The word quit rarely enters the vocabulary of people crazy enough to set out on a month-long motorcycle ride, lace up their shoes for an ultra-marathon, or partake in any other intense demonstration of the power of mind and body. The women interviewed in this work

7. I Cried All the Way Home 169

are no different—quitting is never simple for them. In fact, part of the premise of this book is that women quit the challenge less than men did. Of course, women do quit. Because these women are not only riding their ride, but also enacting an ethic of care, quitting becomes more than letting themselves down. Subsequently these statistics and frames of reference make it even more difficult for women to walk away from the challenge. This chapter discusses the anguish of quitting the challenge. Through three different narratives the steps leading to the decision to leave come to light. Specifically, I highlight accidents, personal health issues, and familial duties as primary reasons women make the difficult choice to leave the Hoka Hey.

As an author, I grappled with proper wording of various passages in this chapter. Although the women who participated in this study infrequently use the word quit, I use the word often. This shows my own desire to pass within the masculine space and (potentially subconscious) association with masculine attitudes. This stems from the stigma I place on not finishing the challenge. Scholars point to stigma as being necessary for solidarity within social groups (see Falk and Goffman). We need a stigma to solidify the binary between "us" and "them." In the Hoka Hey, *we* are finishers, men, warriors; *they* are weak, quitters, others. The stigma of being an outsider (or in this case, a quitter) makes it easier to determine who the "us" is.

While there is some quantitative research on attrition in sport or exercise, it is a struggle to find qualitative research on the subject of quitting.[4] The quantitative studies fail to track the raw emotion associated with leaving a sport or activity. My research adds to the small body of quantitative research on sport and attrition by supplementing with qualitative research. In other words, my work adds voice to existing statistical analysis. Perhaps in part because of their determined spirits, the women with whom I spoke did not leave the road without a reason. Each woman willingly exposes her internal dialogue here on paper in a way that might make most people uncomfortable—a testament to her continued strength. Our experience was not to quit simply because the challenge was difficult, which could open each woman to criticism or expose her as a failure. Regardless of these negative feelings' basis in reality or perceived reality, quitting is something few would do without good reason. We pushed through; but when we did have to quit, it was for a reason. The women of the Hoka Hey have motives to finish and motives to quit, both of which support a feminist ethic of care and socially constructed gender expectations.[5]

Lynne Cox's experience with open water distance swimming mirrors the experiences of women on the Hoka Hey. Her choices and decisions to quit certain swims are no different. Through her narratives about quitting swims, Cox describes the emotional devastation, gendered experiences, and new understandings that emerge after going through these experiences. Her descriptions of quitting, and that of women of the Hoka Hey, resonate as a trauma. Cox describes watching a fellow female swimmer make the choice to leave the swim,

> Her lips were blue, and her voice cracked as she said, "I'm so sorry, you guys. I didn't want to stop. I wanted to stay with you." ... (M)y heart was breaking. To have trained so long and so hard for this and to have to get out.... And then she burst into tears. It was so hard to see her that way. So hard to know that her dream died at that moment (51).

Here, Cox describes watching her friend and teammate, Nancy, leave the Catalina Channel swim. Physical issues forced Nancy to leave the swim, which Cox shows by describing Nancy's blue lips. Nancy's own words describe her desire to keep swimming. Cox, understanding and feeling the same sense of devastation, describes the challenging position in which female athletes find themselves when they must leave the activity for which they train so hard. Nancy's tears are the same as those of the women of the Hoka Hey. They describe a sense of devastation compounded by the time they spent training. Nancy's sorrow and apology to the group reflects the feminist ethic of care woven into the female athletes' core. She cares about the group and sees her inability to finish not just as a reflection on her own abilities but also on that of the group.

Likewise, Cox's second attempt at the Catalina Channel swim highlights experiences felt by women of the Hoka Hey. Here, physical conditions force Cox herself out of the water. The passage below clearly demonstrates gendered emotions coupled with the masculine sporting environment.

> When the crew helped me onto the boat, I completely lost it. I started crying really hard. My father and mother tried to soothe me. I felt so bad to be sobbing in front of Montrella, in front of the reporter for the *Los Angeles Times* and all the lifeguards. It got even worse when I saw Fahmy's face. He knew exactly what I was feeling. I started crying even harder. I had been so scared. I didn't realize it until we were safe, but then I'd let my defenses down. My father tapped me on the cheek with his hand, first gently, then harder, trying to snap me back into reality. He was afraid that I would become hysterical. I hated this scene. Hated giving up. Hated failing. Still, I wasn't fully comprehending the lesson that I should have learned in Egypt: no swim, no athletic venture was worth dying over. There were times when you had to quit. Times when it was too dangerous to continue. Times when you should walk away and try again another day (131).

In this passage, we see Cox struggling with giving up—wanting to continue swimming through all conditions. She shows the gender dance women perform in masculine environments by wanting to prove herself. She feels shame for her emotions as she says she "let her defenses down." These words indicate that the masculine environment of sport is no place for feminine emotions. The "There's no crying in baseball" theme, eloquently stated in the movie *A League of Their Own*, resonates here as Cox's tears force her father to slap her back into the moment. Her father's fear that she will "become hysterical" is a perfect image of the way female athletes are conditioned to tamp down their emotions to appease the masculine space.

Further, Cox's words show the same reality that women of the Hoka Hey (or athletes participating in any endurance/lifestyle sport) face because of the extreme nature of our sports. The element of risk present in endurance sport further complicates gender expectations and performances. At the time of her swim, Cox was a single woman with no children. She could easily choose to be an athlete first. However, women's ethic of care forces riders to favor their identities as mother or wife over athlete. While Cox could assume the identity of athlete first, she remained cognizant that she does not want to jeopardize her life for her sport. While men may feel the same way, the women interviewed show the perceived differences between men and women while making these choices.

Like Cox, women of the Hoka Hey who did not finish the challenge either describe some outside source or responsibilities related to gender expectations forcing them to quit. Rather than being exhausted by a lack of willpower, strength, or desire, these women feel conflicted when leaving the road. Their health, family obligations, and financial concerns are proof of their ethic of care and commitment to their families, supporters, and jobs. These women constantly put others in front of their own desires to continue in the challenge. Here, a different type of challenge takes over as the difficulties of the road force a woman to challenge her own ability to choose between her family and her goals. As such, the decision to quit is in conflict with their identities as Hoka Hey warriors. Simultaneously this can make a female warrior feel like something other than a warrior. This serves as proof that a woman's fight extends from the road into her home and family life. Like other studies focusing on why female athletes terminate their activities, the Hoka Hey women similarly listed the need to return to work as preventing further participation, pointing to her financial responsibilities at home. Women also listed family as a reason to quit or not returning to the challenge. The gendered expectation of women to care for family made the Hoka Hey too risky an endeavor.

The masculine environment of the Hoka Hey promotes the assumption women will not finish the challenge. At the onset, other competitors count women out of the Hoka Hey—and many other sporting environments. Our natural predispositions and socially constructed narratives assume women will be less successful than male challengers. Because women have to prove themselves as equals to men through completion of the challenge, there could be an increase in the perceived pressure to complete. The act of quitting becomes critically important when there is already an assumption you will not be successful. Tristica's feelings about working at the Harley-Davidson proving ground support this idea; she states, "But I've pretty much proven to everybody there that I can do everything that every single male employee can do. And I can also surpass them in most things."[6] Her determination to be seen as an equal precludes her from failing and in fact genders failing as female. While this may be an internalized, perceived pressure, it is pressure nonetheless—a feeling that functions as a motivator and a hindrance. The pressure can increase women's competitive spirit or it could keep women from participating. When a woman quits because of the level of difficulty of the challenge, it could support the stereotype of women as weak, inferior, or less successful. Because one woman rider represents all women riders, there is a fear—or at least an acknowledgment—that if one person quits it will reflect poorly on the entire group.

Further, you can read the action of quitting as a traditionally female gendered action. In sport, common language associates women with lesser positions. "You hit like a girl" and other such phrasing not only keeps women in an inferior position in sport but also connects women to the act of failing. Likewise, derogatory name-calling typically associated with the act of quitting links directly to women. For example, using the term "pussy" to goad a fellow rider who contemplates quitting, or who cannot make a ride, points to an association of women (or, more explicitly, our genitalia) with an act of weakness. Although not born from the Hoka Hey or motorcycle culture specifically, the anti-feminine nature of such expletives contributes to a woman's sense of inferiority and association with failure. This is akin to hostile work environments in which women often feel uncomfortable because of lewd jokes or comments about the female body or mind. As in the workplace, which requires a woman to defend her gender, the Hoka Hey requires women to set themselves apart from men. It is no wonder women feel a need to complete the challenge and thus defend our gender as equal to men.

As the composite narrative at the beginning of this chapter shows, women who participate in the Hoka Hey are determined to finish thus making it harder to fathom quitting. Gender expectations and intrinsic motivation push the women. There is a sense of guilt associated with leaving the road, stemming from the women's sense of determination. Failure to complete the challenge not only means letting down their family or people they met along the way but also letting down the other women on the challenge. In this masculine environment, women are tokens. We represent more than just ourselves as an individual rider. Women must be defendants and champions of the entire gender. Moreover, the act of speaking or writing about quitting exposes you as a quitter, which could extend feelings of guilt, shame, or regret. Because of this gendered experience, women feel a need to justify the action of quitting the challenge. Women tend to carry that sense of determination and grit with them through the challenge. Embodying their ethic of care, they stay on the road at all costs to waylay their sense of guilt. In other words, wanting to leave the road is not enough to quit; rather, the road must force you to quit.

Accidents and Wrecks

The deer came from nowhere. The flash of its translucent blue eyes stick in my lights. In front of me, Mark missed the deer. I swerve. The deer zigzags. Bam. I can't stop it. Fur, antlers, hooves, handle bars, spokes, brakes. My eyes slam shut, an unconscious reaction. I don't want to see what comes next. We collide into a mesh of chrome and flesh and pavement. Breathless. It happens fast but seems like an eternity. My mind watching in slow motion; the cacophonous sound of the crash, the piercing last screams of the deer, and the scorch of metal ring in my ears while I slide on my side, feeling leather burn through to flesh. Bike and body skidding together down the road in a wash of sparks past the twitching carcass. My bike and I are in this together. The purpose for this trip flashes in my mind as I skid to a halt into the cold metal guardrail— just missing the terrifying ride off the cliff. This is not *how this story is supposed to end. This is* not *how this is supposed to end. "You're supposed to be bringing home money for the Northern Nevada Children's Cancer Foundation. You're supposed to be seeing the country." Just beating myself up.*[7] *Then a calm washes over me as I climb my way out from under the bike and peer into the dark abyss I narrowly escaped. I'm fine. No harm done to me. My bike protected me and took the brunt of the accident. But it did. I can keep going. I'm not dead.*

Mark stopped down the road after hearing the crash. He hopped from his bike and sprinted towards me through the rain. I yank on my handle bars and scream to him, "Help me get this bike up, we gotta go, we gotta GO!" My panicked voice reflects the adrenaline of surviving the crash and the extreme sleep deprivation. I couldn't get the words out fast enough. My hands, slick from the rain, melt off the bike as I try to pull it from the ground alone. As he approaches he spits out his blunt command, "Sit your ass down." He made me sit down. And of course, he's Mr. EMT, he went through all that stuff with me. And he spent quite a bit of time trying to pick the bike back up thinking that quite possibly we could duct tape and zip tie it back together. That ends up not to be the case.[8] *Thankful I am fine but disappointment and sadness flood over me. Maybe this is exactly how this story is supposed to end. Obviously. Who am I to have control over it? I'm alive. I did not get hurt. I have no idea why that deer was supposed to jump out at me, out in front of me the way it did. I have no clue why my chapter ended there.*[9]

We call for help. Truck is on the way. Mark gets back on his bike and keeps going. I urged him to continue. Finish for us. When he finally takes off, I sit on the guardrail and just start to cry.[10] *Forced from the road. The rain pours over me, drowning out my tears. His taillight fades as he rounds the next corner, off to attempt and finish what I could no longer do.*

The experience above shows a woman forced from the road. Accidents and wrecks are common on the Hoka Hey, but not all result in a rider's inability to complete the challenge. Some riders whose motorcycles sustain significant damage rent or purchase a new motorcycle to continue riding. This denotes a high-level socioeconomic stability, which is not accessible to all riders and specifically is unattainable to the majority of the women interviewed. Riders shake off other accidents not resulting in injury or excessive damage and return to the challenge. However, when an accident forces a rider from the road, they view it as a justifiable reason to leave. Rather than being perceived by other riders as an excuse to quit, accidents are seen by many as circumstances outside of riders' control and thus acceptable within the culture. This "It wasn't me, it was the road" attitude preserves feelings of masculinity and strength. Quitting because of an outside, inexplicable force takes the onus off the rider and takes out of question the rider's ability to ride hard and be competitive. Beyond taking the responsibility off the rider, some accidents can make a rider seem more masculine. In particular, surviving an accident increases a rider's perceived toughness.

Further, when a woman rider leaves the challenge due to an outside force, she is not weak, but a fellow competitor who succumbed to the road. Here, another form of gender bending takes place and the woman becomes a gender-neutral rider affected by external conditions. Men who dominate the culture dictate the terms upon which riders deem quitting acceptable. Here, riders view leaving the challenge as a lost battle rather than an event that deems a rider a "pussy" or a quitter. When a rider wrecks because of something out of their control they leave the challenge with honor, dignity, and masculinity intact. Contributing to this is the knowledge the road can force any rider to leave at any time. In this sense, riders see the road as a worthy adversary, an unforeseen enemy on the field of battle. Here the wounded warrior imagery comes to mind. The fallen female rider becomes a true warrior rather than a weakling or a coward, further masculinizing her as a tough rider.

Personal Health and Safety

I sat down in North Carolina and cried like a baby because I had to come home.[11] *I knew I couldn't finish the challenge. It is too long. I don't feel well. It's probably just because I'm tired. My legs are so swollen. Probably just from sitting. I didn't anticipate having the swellingness that I had. I'm used to riding in heat. I am consuming a lot of water. But when you're not moving other than getting off your bike, putting gas in it, and an occasional walk to the convenience store—my legs are ENORMOUS.*[12] *I'll walk more often.*

It is so long. They didn't tell us how long it was going to be. No one expected it to be this long. I have to be back at work. I have taken all of my time off and my sick days and everything to accomplish this. I'm into Raleigh, North Carolina. I still have about 3,000 miles to go. It is Tuesday. I have to get into Vermont and then I have to get into Canada. And then I need to turn around and come all the way back to New Mexico and be home by next Tuesday to go to work.[13] *That's only a week. It's not enough time. I have to admit it. Because there is no way I am going to be able to accomplish this. But finishing means so much to me. Tears stream down my face. I try to reason the other way. I'll just call off work. I'll get home when I get home. That's crazy. Crazy. Not reality. I have a home and a mortgage payment and everything else. And my boss, the owner of the dealership, has been extremely good to me and my husband. I couldn't do that to him. I have to go back to work. I'll let him down one way or another—the letdown of not finishing is better than the letdown of not coming back at all. He was my sponsor also and as much as it hurts me to come home, I have to come home.*[14]

I will be completely up front, I cried All. The. Way. Home. Like a baby. I cried. And nothing in life has made me cry like that did.[15] *And then of course when I got home, it's a good thing I left the challenge. That's when it was all said and done that my doctors started doing some other stuff, other tests, they thought I had a heart blockage and then they found out that it wasn't a blockage. That I had an actual congenital heart defect that I shouldn't have lived past the first year of life with.*[16] *Leaving the Hoka Hey ended up saving my life. I wouldn't have known about the defect if I hadn't had my legs swell up so much in North Carolina. If I hadn't turned around then. If I hadn't left the road.*

Carla Dubois's story is an unbelievable triumph in the face of adversity, push-until-you-can't-go-on tribute to life. Participating in two Hoka Hey challenges, she has yet to cross the finish line but remains undaunted. Her scenario is akin to the many men who attempt the challenge more than once but do not finish. Beth Durham, co-founder of the Hoka Hey, says more men than women try the challenge multiple times but never complete it. The road keeps nailing Carla and she keeps coming back for more. She is the embodiment of grit. Her first Hoka Hey ended in a lifesaving diagnosis but felt like debilitating failure. On her second attempt, she blew out a tire and had an accident that landed her in the hospital for weeks. Much like Lynne Cox, Carla realizes that no athletic feat is worth losing your life over. Her grit kept her moving and hospitalization did not stop Carla; she recovered and jumped back on her bike. She will ride again in the 2018 ride, remaining undaunted.

While Carla's injuries can be associated with masculinity, her desire to care for her own health was an extension of her love for her family. An ethic of care informed her decision. As a woman, Carla had to take care of herself so she could care for her family. In her interview, Carla described feeling as if she would let people down "one way or another," indicating that leaving the challenge or not leaving the challenge would affect those around her in different ways. For example, she would let her boss down if she did not return to work but would also let him down because she felt he would be disappointed if she did not finish the challenge. While caregiving does not preclude men, women are traditionally situated as *the* primary caregivers. Choosing to leave the road during her first Hoka Hey to care for her family fulfills the female gender role. As she made the decision to leave the road, she thought first of her family and support group. Her sense of duty to her employer/sponsor and her family took precedence over her own desires to finish the challenge. Tears show how conflicted she was making the decision to leave the course. Carla describes this as not only a personal struggle, but also a decision she made with the thoughts and feelings of others in her life in mind. Women do not make the decision to leave in isolation. Instead, the need to care for her family informs her actions. Trapped in the binary between a feminine desire to be a caregiver and a masculine desire to complete a difficult ride, Carla's situation shows the balance women in endurance sport face.

I should note that like many social constructions, Carla's perceptions might not be the reality. Her family and friends likely would not feel let down because Carla did not finish the challenge. Very few people probably remember that she did not finish. When we are in a (seemingly) shameful situations, we automatically assume the worst. This feeling that everyone is looking at you intensifies when you are one of a small number. I point again to women riders feeling representative of all women riders and to the Panopticon-like effect of the GPS tracking system. However, our perceptions quickly become our realities under the severe mental and physical pressure of the challenge (even if only in our own minds) and the way women think about others shows our desire to preform care-based femininity.

The near-fatal accident on her second Hoka Hey transitioned Carla from woman rider to warrior within the context of the challenge. Rather than surrounding her female body with shame and weakness, members of the group venerate her as a warrior for returning to the road after her recovery. While this distinction may prove that hegemonic masculinity does not only apply to men, it also shows masculinized strength to be the desired goal. Carla identifies as a Hoka Hey warrior woman; by doing so she furthers her connection with the masculine world. Likewise, the image of the wounded warrior creates delineation between a valid and invalid reason to leave the challenge. The physicality of Carla's injuries creates a sense of masculinity.

Her physical wounds bring her closer to the culture, more an insider than if she had left the challenge for emotional reasons. She escapes the stigma of quitting by sustaining physical injuries. It is possible here to draw a clear connection between the masculinity of body/physicality and femininity of emotions.

The space between masculinity and femininity the women of the Hoka Hey occupy allows for feelings of great triumph but also of great shame. Many successful women similarly occupy this space between being high achieving and being dutiful. This is easily expressed with the troupe of the successful woman who rises to a high level in the workplace and is subsequently seen as a gender bender because she does not care for her children. The masculine space of success for achieving her goal and the feminine space of needing to care for her family and employer pull Carla in multiple directions. Neither scenario would easily fulfill societal and cultural expectations of her. She's damned if she does, damned if she doesn't here. In some ways, the gender-neutral zone between remaining in the challenge and leaving is the "appropriate" place for women. Women succeed within the confines of the Hoka Hey culture by finishing and then go on to succeed as women by fulfilling traditional roles. It is not enough to finish, you have to finish and still be a good mom/employee/daughter. As gender bending women of the Hoka Hey, we are both masculine and feminine, further evidence that the logic of a binary is ill-suited for our multiple layers of identity.

Familial Duty

I stood in the parking lot of the Canadian truck stop, mouth agape. It came from nowhere like a fist to the head. Was he serious? His unnervingly demure voice rang through my head, now cleared of any other thoughts but those seven words. "Well, what do you want to do?" He asked me as if we were taking a leisurely ride through the countryside or choosing between eating dinner at home or in a restaurant. We were doing anything but. I didn't know there was another option. We were going to get on the road and ride another six hundred miles toward the next checkpoint. That's all there was to do. He was serious. Seriously posing another option, seriously insinuating that we could—no, should—quit.

Speechless. Dumbfounded. Head reeling. Still speechless. Now stuttering. Stammering to get anything out. "Whaa.... What.... What do you mean?" I know I had just dropped my bike for the second time in two consecutive days, but that was no reason to quit! So what, I did that last year. This felt like my fault. "Is this my fault?" I asked pointedly. He denied it. Again. Again. Like Peter denying Jesus. "No, my foot hurts." He looked disappointedly down at his presumably ailing appendage. An unfathomable problem keeping us from moving on, it seemed so small. I squinted as the sun flooded over his wide shoulders. Holding my hands over my eyes as a visor I began to process what he was saying, desperately putting pieces of the last few days together to make sense of this asinine request. "Is this new? You haven't said anything about it since we left. I can tape it." Was that a smirk on his face? Disappointment perhaps? Too hard to tell through the ever-growing mustache and now beard. *"It's going to be hot when we get down south too, I don't think it will do well in the heat…. Sault Saint Marie is just down the road, we could go home through Michigan."* Still trying to make sense of what was happening, I shot back into reality, remembering that our riding party was baking in the hot sun waiting for us to mount our bikes. *"Let's just go inside and talk about this. I guess I'll tell them to get on the road?"*

I staggered over to Wendy and Bill. They looked expectantly in my direction but still carried on their conversation as if to indicate that they hadn't just heard our interaction. "He wants to go, I think. Says his foot hurts, but it feels like my fault, but he says it's not. You guys can go ahead. I'm not sure what's going on." My eyes were dry for the moment, having cried for the better part of an hour after my spill; the anger, bewilderment, and disappointment boiling inside kept the tears at bay. "Are you sure?" Wendy asked. "I guess…" Seeing Bill look away from me, I noticed my dad wandering over. "You not feeling well?" Bill asked as he accepted my dad's extended hand. "Nope. Think this is it for us. You guys have a good ride." Everyone looked surprised and simultaneously blank. He gave Wendy a hug. She turned to embrace me next. Through pursed lips she whispered in my ear, "Call me, we're just an hour down the road, two hours down the road, you can catch up." "Thanks, Wendy," I replied, contemplating the options. "I can't leave my dad." We said goodbye to KC, our fifth group member, and now down to three, they rode off down the course.

Taking the maps in our hands, we went inside the restaurant. "We don't have to go that hard, we can stop more often, sleep in hotels, whatever you want." I was pleading with him, frantically hoping it was truly not my fault that we were stopping. I felt the all-too-familiar-tears welling up in my eyes as I chose a booth in the far corner and ordered an ice water. The air-conditioning offered relief from the heat; I foolishly thought it might help him refocus. The table seemed to dwarf as he unfurled the large map of expansive Ontario. He was on a mission. Find our way home. Looking at a map to find a route on our own felt foreign. Crying louder now. Hyperventilating. Hate the way I cry. "It's not your fault." He looked over his rectangular glasses at me. "Do you believe me?" His voice was calm for the first time in days. The passion and heat of the challenge turned into serene composure. He seemed at peace. "Half…. I half believe you." His shoulders shrugged, letting out a single deep-sighing chuckle, shaking his head and staring down at the table. "It's not you." He continued looking at the map. "I'm sorry." Softer this time. His sereneness juxtaposed against my breathless sobs. My booming reply thrusting me back to childhood, helplessly wanting to care for the large man across from me, "No, daddy, don't be sorry. If you're hurt we should stop. I don't want you to be hurt." I saw tears beginning to well in his eyes too; he quickly picked up his dark sunglasses and fumbled them onto his head, skirting quickly from the table, leaving me behind with the map and my tears.

I exited the restaurant still in disbelief, still crying. It all made no sense. It was as if we were breaking up with one another, with the Hoka Hey, with the road. Frenzied, he threw his seat across the parking lot. "What are you doing?!" I asked, shocked as my stride lengthened to reach him faster. "I'm taking the tracker off. I don't need anyone to know where I am." It seemed like an act of desperation and disappointment in himself, or worse, in me. "Do you want yours off?" "No, it's ok," I responded, thinking it was far too hot to start taking seats off of motorcycles to unhook a GPS tracker. A look of shock struck his face, as if I told him I no longer wanted to be his daughter. Betrayal at its best. I hurried to redact my betrayal and appease his wishes, "Ok! Yes! Let's take it off! How does this come off?" I fumbled around the seat, as if I could take it off with my bare hands. Confused but still trying to please him and placate his desire to quit. He didn't say a word as he strode over to my bike and began pulling out tools to remove the sun-warmed leather seat. He hastily cut the wires from my tracker. Just like that, with the quick snip of side cuts slicing through plastic and metal like nothing, it's over. Little hope now. Silence. Deafening silence between us with only the whir of trucks going by on the road. No more words were spoken. We returned to the road toward Sault Saint Marie and the end of our journey, on the same road as the challenge, two hundred miles of thunderous silence ahead.

Forcing my thumbs to move across the small keypad, I pushed out one last blog post to sign off and end the chapter. Admitting I lost the challenge. Admitting I could not do it. This is the agony of defeat. The weight of an entire year building up to this moment fell on me as I succumbed to the notion that this last post was not a triumph but a defeat. "This will not make the book," I think as I carefully crafted the ambiguous words. I am not ready to face the shame. But I have to tell people we're leaving. Have to show my supporters I'm at least alive:

"Until Next Year...

Seems like this one just wasn't our year. More great memories, new friends, and lots of lessons learned.

Thanks for following along. Stay happy, healthy, and keep it shiny side up! We'll see you on the next big one" (Blog Post, June 27).

We return to our house without a hero's welcome. My mom isn't even home. We pull into the garage. I text her, begging her to come home and figure out what is wrong with him. He immediately begins unloading his bike. Bags, bungees, and squashed packs of Oreos fly through the air. His disdain for leaving the road shows through while he aggressively flings things across the garage in unorganized piles. I follow his lead. Taking things from my bike but putting them back where they belong. We unpack differently. Then he sidesteps past me, averting his eyes to the ground so as not to see me and disappears out of the garage. I see the white suburban barreling down the one lane road. My mom finally arrives. A warm hug feels good after the chilling silence of the past twenty-four hours. I want to cry but can't, unsure if my eyes are drained or if the raw emotion and hatred for our being home won't allow me to produce tears. My entire world changed in just a day. She goes inside the house to find my dad. I continue laying my wet belongings out in the driveway for the sun to eek the moisture out. After a short time, I decide to venture into the house; I need the bag for my sleeping bag. He sits on the bench in our kitchen, hidden by the stub wall. I can only see his feet stretched out into the walkway. My mom leans up against the counter facing him head on. Then I hear it. "She looked scared. I didn't think she could do it. I didn't want another eight days of her dropping that bike." Knocked in the chest. Breathless. Swaying. Dizzy. I stumble back down the hall toward the door, quickening my pace until I am back safely in my cabin, a few doors down from my parents on the lake we both call home. The tears return, stronger, faster, harder. I have been the one betrayed. I heard him! He said it was my fault. And he lied. Fuck him. Fuck that. I am never riding with him again. I want to rip the "My Dad's Biker Buddy" patch off my cut.

 The next hours are a blur. I stood lifeless in the shower, my tears mixing with the hot water until I was drained. My mom comes to the cabin. There are many hugs, many tears, and many passionate words exchanged out of exhaustion, disappointment, and betrayal. We are upset, hurt, and mad beyond words. She felt as betrayed as I did. She believed in me. He doesn't even realize he just lost his daughter, and his biggest supporter! Do you know how much I stick up for him when he's being a dick?! That's all over now. We will never come back from this. After we talked my mom said she told my dad to come down and talk. Get it out in the open or it's going to be very bad.

 My dad comes to my house. I am lying on the deck in my polka dot bikini sunning myself—a desperate attempt to soak up enough Vitamin D to change my disposition and symbolically be as far from motorcycling as I could possibly be. He comes through the screen door onto the porch as it slams behind him, sits on my teal Adirondack chair. I remain on the ground. I will not look at him. I will not speak first. "So, are we going to have this out?" There is a tinge of a snicker in his voice. This infuriates me. Somewhere inside me, I know his is a chuckle of desperation and guilt, not malice. We talk. I cry. He tries to defend himself in the only way he knows how, by diverting the topic and never *taking full responsibility for his actions. He only begrudgingly admits that he may have been wrong. This is an important "may," alleviating his guilt. This conversation becomes about something else. I do not know how we have taken this course. We talk in circles and confuse one another with illogic. We are both exhausted, more than we were the day before; this conversation compounds physical and mental exhaustion with emotional exhaustion. I tell him I am going to leave for a few days. Mom and I are going to go somewhere. This is my only vacation and I intend on using it. I do not want to speak to him. I do not want to look at him; but, I do what is right and I invite him to come along. He is not allowed to make any decisions. He will go where we want and will not complain. None of this happens.*

I struggled greatly with writing this chapter. In part because I still feel the act of telling my own story exposes myself as a quitter and because I continue to feel guilty about presenting my dad in this light. My desires to protect my dad as a man and as a great father remain in my thoughts and show my continued, and expected, role of woman serving the needs of another. Juxtaposed against this sense of duty and ethic of care, pushed on me by cultural gendered expectations, is my desire to prove myself as a warrior within the context of the Hoka Hey. Ashamed to tell people we left the road, I felt my own desire to fulfill the masculinized expectations of the challenge. Likewise, I felt stigmatized as a quitter, which placed a (perceived) divide between myself and the other riders. Sociologist Gerhard Falk discusses the trauma of stigma in his work, *Stigma: How We Treat Outsiders*. According to Falk, "all societies will always stigmatize some conditions and some behavior because doing so provides for group solidarity delineating 'outsiders' from 'insiders'" (13). The delineation between challenge finishers and all others emphasizes the need to finish and the stigma of quitting. Here it is possible to see a further development of group association because I viewed myself as an outsider; the desire to be a part of the culture was so strong, I thought ill of myself for not completing the challenge. While others may not have looked at me as a quitter, I viewed myself as such. I let myself down. I could not hack it. Because I hoped to not be fully stigmatized, I desperately clung to the notion that I did not leave the road because the challenge was difficult but rather I left the road because my dad did; because he was hurt; because I could not leave him; because I was his caretaker; because I remained loyal; because I enacted my ethic of care. These thoughts helped lessen the stigma and shame associated with my perceived inability to complete the challenge.

As a feminist, I know I did not need to fulfill the societal expectations of my gender; but as a daughter, I could not leave my dad. I had the power to remain on the road and finish the challenge. I could have ridden with the others in our group and kept going without him. However, my desire to remain dutiful to my family erased any other option than following my dad back home to Indiana. My desire to bend and break the gendered expectations of women paled in comparison to the strong feelings of completing my role as a woman. Leaving my dad is not part of my identity. Riding as a team, we carried a no-man-left-behind attitude. While quitting is not part of who I am, more importantly I would not go back on my promise to remain together.

Despite my autonomy, I feel indebted to my father as his caretaker. Ann Burack-Weiss describes the pull of a family caretaker in her work *The Caregiver's Tale: Loss and Renewal in Memoirs of Family Life*. Burak-Weiss describes this by saying, "A feeling of being robbed and cheated of the life one expected to lead is common, sometimes resulting in an angry outburst directed at the ... family member" (148). In some ways, caring for my father on the Hoka Hey when he said his foot caused him problems foreshadowed my role as his caretaker later in life. Taking this responsibility and his pain seriously, I (un)consciously transitioned from daughter in need of protection to adult woman offering care and support. As a researcher, I pushed through the feelings of shame as well as the guilt of exposing my dad to complete the narrative of hegemonic gender roles. In addition to the shame associated with quitting the challenge, my sensitivity to my dad's masculinity entwines with my ethic of care. Moreover, telling my story exposes my dad's feelings. I contemplated the consequences of sharing this narrative and chose to leave specific details out to protect him while also being true to my experience.

Gender obligations similarly shroud my dad's decision to leave the road. He felt the need to protect me as a man and as a father. His desire to be the protector showed itself in multiple forms. First, he felt he protected me by forcing me to leave the challenge. Although I did not see it as such, he felt it his responsibility to tell me to leave the road because he feared for my safety. Secondly, he protected my feelings by telling me that leaving the road was not my fault. Because he showed compassion for my feelings, he offered an ulterior motive for quitting the challenge. By saying he did not feel well, he gave up his sense of masculinity for my desire to break gender expectations and complete the challenge. While he could admit to me that he did not feel well, that he, not I, wanted to leave the challenge, he subsequently told others we left the road because I could not handle the ride. This shows a need to restore his masculinity.

While he may not see it this way, I perceived his actions to be proof that his masculinity meant more to him than his relationship with his daughter. He chose the façade of virility over my actual feelings and desire to finish the challenge. My dad might seem like a not-so-great guy in this scenario, and I certainly do not pretend that he is an angel; but in reality he is an advocate for women's issues or at least issues affecting the women in his life. Part of my hesitance to write this chapter comes from my desire to protect my dad's reputation. The fact that I am exposing our family trauma flies in the face of my desire to care for my dad and protect his masculinity. You could also interpret my telling of our story as further assertion of my dad as a hegemonically masculine misogynist. By choosing his own desire over mine, he reinforces the dominant narrative that men make decisions and women follow. Within motorcycle culture, this behavior is lauded rather than loathed.

In this case, the execution of my dad's actions perpetuated his masculinity, perhaps despite his intentions. Rather than speaking to me as a fellow rider and equal partner, he made a choice for me, relegating me to an inferior position. However, his masculinity may not have been the true crux of making me leave the road. My dad may have felt he enacted his own ethic of care by removing me from the challenge. Like my divergence from woman warrior to dutiful daughter, he may have felt a pull between performing his masculinity by completing the challenge and his own ethic of care as a father protecting his daughter. He likely viewed this as an act of kindness and his fatherly obligation; however, the manner in which he executed the removal reinforced his role as masculine protector. The Hoka Hey continually pulls riders between worlds and across boundaries. This event is likely no different. His own fear of losing his daughter trumped his desire to complete the challenge, blurring the boundary between masculine and feminine.

Much like our gender performance is part of who we are, the act of quitting or leaving the challenge becomes wrapped in our identities. The Hoka Hey, like many endurance challenges, develops into a significant part of challengers' lives. For many, training, raising funds, and spending time on the ride take so much of our time it is hard to identify ourselves outside of the challenge. When we are forced, or choose, to leave the road, it is like leaving a part of ourselves. Taking on a challenge like the Hoka Hey requires a grit mindset that precludes quitting. When that happens, we are in uncharted territory, abandoning who we thought we were, leaving ourselves on the side of the road to chart a new path. The stigma associated with leaving the challenge remains with us until we realize quitting and finishing are another binary with little relevance on reality.

The binary of right and wrong plays into our decisions to leave the road as well. Because of our position in the community and need to defend ourselves as women riders, we assume there to be valid and invalid reasons for leaving the challenge. Women of the Hoka Hey listed female gendered reasons for leaving the road such as familial duty and health. Situated in opposition of these reasons is being forced from the road by an outside force such as a wreck or an accident, which increase the rider's toughness. Although other challengers might not perceive them as such, both the feminized and masculinized reasons to leave the challenge become valid in the minds of the women of the Hoka Hey. Further, the masculinized perceptions of validity permeate the attitudes of the men and women who ride the Hoka Hey. While we may all claim to ride our own rides, we also feel the need to justify our actions with some sort of higher power, valid reason, or redemptive purpose. The fact that we remind ourselves to ride our own rides proves the distrusting nature of the culture. We tell ourselves we are on the road, competing against ourselves, but also compare ourselves to other riders when we fail to reach our own goals. This shows the in-betweenness of the Hoka Hey—a challenge fighting binaries of masculine/feminine, affluent/poor, white/Native, and strong/weak.

The act of qualifying the reason or excuse to quit is in itself a chauvinistic act. This assumes that a person cannot quit the challenge simply because they want to quit or because it is difficult. It assumes the existence of a righteous path and a fallible path. The sense of reasoning is born from a storytelling culture where you must explain what happened on your journey. Motorcycle culture is a culture of one-upmanship, of power, and of proving worthiness. Within this culture, you must prove yourself part of the club rather than receiving acceptance for who you are intrinsically. Acceptance comes in part from explaining yourself to the larger group; by telling about an amazing ride, by proving you had a reason to take a certain action. However, accidents, health issues, and familial duties are not simply reasons to leave the Hoka Hey, they are reactions fueled by a gendered experience—even a run in with an animal turns into a situation forcing women to question her responsibilities and ethic of care. We cannot just hit the deer and move on; we must first contemplate what our actions mean for the larger community of women, family, and supporters. When push really comes to shove, we take the role of women first and rider second.

Conclusion

Scholarly literature on motorcycling and sport indicate sport and motorcycling as sources of empowerment for women (here I refer again to Theberge, Jansen, Mullins, and Ferrar). Likewise, as the narratives woven throughout this work suggest, women find empowerment through participating in motorsports such as the Hoka Hey. Cyclically, empowerment and identity (re)formation inform one another, creating nomadic, gender nonconforming identities of challengers as riders, warriors, and women. Through negotiating and navigating the masculinized environment and overcoming social restraints, women challengers have the ability to effect individual change. These processes of empowerment, the gendered experience, change, and transgression make clear the need for an elimination of such binaries as feminine/masculine, white/Native American, rich/poor, and a larger shift in perception toward an increasingly grey area.

Postmodern scholars Deleuze and Guattari suggest the rhizome (a biological reference—think about a web or a root system) as a conception of power to support an integrated network in which no one thing or person is more important than another. Rather than a traditional hierarchy, postmodernism supports an interrelated power structure through which all things, choices, people, and situations impact and connect to one another. The perception shift suggested throughout this book should incorporate an overall acceptance of the women challengers as empowered, confident motorcyclists, and a formative change in how we, as scholars, participants, and onlookers, view sport. Overall, the Hoka Hey emerges as an example of extreme lifestyle sport, acting as a meaningful event[1] and gendered experience[2] with the ability to create and effect change as is possible in sport.

Restrictive gender roles may not keep all women from participating, but it does bring their participation and intentions constantly into question. "Why are they these women participating?" and "How are these women going to succeed?" are questions asked—sometimes aloud but often unspoken—by their families and the public, as well as other riders, affecting women's participation in all lifestyle sports. Because we currently view sport as a hierarchical system in which women athletes are less valued than men, these questions remain. However, a postmodern view of sport reinforces the interconnections between genders, potentially eliminating questions of participation based on gender. The flimsy gender binary evaporates when we conceptualize sports as relational. Regardless of their chosen identities or their level of participation, women's involvement in motorcycling culture is a gendered experience with the ability to create change.

As you have read throughout this work, women's participation and presence in a masculine culture has the ability to effect change. Specifically in regards to the Hoka Hey, the idea that the toughest rider on Earth might be a woman is paramount in masculine cultures. The presence of women in the challenge nullifies the simple notion that a man must be the toughest rider on Earth and challenges our perceptions of the masculine environment. Here, women's acceptance and ability to enter the competition takes an important stance on women's ability and legitimacy as expert riders. In an arena where simply showing up would make a difference, the women who participate in the Hoka Hey are doing far more than the minimum; they excel in this world. While participation may be sufficient, women's success in the Hoka Hey furthers the acceptance and appreciation of women as skilled and confident riders.

A direct result of women's participation in the Hoka Hey, the public's and male riders' perceptions about women riders alter. On a number of levels, women create change by changing minds. First, women who participate in the Hoka Hey have the ability to push boundaries of generally accepted principles of femininity. Be it through seeing themselves as non-gendered, or appreciating their "otherness" or "specialness" in a male work environment, or riding a motorcycle, these hard-riding, tough-it-out women riders shift culturally accepted norms of women as demure, soft, and fragile creatures who must remain indoors. Riding enables them to become a more complete person—not just a man or woman riding a motorcycle. Motorcycle scholars such as Joans, Ferrar, and Jansen already support this notion by understanding women riders as "the perfect psychic balance of feminine and masculine" (Jansen 11). Rather than inflexible identities, their gender performances are fluid and dynamic.

Second, because of women's high levels of success in the Hoka Hey, male challengers' opinions of female riders change. After completing the challenge, male counterparts see women riders not as an appendage to the culture but instead as Hoka Hey sisters who can keep up, ride, and make it just as well as, if not better than, some men can. This further blurring of the male/female binary makes clear the connection to postmodernism. As women enter the challenge, they touch male challengers' lives, whose altered perceptions in turn effect change within their own communities. The burst of energy created through women's participation in the Hoka Hey blazes new paths within the construction of alternative understandings of sport, sending shock waves of change through larger motorcycle culture and beyond.

Third, as perceptions of ourselves and men's perceptions of us change, so do the public perceptions of female riders. By serving as role models, and with the influx of women riders in motorcycle culture more generally, women riders of the Hoka Hey have the unique ability to effect change on a national (and international) scale. As we travel across the country during the challenge, people adore, laud, and encourage women for their participation. Rather than their riding ability being a detriment to their femininity, women interviewed stated people were "impressed" by their ability to execute the challenge and largely viewed participation in the Hoka Hey as positive. This post-challenge success shows a divergence from previous notions and feelings that women should feel guilty because of their participation in the event and increases women's interconnectivity to those around them. Again, the ethics of care reinforce the connections between athlete/fan/supporter/coach. By touching lives through their sport, the women of the Hoka Hey add to a nonhierarchical conception of sport.

It is particularly important to note the Hoka Hey culture has changed since I began working on this book in 2011. As a microcosmic example of the larger culture, I believe the challenge operators, specifically Jim Red Cloud, became more accepting of women riders. While I am unsure of Jim's personal stance on women riders prior to my meeting him, there is evidence of change within the culture. For example, while I detail an advertisement in which Jim refers to the Hoka Hey as a ride for the "toughest men on Earth," the Hoka Hey website and other documents now identify the challenge as one for the "toughest riders on Earth." There is a marked difference in the use of gender-neutral language to describe riders rather than masculine language. This type of change makes the challenge more accepting and welcoming of women riders and eliminates gender-based hierarchies. The breakdown of gender differences is a step toward a new understanding of sport. Here, as Mary Jo Kane's continuum of sport suggests, ability can supersede gender as a marker of success. This simple change in language is a small step toward inclusivity that might someday permeate motorcycle culture.

Today, the Hoka Hey functions in a similar nonhierarchical model. Prior to his death in 2017, founder Jim Red Cloud took a different role in the challenge. Focusing more on the Pine Ridge reservation and his work with the Lakota people, Jim stepped away from directing and running the challenge before he passed away in the summer of 2017. I recall a rider meeting before the 2013 ride in which Jim explained his need to step back. He questioned the participants about what we wanted to see from the challenge. Where did

Jim Red Cloud (left) and Abby Van Vlerah (right) at the finish of the 2012 HHMC in the Seneca Nation. (Author photo.)

we see the future of the Hoka Hey? Passionate about the Hoka Hey, there was a resounding yes in response to the question "Should we continue to do this?" Participants made various suggestions on how to move forward. Perhaps we should only run a big challenge every other year? Perhaps we should make it shorter or less expensive so more people could participate? The challenge operators' decision and ability to ask and listen to the challengers is in itself a feminist act. White hetero capitalist patriarchy rarely uses this collective style of leadership; and it shows the grey area between masculine and feminine and/or white and Native American cultures.

While operators made no official decisions at the rider meeting in 2013, a dedicated few came together in the years after to form the Hoka Hey Board of Directors. This consortium (maybe they will become feminists after all) plans the route, recruits new riders, and connects with the community. The collective consists of both male and female riders from previous challenges. Continuing the spirit of the challenge, the newly revised Hoka Hey website displays a more prominent donation request for the Pine Ridge reservation. Those running the challenge seem to have fully embraced the ethic of care model typical of the women riders. Although the new operators of the Hoka Hey may not think of themselves in this way, they are creating change for women in the motorcycling community. These simple changes to be more inclusive have the opportunity to make a significant impact on women riders.

While women have great capacity to create change in masculine environments, it is important to note women should not solely be required to spur these changes. In other words, women should not have to teach the world about women's oppression. Rather, we should all work together to make fundamental changes (albeit small at first) in the way we interact, present ourselves, and understand the limits of gender roles. For change to truly take effect, male riders must not only profess to others that women are skilled and competent riders but also truly believe this themselves, and show it through their words and actions—a concept with which even my own father still struggles. We might not be there yet, but by working together (as seen through the new model of the Hoka Hey), substantive changes can permeate masculine spaces.

This work makes clear that rigid binaries and hegemonic gender roles do not include an interpretation of identities that are nomadic or fluid. As more and more women and men move away from traditional femininity and masculinity we must continue to challenge and change our conception of what is "right" or "best." By understanding that there is no singular or correct way to be masculine or feminine, we grow in our appreciation of others and ourselves. Motorcycle culture, which tends toward being anti-establishment and promotes anarchy and individualism, can be a cultural incubator for establishing change and eliminating restrictive binaries. However, because it is so steeped in masculinity, effecting change within this space is difficult and slow-moving. Regardless, women riders of the Hoka Hey add to this potential elimination of rigidity by embracing their fluid identities as women, riders, and women riders.

Women and women riders should note empowerment does not come only through taking on the Hoka Hey. Empowerment can come from any number of sources including many leisure activities other than motorcycling. Potentially the most important quality among the women who rode the Hoka Hey is their ability to change their minds about themselves. They adapted to difficult situations and were able to feel good about their decisions no matter the situation. They show an enormous amount of determination, grit, and passion. Harnessing the power within you to take on any challenge should be empowering. Many women of the Hoka Hey advised taking up motorcycling, running, cooking, or any other new challenge. Each woman found that taking on those challenges could change her world and the world around her.

In addition to creating change and transgression within the motorcycling community, this work has implications for (re)conceptualizing sport to include the ever-changing and multi-layered understandings of gender. I propose, and suggest further research be done on, creating more postmodern models for understanding sport. Rather than a linear continuum, a postmodern (potentially rhizomatic) model would appreciate all sports as valid and equally worthy. No longer stacked from best to worst, the interconnected model would clearly show that all sports touch, intersect, diverge, and converge to create an intricate web of ability, gender, competition, and success. If we think of sport in other ways then we are better able to conceptualize a world in which each sport has its own unique value. This model also allows us to decouple monetary value from perceived value; in other words, greatness is not dependent on how much an athlete makes or how much money a single group spends on a sport through ticket sales, advertising, and aftermarket promotions. In a postmodern understanding of sport, simply because football brings in a large amount of revenue does not automatically position it as the most important sport. Likewise, the performance, ability, or greatness of an athlete need not link directly to how much money he or she makes; rather, an athlete's value is derived from alternative means, such as personal growth. In this model, by embracing alternative competition styles, the Hoka Hey, like other lifestyle sports, challenges the center of sport.

Eliminating binaries and embracing permeable gender identities adds to the changing perceptions that enable masculine culture to be more inclusive. While there is a distinct possibility that the majority of people who make up motorcycle culture do not *want* to change, the presence of few but strong women and other minorities within the boundaries of the culture push all riders toward a change in attitudes and perceptions. As the economic landscape continues to change and motorcycling sees an influx of new riders (including more women), cultural shifts are inevitable. What motorcycling needs now is to keep up with its changing clientele and discontinue harboring the center of this sport, which steeps itself in sexual oppression, racism, and antiquated notions of masculinity and femininity. Although still present in the news, on television, and in the media, gone are the days of one-percenter outlaw motorcycle gangs ruling large over the motorcycling world. As more people take to the roads on two wheels, these pervasive images continue to simultaneously depreciate and appreciate in cultural value. Cultural change and growing acceptance must come from within; women riders of the Hoka Hey are at the forefront of this change.

Chapter Notes

Introduction

1. In his 2002 work, *Taking the Field: Men, Women, and Sports,* Michael Messner discusses the concept of the center of sport. We laud the most elite players of the most culturally valued sports, therefore creating a "center of sport." These athletes hold a position of power over other athletes. Hegemonic masculinity in sport often manifests itself in the denigration of others and can come in the form of misogyny, homonegativism, racism, classism, or violence. Messner's work suggests that being at the "center" of sport requires strength, dominance, a "rough and tumble" attitude, and a relentless sense of competition—all traits associated with masculinity. The "center" of sport "is a position occupied by the biggest, wealthiest, and most visible sports programs and athletes" (xviii). The center is considered best and results in all other sports and athletes who do not fit into this category being marginalized or seen as less valuable. In other words, if you're not on the winning football team, you do not matter as much.

2. Feminist Cultural Studies combines feminist theories and cultural studies theories (Krane). Using this framework, I examine the multifaceted challenges faced by women participants of endurance challenges through an intersectional lens. Intersectionality, the understanding of multiple forms of oppression such as race, class, gender, and sexuality, allows feminist cultural studies scholars to view power structures as hierarchical, layered, and converging. In other words, by applying an intersectional lens, scholars see that it is not only our gender, but also our race and class which affect our daily lives. Intersectionality is paramount throughout my analysis, as I remain cognizant of and reflexive toward the fact that the women involved in this study may be subject to multiple forms of intersecting oppression. Specifically, I look at how race, class, and gender intersect in the Hoka Hey Motorcycle Challenge. Furthermore, cultural studies analyze lived experiences of daily life critically and reflexively. In researching everyday behaviors--such as our leisure activities--cultural studies seeks to further understand ideological apparatuses, cultural assumptions, and daily oppressions, all of which inform our worldview. Building on these ideas, feminist cultural studies applies an intersectional (gendered/raced/classed) perspective to everyday experiences of individuals, which often include fluid understandings of the self and other. By understanding that identities are multilayered, feminist cultural studies seeks to uncover the injustice, oppression, and opportunities for growth and transformation in everyday life. Krane notes that "sport researchers employ feminist cultural studies to explore women's lived experiences in sport and physical activity and to understand the cultural conditions that confront them" (406). As applied to motorcycling, I use feminist cultural studies to explore women's experiences as motorcyclists in an effort to understand the challenges they face as women in a masculine culture. This requires an intersectional analysis and must specifically deal with hegemonic structures that we take for granted in daily life. In this study specifically, I look at the gendered, classed, and racial experiences of female motorcycle riders. In an effort to create an increasing awareness of

otherwise silenced voices, I highlight opinions and stories from marginalized populations (women in motorcycling). This work seeks to expose the issues related to gender, class, and race in motorcycling that are taken for granted or go unquestioned. Throughout this project, I rely on feminist cultural studies to inform and guide my purpose and research.

Chapter 1

1. Sheila, 2010 (548–550).
2. Kelly Quinn, 2012 (227–230).
3. Junie Rose, 2010–2014 (643–645).
4. Sherie, 2010 (145–146).
5. Wendy, 2011–2014 (219–222).
6. In 2010, riders received a small pictorial representation of the route on the first page of each direction set; however, they did not receive specific mileage between turns, as was the case in subsequent years.
7. Schatzi, 2011–2013 (617–620).
8. Sheila, 2010 (335–336).
9. Carla, 2011, 2013 (277–281).
10. Tristica, 2010 (504–511).
11. Wendy, 2011–2014 (301–303).
12. Debra, 2011 (129–132).
13. Sheila, 2010 (321–323).
14. Bryana, 2010 (228).
15. The phrase "myth and symbol" emerged in the 1950s and came to mark the discipline of American Studies. Simply put, myth and symbol is both a theoretical concept and method that imbues images with meaning and value. In this context, the images of both the motorcycle and the natural environment conjure meaning far beyond their material being.
16. Gloria Anzaldua describes this "inbetweenness," this process of embodying multiple cultures, as "floundering in uncharted seas" (McCann and Kim 255). She goes on to note, "in perceiving conflicting information and points of view, she is subjected to a swamping of her psychological borders" (255).
17. Eden, 2010, 2011 (206–285).

Chapter 2

1. As noted by Patricia Maguire in her work, "Feminist Participatory Research," "participatory research insists on an alternative positioning regarding the purpose of know-ledge creation…the intent is to transform reality 'with' rather than 'for' oppressed people" (417).
2. I refer here to work by Connell, Messner, Allain, and Whannel.
3. As Eduardo Bonilla-Silva suggests in his article "Color-Blind Racism," "today most whites assert that they 'don't see any color, just people,' that although the ugly face of discrimination is still with us, it is no longer the main factor in determining minorities' life chances…. But regardless of whites' 'sincere fictions,' racial considerations shade almost everything that happens in this country" (133).
4. This memoriam comes from Jim Red Cloud's funeral service held in South Dakota in 2017.

Chapter 3

1. Junie Rose, 2010–2013 (325–328).
2. Junie Rose, 2010–2013 (331–336).
3. Junie later learned the blankets reached 132 tribes.
4. Junie Rose, 2010–2013 (939–944).
5. Tristica Kendall, 2010 (36–37).
6. Tristica Kendall, 2010 (65–70).
7. Sheila, 2010 (82–86).
8. Sheila, 2010 (162–166).
9. Sheila, 2010 (659–665).
10. Carla, 2011, 2013 (69–73).
11. Carla, 2011, 2013 (249–252).
12. Kristin, 2010 (180–182).
13. Kristin, 2010 (211–218).
14. Bryana, 2010 (689–695).
15. Bryana, 2010 (422–425).
16. Kelly Quinn, email, 16 June 2015.
17. Kelly Quinn, 2012 (416–423).
18. Debra, 2010 (3).
19. Debra, 2010 (92–98).
20. Debra, 2010 (339–347).
21. Wendy, 2011–2014 (183–189).
22. Tail draggers are riders who latch onto another rider or group of riders and slow them down.
23. Jane and Schatzi, 2011–2013 (166–168).
24. Jane and Schatzi, 2011–2013 (190–192).
25. Jane and Schatzi, 2011–2013 (172–175).
26. Jane and Schatzi, 2011–2013 (411–417).
27. Debby, 2011 (238).
28. Debby, 2011 (240–242).
29. Debby, 2011 (250).
30. Debby, 2011 (221–227).
31. Debby Pearson, email, 17 June 2015.

32. Debby Pearson, email, 17 June 2015.
33. Eden, 2010–2011 (490–498).
34. Eden, 2010–2011 (506–508).
35. Sherie, 2010 (176–185).
36. Sherie, 2010 (313–314).

Chapter 4

1. Debra, 2011 (84–87).
2. Junie Rose, 2010–2014 (392–395).
3. Jane, 2011–2013 (306–307).
4. Wendy, 2011–2014 (78–81).
5. Junie Rose, 2010–2014 (372–402).
6. Debby, 2011 (351–354).
7. Junie Rose, 2010–2014 (381–386).
8. Kelly Quinn, 2012 (401–406).
9. Tristica, 2010 (230–232).
10. Bryana, 2010 (193–209).
11. Kelly Quinn, 2012 (520).
12. Debby, 2011 (262–265).
13. Kelly Quinn, 2012 (174–176).
14. Tristica, 2010 (792–795).
15. Tristica, 2010 (276).
16. Junie Rose, 2010–2014 (520–521).
17. Sheila, 2010 (246–248).
18. Bryana, 2010 (210–217).
19. Tristica, 2010 (548–550).
20. Sheila, 2010 (291–293).
21. Wendy, 2011–2014 (316–317).
22. Jersey Pearl, 2010 (542–546).
23. Junie Rose, 2010–2014 (328–330).
24. Junie Rose, 2010–2014 (331, 295–297).
25. Jersey Pearl, 2010 (314–316).
26. Eden, 2010, 2011 (315).
27. Tristica, 2010 (688–694).
28. Tristica, 2010 (277–280).
29. Jersey Pearl, 2010 (699–706).
30. Sheila, 2010 (67–70).
31. Sheila, 2010 (82–87).
32. Kelly Quinn, 2012 (326–329).
33. Sherie, 2010 (120–122).
34. Debby, 2011 (259–261).
35. Wendy, 2011–2014 (204–207).
36. Eden, 2010, 2011 (490–492).
37. Debby, 2011 (325).
38. Tristica, 2010 (207–214).
39. Jersey Pearl, 2010 (190–192).
40. Bryana, 2010 (181–184).
41. Bryana, 2010 (680–685).
42. Tristica, 2010 (140–144).
43. Jersey Pearl, 2010 (449–451).
44. Eden, 2010, 2011 (389–396).
45. Bryana, 2010 (362–367).
46. Eden, 2010, 2011 (511–515).
47. Carla, 2011, 2013 (394–395).
48. Tristica, 2010 (254–259).
49. Sheila, 2010 (375–380).
50. Sheila, 2010 (374).
51. Jersey Pearl, 2010 (628–631).
52. Sheila, 2010 (562–564).
53. Junie Rose, 2010–2014 (804–808).
54. Debby, 2011 (692–696).
55. Sheila, 2010 (420–422).
56. Tristica, 2010 (644–647).
57. Tristica, 2010 (275–281).
58. Debby, 2011 (646–649).
59. Wendy, 2011–2014 (96).
60. Junie Rose, 2010–2014 (810–813).
61. Eden, 2010, 2011 (461–468).
62. Junie Rose, 2010–2014 (775–779).
63. Debby, 2011 (172–174).
64. Schatzi, 2011–2013 (1524).
65. Jersey Pearl, 2010 (615–617).
66. Wendy, 2011–2014 (232–234).
67. In *An Ethics of Care*, Carol Gilligan describes this gendered performance. She states, "the ideal of care is thus an activity of relationship, of seeing and responding to need, taking care of the world by sustaining the web of connection so that no one is left alone" (62).
68. As Markula and Pringle suggest, the Panopticon in connection to sport normalizes behavior through external influencers; more specifically, they discuss how "in this broad manner we can consider fitness instructors, physical education teachers, sport scientists, and coaches as 'agents of normalization'" (45). In this instance, the agents of normalization are the women's support networks and fans.
69. Feminist theorist Rosemary Tong discussing Carol Gillian's ethics of care speaks to this type of connected decision-making. Gillian suggests women "reason toward moral decision making" in her study of pregnant women and abortion. Describing this caregiving ethic, Tong paraphrases Gillian's description of how the women worried about their decisions affecting themselves in "connection to their partners, parents, friends and so on" (165).
70. Feminist scholars like Peggy McIntosh show how men's attitudes differ from women's attitudes. In her article "Gender Perspectives on Educating for Global Citizenship," she states, "What is rewarded in them [young men], however, is a solo risk-taking and individualism, and if they are white male a go-it-alone and 'damn-the-torpedoes' kind of bravery without regard for, or awareness of, the outcomes for other people of one's behaviors" (26).

Chapter 5

1. Junie Rose, 2010–2014 (250–253).
2. Carla, 2011, 2013 (417–418).
3. Schatzi, 2011–2013 (846–848).
4. Jersey Pearl, 2010 (638–646).
5. Bryana, 2010 (55–59).
6. Wendy, 2011–2014 (51–52).
7. Eden, 2010, 2011 (30–31).
8. Tristica, 2010 (461–464).
9. Carla, 2011, 2013 (241–251).
10. Eden, 2010, 2011 (398).
11. Debby, 2011 (534–539).
12. Carla, 2011, 2013 (233–235).
13. Debby, 2011 (388–389).
14. Jane, 2011–2013 (813–817).
15. Sheila, 2010 (463–467).
16. Carla, 2011, 2013 (265–272).
17. Carla, 2011, 2013 (272–276).
18. Tristica, 2010 (430–432).
19. Jane, 2011–2013 (593–594).
20. Junie Rose, 2010–2014 (574–577).
21. Jane, 2011–2013 (1322–1324).
22. Jane, 2011–2013 (1302–1307).
23. Debby, 2011 (767–775).
24. Bryana, 2010 (468–472).
25. Sheila, 2010 (252–271).
26. Sherie, 2011 (342–343).
27. Jane, 2011–2013 (509–511).
28. Schatzi, 2011–2013 (507–513).
29. Jersey Pearl, 2011 (466).
30. Bryana, 2011 (348–357).
31. Kelly Quinn, 2012 (730–734).
32. Sherie, 2010, 2011 (277–282).
33. Debby, 2011 (404–408).
34. Junie Rose, 2010–2014 (553–555).
35. Schatzi, 2011–2013 (1631, 1632).
36. Junie Rose, 2010–2014 (746–748).
37. Jane, 2011–2013 (1635).
38. Bryana, 2010 (394–398).
39. Junie Rose, 2010–2014 (683–686).
40. Debra, 2011 (121–123).
41. Eden, 2010, 2011 (379).
42. Tristica, 2010 (158–162).
43. Eden, 2010, 2011 (496–498).
44. Wendy, 2011–2014 (130–132).
45. Jane, 2011–2013 (190–192).
46. Eden, 2010, 2011 (114–117).
47. Wendy, 2011–2014 (98–99).
48. Debra, 2011 (507–510).
49. Wendy, 2011–2014 (393–395).
50. Eden, 2010, 2011 (145–146).
51. Sherie, 2010 (339–340).
52. Sherie, 2010 (104–116).
53. Debby, 2011 (791–792).
54. Carla, 2011, 2013 (82–84).
55. Eden, 2010, 2011 (331–337).
56. Carla, 2011, 2013 (219).
57. Debra, 2011 (48).
58. Bryana, 2010 (233).
59. Schatzi, 2011–2013 (503–505).
60. Junie Rose, 2010–2014 (790–796).
61. Sheila, 2010 (307–310).
62. Debra, 2011 (346–347).
63. Sherie, 2010 (424–425).
64. Debra, 2011 (425–427).
65. Junie Rose, 2010–2014 (421–428).
66. Sheila, 2010 (661–665).
67. Wendy, 2011–2014 (376).
68. Sherie, 2010 (81–89).
69. Wendy, 2011–2014 (72–74).
70. Wendy, 2011–2014 (418–421).
71. Eden, 2010, 2011 (134–135).
72. Jersey Pearl, 2010 (665–666).
73. Jane, 2011–2013 (1083–1087).
74. Debra, 2011 (109–111).
75. Carla, 2011, 2013 (485–498).
76. Sherie, 2010 (562–584).
77. Tristica, 2010 (620–624).
78. Bryana, 2010 (292–296).
79. Junie Rose, 2010–2014 (409–415).
80. Jane, 2011–2013 (577–579).
81. Schatzi, 2011–2013 (595).
82. Jane, 2011–2013 (612–613).
83. Schatzi, 2011–2013 (614–616).
84. Schatzi, 2011–2013 (1884–1890).
85. Carla, 2011, 2013 (182–188).
86. In describing the Foucauldian concept of disciplined bodies, which sport scholars describe in terms of forcing our bodies to perform at extreme levels by justifying pain, Markula and Pringle suggest that some athletes recognized and ignored pain as they "simultaneously normalized and problematized injury" (118).
87. As Nancy Theberge notes in "Sport and Women's Empowerment," "regular physical activity is not only appropriate but desirable and can lead to a more positive sense of self and physical well being" (390).
88. In "White Privilege: Unpacking the Invisible Knapsack," Peggy McIntosh describes white privilege as "an invisible weightless knapsack of special provisions, maps, passports, codebooks, visas, clothes, tools, and blank checks" (175).
89. Debra, 2011 (443).
90. Junie Rose, 2010–2014 (988–989).
91. Jersey Pearl, 2011 (673–675).

Chapter 6

1. Debra, 2011 (177–179).
2. Sherie, 2010 (140–147).

3. Debra, Sheila, Schatzi, Jane, Wendy, Kelly
4. Debra, 2011 (21–23).
5. Kelly Quinn, 2012 (258–260).
6. Sheila, 2010 (107–108).
7. Debby, 2011 (238–242).
8. Jane, 2011–2013 (439–451).
9. Schatzi, 2011–2013 (416–417).
10. Debby, 2011 (365–368).
11. Wendy, 2011–2014 (275–277).
12. Carla, 2011, 2013 (441–444).
13. Eden, 2010, 2011 (422–423).
14. Bryana, 2010 (248–257).
15. Eden, 2010, 2011 (161–166).
16. Wendy, 2011–2014 (381–382).
17. Wendy, 2011–2014 (146–147).
18. Carla, 2011, 2013 (68–70).
19. Debra, 2011 (124).
20. Bryana, 2010 (163); Kelly Quinn, 2012 (337).
21. Eden, 2010, 2011 (54–55).
22. Debby, 2011 (684).
23. As Braidotti suggests, I find that our multiple nomadic identities "are seldom synchronized" and thus "one may for a period of time, coincide with some [identity] categories, but seldom with them all" (94).
24. In a postmodern age, these collectively and individually constructed identities are constantly in flux. Scholars such as Wheaton (2004) and Kellner (1992) suggest that identities formed around more fixed or stable social markers––work, gender, ethnicity, and age––become fluid based on multiple self-reflexive markers, which are subject to constant change. Rosi Braidotti expands this notion through her idea of nomadic identities and becoming(s). According to Braidotti, the mobile, self-reflexive identities that Wheaton describes place us in a situation of always "becoming"—our identities are continuously growing, changing and morphing into something else. For example, Braidotti states, "what the process of becoming stands for is the qualitative shift of perspective…there is a becoming woman, for instance, which refers to established counter-ideologies and theoretical frameworks and emancipatory ideals and practices" (133).
25. Junie Rose, 2010–2018 (272).
26. In attempting to define female masculinity or even masculinity itself, Halberstam notes, "masculinity must not and cannot and should not reduce down to the male body and its effects" (1). She further notes, "the suppression of female masculinity, [either in the form of tomboyism, drag kings, or other gender nonconforming identities], allows for male masculinity to stand unchallenged as the bearer of gender stability and gender deviance" (41).
27. In her work, *Female Masculinity*, Judith Halberstam notes, "tomboyism generally describes an extended period of female masculinity" (5). According to Halberstam, parents generally accept this blurring of the gender binary—as long as their child eventually "grows out of it" and continues to assume some female characteristics.
28. Tristica, 2010 (475–479).
29. Bryana, 2010 (680–685).
30. Bryana, 2010 (160–162).
31. Kelly Quinn, 2012 (282–285).
32. Debby, 2011 (657–660).
33. Junie Rose, 2010–2014 (256–260).
34. Tristica, 2010 (445–448).

Chapter 7

1. Carla, 2011, 2013 (404–406).
2. Debby, 2011 (762–764).
3. Jane and Schatzi, 2011–2013 (1523–1524).
4. I point here to Kendzierski and Johnson 1993, Anderson 2003, and Nuviala et. al 2013.
5. Sport and leisure scholars writing about termination of activities point to gendered differences between men and women (Stewart, Kendzierski and Johnson, and Anderson). Specifically men and women reported different reasons for quitting a sport or leisure activity. These reasons (or excuses) range from financial constraints to injury to coaching styles to decreasing intrinsic motivation. Although varied, many studies found women linked an excuse to the termination of the given sporting activity. Further, Kendzierksi and Johnson found women reported a higher frequency of thoughts involving reasons or excuses for not exercising than men. Harris and Smith's work on college athletes and Boulware's writings about backpackers found women quit or burned out more often and earlier than their male counterparts did. These studies both support and are contrary to my own research. As previously stated, women tend to finish the Hoka Hey at higher percentage rates than men. This contrasts with the studies pointing to higher cessation rates among women. It's important to note that the sport

and leisure studies regarding the termination of activity spoke of continuous activity over time. In the context of this work, the activity, while prolonged, is not sustained over the course of multiple months, years, etc.; rather, it is limited to a specific time frame. This difference may affect the rates at which women involved in each study left their respective activities. Despite this difference, research points toward a higher need for reason(s) to quit among women. The women in these studies needed to justify their termination either to themselves or to their communities.

6. Tristica, 2010 (118–120).
7. Kelly Quinn, 2012 519–522.
8. Kelly Quinn, 2012 (505–510).
9. Kelly Quinn, 2012 (522–526).
10. Kelly Quinn, 2012 (517–519).
11. Carla, 2011, 2013 (387–388).
12. Carla, 2011, 2013 (241–246).
13. Carla, 2011, 2013 (382–387).
14. Carla, 2011, 2013 (388–395).
15. Carla, 2011, 2013 (207–209).
16. Carla, 2011, 2013 (246–251).

Conclusion

1. Seen through Gilligan's feminist ethics of care and Braidotti's nomadic subjectivities.
2. Supporting Halberstam and Butler's notions of gender nonconformity and the idea of forming a more complete person.

Bibliography

Alford, Steven E., and Suzanne Ferriss. *Motorcycle.* London: Reaktion Books, 2007. Print.
Allain, Kristi. "'Real Fast and Tough': The Construction of Canadian Hockey Masculinity." *Sociology of Sport Journal* 25 (2008): 462–481. Print.
Anderson, Cheryl. "When More Is Better: Number of Motives and Reasons for Quitting as Correlates of Physical Activity in Women." *Health Education Research Theory and Practice* 18.5 (2003): 525–537. Print.
Auster, Carol J. "Transcending Potential Antecedent Leisure Constraints: The Case of Women Motorcycle Operators." *Journal of Leisure Research* 33.3 (2001): 272–298. Print.
Barker-Ruchti, Natalie, and Richard Tinning. "Foucault in Leotards: Corporeal Discipline in Women's Artistic Gymnastics." *Sociology of Sport Journal* 27 (2010): 229–250. Print.
Birrell, Susan, and Nancy Theberge. "Feminist Resistance and Transformation in Sport." *Women and Sport: Interdisciplinary Perspectives.* Champaign, IL: Human Kinestics, 1994. 361–376. Print.
Bonilla-Silva, Eduardo. "Color-Blind Racism." *Race, Class and Gender in the United States.* 9th ed. New York: Worth Publishers, 2014. 133–140. Print.
Boulware, David. "Gender Differences Among Long-Distance Backpackers: A Prospective Study of Women Appalachian Trail Backpackers." *Wilderness and Environmental Medicine* 15: 175–180. Print.
Braidotti, Rosi. *Transpositions.* Cambridge: Polity Press, 2006. Print.
Briscoe, Steve. *Solitary—Without the Confinement: A Rider's Life-Changing Experience During the 2013 Hoka Hey Motorcycle Challenge.* Bloomington: WestBow Press, 2015. Print.
Brown, Ruth. "Formal complaint filed against Hoka Hey Motorcycle Challenge." *Rapid City Journal.* 2 July 2010. Web.http://rapidcityjournal.com/news/formal-complaint-filed-against-hoka-hey-motorcycle-challenge/article_a5b791e0-8628-11df-a447-001cc4c03286.html?utm_medium=social&utm_source=email&utm_campaign=user-share.
Bruack-Weiss, Ann. *The Caregiver's Tale: Loss and Renewal in Memoirs of Family Life.* New York: Columbia University Press, 2006. Print.
Brymer, E., and L.G. Oades. "Extreme Sports: A Positive Transformation in Courage and Humility." *Journal of Humanistic Psychology* 49.1 (2009): 114–126. Print.
Butler, Judith. *Gender Trouble: Feminism and the Subversion of Identity.* New York: Routledge, 1990. Print.
_____. *Undoing Gender.* New York: Routledge, 2004. Print.

Chananie-Hill, Ruth A., Shelly A. McGrath, and Justin Stoll,. "Deviant or Normal? Female Bodybuilders' Accounts of Social Reactions." *Deviant Behavior* 33.10 (2012): 811–830. Print.
Chang, Heewon. *Autoethnography as Method*. Walnut Creek, CA: Left Coast Press, Inc., 2008. Print.
Chappell, Ben. "Lowrider Style: Cultural Politics and the Poetics of Scale." *Cultural Studies: An Anthology*. New York: Wiley, 2008. Print.
Conner, M. Shelly. "First-Wave Feminist Struggles in Black Motorcycle Clubs." *International Journal of Motorcycle Studies* 5.2 (2009): n. p. Web.
Cox, Lynne. *Swimming to Antarctica: Tales of a Long-Distance Swimmer*. New York: Harcourt Books, 2004. Print.
Deleuze, Gilles, and Felix Guattari. "The Rhizome/A Thousand Plateaus." *Social Theory: The Multicultural and Classic Readings*. 4th ed. Boulder, CO: Westview Press, 2010. 671–673. Print.
Di Leonardo, Michaela. "Mixed and Rigorous Cultural Studies Methodology—an Oxymoron?" *Questions of Method in Cultural Studies*. Malden, MA: Blackwell Publishing, 2006. 205–220. Print.
Durham, James G., and Virginia Thomas. *Sacred Buffalo: The Lakota Way for a New Beginning*. Boulder, CO: Sycamore Island Books, 1996. Print.
Falk, Gerhard. *Stigma: How We Treat Outsiders*. Amherst, NY: Prometheus Books, 2001. Print.
Ferrar, Ann. *Hear Me Roar: Women, Motorcycles, and the Rapture of the Road*. New Hampshire: Whitehorse Press, 2000. Print.
Finley, Nancy. "Skating Femininity: Gender Maneuvering in Women's Roller Derby." *Journal of Contemporary Ethnography* 39.4 (2010): 359–387. Print.
Goffman, Erving. *Stigma: Notes on the Management of Spoiled Identity*. New York: Simon & Schuster, 1963. Print.
Guillet, Emma, et al. "Understanding Female Sport Attrition in a Stereotypical Male Sport Within the Framework of Eccles's Expectancy-Value Model." *Psychology of Women Quarterly* 30: 358–368. Print.
Hall, Stuart, et al., eds. *Culture, Media, Language*. New York: Routledge, 1980. Print.
Hammermeister, Jon. "Gender Differences in Coping with Endurance Sport Stress: Are Men from Mars and Women from Venus?" *Journal of Sport Behavior* 27.2: 148–164. Print.
"Harley-Davidson Tackles Stereotypes in New Advertising Campaign." *Harley-Davidson News*. Mar. 2012. Web.
Harris, Brandon, and Meredith Smith. "Influence of Motivational Climate and Goal Orientation on Burnout: An Exploratory Analysis among Division I Collegiate Student-Athletes." *Introduction to Sport Psychology*. Robert Schinke, ed. Hauppauge, NY: Nova Science Publishers, Inc., 2011. Print.
Hebdige, Dick. *Subculture: The Meaning of Style*. London: Methuen, 1979. Print.
Heywood, Leslie. "A New Look at Female Athletes and Masculinity." *Built to Win: The Female Athlete as Cultural Icon*. Heywood, Leslie, and Shari L. Dworkin, eds. Minneapolis: University of Minnesota Press, 2003. Print.
"History of the Hoka Hey Motorcycle Challenge." Web. 13 Dec. 2012.
Hogarth, Robin, Natalia Karelaia, and Carlos Andres Trujillo. "When Should I Quit? Gender Differences in Exiting Competitions." *Journal of Economic Behavior and Organization* 83 (2–12): 136–150. Print.
"Hoka Hey Motorcycle Challenge." Web. 13 Dec. 2012.
HokaHey Challenge. *Hoka Hey Discusses Cee Bailey Windshield*. n. p. Film.
Hokaheychallenge.com. Web. 21 Nov. 2015.
Jansen, Liz. *Women, Motorcycles and the Road to Empowerment: Fifty Inspirational*

Stories of Adventure and Self Discovery. Orangeville: Trillium Wordworks, 2011. Print.
Jeffery, Karin A., and Ted M. Butryn. "The Motivations of Runners in a Cause-Based Marathon-Training Program." *Journal of Sport Behavior* 35.3 (2012): 300–319. Print.
Joans, Barbara. *Bike Lust: Harleys, Women, and American Society.* Madison: University of Wisconsin Press, 2001. Print.
Johnson, Corey W., and Beth Kivel. "Gender, Sexuality, and Queer Theory in Sport." *Sport and Gender Identities, Masculinities, Femininities and Sexualities.* New York: Routledge, 2007. 93–105. Print.
Kane, Mary Jo. "Resistance and Transformation of the Oppositional Binary: Exposing Sport as a Continuum." *Journal of Sport and Social Issues* (1995): 191–218. Print.
Kauer, Kerrie J., and Vikki Krane. "'Scary Dykes' and 'Feminine Queens': Stereotypes and Female Collegiate Athletes." *Women in Sport and Physical Activity Journal* 15.1 (2006): 43–56. Print.
Kay, Joanne, and Suzanne Laberge. "'Mandatory Equipment': Women in Adventure Racing." *Understanding Lifestyle Sports: Consumption, Identity, and Difference.* New York: Routledge, 2004. 154–174. Print.
Kellner, D. "Popular Culture and the Construction of Postmodern Identities." *Modernity and Identity.* Lash, S., and J. Friedman, eds. Cambridge: Blackwell Publishing, 1992. Print.
Kendzierski, Deborah, and Wendy Johnson. "Excuses, Excuses, Excuses: A Cognitive Behavioral Approach to Exercise Implementation." *Journal of Sport and Exercise Psychology* 15 (1993): 207–219. Print.
King, Wesley C., Jr., Edward W. Miles, and Jane Kinska. "Boys Will Be Boys (and Girls Will Be Girls): The Attribution of Gender Role Stereotypes in a Gaming Situation." *Sex Roles* 25.11 (1991): 607–623. Print.
Koo, Vera, with Justin Pahl. *The Most Unlikely Champion: A Memoir.* Bloomington: Balboa Press, 2017. Print.
Krane, Vikki. "Gendered Social Dynamics in Sport." *Group Dynamics in Exercise and Sport Psychology: Contemporary Themes.* Routledge, 2008. 159–176. Print.
_____. "One Lesbian Feminist Epistemology: Integrating Feminist Standpoint, Queer Theory, and Feminist Cultural Studies." *The Sport Psychologist* 15 (2001): 401–411. Print.
Krane, Vikki, and Shannon Baird. "Using Ethnography in Applied Sport Psychology." *Journal of Applied Sport Psychology* 17.2 (2005): 87–107. Print.
Krane, Vikki, et al. "Living the Paradox: Female Athletes Negotiate Femininity and Muscularity." *Sex Roles* 50.5/6 (2004): 315–329. Print.
Lowes, David. "Women and Endurance Running: Should Female Endurance Athletes Train Differently Than Their Male Counterparts?" *Athletics Weekly* 17 (2009): 40–41. Print.
Lyotard, Jean-Francois. "The Postmodern Condition." *Literary Theory: An Anthology.* 2nd ed. Malden, MA: Blackwell Publishing, 2004. 355–364. Print.
Maguire, Patricia. "Feminist Participatory Research." *Just Methods: An Interdisciplinary Feminist Reader.* Jaggar, Alison, ed. Boulder, CO: Paradigm Publishers, 2008. 417–432. Print.
Maharam, Lewis G. "Running Doc: Are Women More Suited for Endurance Than Men?" *Competitor.* n. p., n. d. Web. 14 Mar. 2012.
Markula, Pirkko, and Richard Pringle. *Foucault, Sport and Exercise: Power, Knowledge, and Transforming The Self.* New York: Routledge, 2006. Print.
Marx, Leo. *The Machine in the Garden: Technology and the Pastoral Ideal in America.* Oxford: Oxford University Press, 1964. Print.
McCann, Carole, and Seung-Kyung Kim. *Feminist Theory Reader: Local and Global Perspectives.* 2nd ed. New York: Routledge, 2010. Print.

McDougall, Christopher. *Are We Born to Run?* n. p. Audio Recording.

_____. *Born to Run: A Hidden Tribe, Superathletes, and the Greatest Race the World Has Never Seen.* 2nd ed. New York: Vintage Books, 2011. Print.

Messner, Michael. "Playing Center: The Triad of Violence in Men's Sport." *Taking the Field: Women, Men, and Sports.* University of Minnesota Press, 2002. 27–62. Print.

"The Movement." *The Hoka Hey Experience.* Film.

Mullins, Sasha. *Biker Lady Living and Riding Free!* New York: Citadel Press, 2003. Print.

Neihardt, John C. *Black Elk Speaks.* Premier Edition. Albany: SUNY Press, 2008. Print.

Nuviala, Alberto, et al. "Duration of Membership at Sports Centers and Reasons for Quitting." *Perceptual and Motor Skills: Exercise and Sport* 117.3: 733–741. Print.

Parr, H. *The Deleuze Dictionary.* 2nd ed. Edinburgh: Edinburgh Press, 2010. Print.

Pflugfelder, Ehren Helmut. "Something Less than a Driver: Toward an Understanding in Gendered Bodies in Motorsport." *Journal of Sport and Social Issues* 33.4 (2009): 411–426. Print.

Pierson, Melissa Holbrook. *The Perfect Vehicle: What It Is about Motorcycles.* New York: Norton, 1997. Print.

Red Cloud, Jim. Personal Conversation with Author. 15 Feb. 2011.

Richardson, Laurel. "Skirting a Pleated Text: De-Disciplining an Academic Life." *Qualitative Inquiry* 3 (1997): 295–303. Print.

Roster, Catherine. "'Girl Power' and Participation in Macho Recreation: The Case of Female Harley Riders." *Leisure Sciences* 29 (2007): 443–461. Print.

Rothenberg, Paula S., and Kelly S. Mayhew, eds. *Race, Class, and Gender in the United States.* 9th ed. New York: Worth Publishers, 2014. Print.

Rouen, Ethan. "Taking It to the Limit." *American Way* (2013): 50–57. Print.

Russell, Kate. "'Queers Even in Netball?' Interpretation of the Lesbian Label among Sportswomen." *Sport and Gender Identities, Masculinities, Femininities and Sexualities.* New York: Routledge, 2007. 106–121. Print.

Sabo, Don. "Pigskin, Patriarchy, and Pain." *Race, Class and Gender in the United States.* 9th ed. New York: Worth Publishers, 2014. 448–451. Print.

Shaw, Susan M. "Gender, Leisure, and Constraint: Towards a Framework for the Analysis of Women's Leisure." *Journal of Leisure Research* 26.1 (1994): 8–22. Print.

Sisjord, Mari Kristin, and Elsa Kristiansen. "Serious Athletes or Media Clowns? Female and Male Wrestlers' Perceptions of Media Constructions." *Sociology of Sport Journal* 25 (2008): 350–368. Print.

Sparkes, Andrew. "Autoethnography and Narratives of Self: Reflections on Criteria in Action." *Sociology of Sport Journal* 17 (2000): 21–43. Print.

Stewart, Craig, and Joan Taylor. "Why Female Athletes Quit: Implications for Coach Education." *Physical Educator* 57.4 (2000): n. p. Print.

Stock, Kyle. "Can Harley-Davidson Finally Woo Women?" *Bloomberg Business.* 2 June 2014. Web. 21 Feb. 2015.

"Terms and Conditions of Participation in the Hoka Hey Motorcycle Challenge." Web. 13 Dec. 2012.

Theberge, Nancy. "Reflections on the Body in the Sociology of Sport." *Quest* 43 (1991): 123–134. Print.

Theberge, Nancy. "Sport and Women's Empowerment." *Women's Studies International Forum* 10.4 (1987): 387–393. Print.

Thompson, William. "Don't Call Me a 'Biker Chick': Women Motorcyclists Redefining Deviant Identity." *Deviant Behavior* 33.1 (2012): 58–71. Print.

Tong, Rosemary. *Feminist Thought: A More Comprehensive Introduction.* 3rd ed. Charlotte: Westview Press, 2009. Print.

"True Pioneers." *American Motorcyclist* (2006): 52–56. Print.

Walker, L. "Under the Bonnet: Car Culture, Technological Dominance and Young Men of the Working Class." *Journal of Interdisciplinary Gender Studies* 3.2 (1998): n.p. Print.

Whannel, Garry. "Mediating Masculinities: The Production of Media Representations in Sport." *Sport and Gender Identities, Masculinities, Femininities and Sexualities.* New York: Routledge, 2007. 7–21. Print.

Wheaton, Belinda. *Understanding Lifestyle Sports: Consumption, Identity, and Difference.* New York: Routledge, 2004. Print.

White, Renee. "Talking about Sex and HIV: Conceptualizing a New Sociology of Experience." *Just Methods: An Interdisciplinary Feminist Reader.* Jaggar, Alison, ed. Boulder: Paradigm Publishers, 2008. 282–289. Print.

Wise, Gene. "'Paradigm Dramas' in American Studies: A Cultural and Institutional History of the Movement." *American Quarterly* 31.3 (1979): n. p. Print.

Zaslow, Emilie, and Judy Schoenberg. "Stumping to Girls through Pop Culture: Feminist Interventions to Shape Future Political Leaders." *Women and Language* 35.1 (2012): 97–116. Print.

Zheutlin, Peter. *Around the World on Two Wheels: Annie Londonderry's Extraordinary Ride.* New York: Citadel Press, 2007. Print.

Index

American Motorcyclist Association 5–6, 47

Battles, Wendy 18, 26, 70, 84–86, 109, 120, 136, 139–140, 147–150, 153–155, 157–160, 178
binary 27, 37, 47, 61–62, 113, 118, 131–132, 134, 155, 166, 169, 176–177, 183, 186
Bixby, Jane 70, 86–88, 91, 120–124, 143–144, 153, 156–157, 160, 163
Briscoe, Steve 161–162
Brown, Schatzi 24, 55–56, 70, 86–88, 91, 120–123, 144, 153, 156–157, 160, 163

competition 5–6, 16–17, 19, 33–34, 36–38, 40–41, 44, 102, 105, 107–110, 131, 135, 137, 156, 162, 186, 190
continuum 163, 187, 190
Cox, Lynne 106–107, 114, 168–169, 175

dragon boat racing 137–138
Dubois, Carla 24, 70, 77–79, 120–122, 126, 131, 140, 149, 153, 175–177
Durham, Beth 32, 42, 58–59, 66, 103, 133, 142–142, 145, 153, 175
Durham, Jim Red Cloud 11, 36, 42, 52–55, 58–61, 64–67, 103, 120, 129, 133, 187–188

empowerment 1, 4, 18–19, 37, 42, 82, 86–88, 92, 106, 109, 110, 115, 119, 130–132, 134–135–137, 139–141, 159, 163, 165, 185, 189
endurance motorcycle; challenges 1, 4, 19, 40, 163; riders 4, 6, 117, 154–155
ethics of care 62, 98, 106, 108, 112, 134, 137, 187

female masculinity 75, 80, 95, 131, 156–157, 163, 166
femininity 7–9, 19, 38–39, 44, 46–48, 51, 80–81, 83, 97, 108, 110, 113, 115, 118, 131, 134, 150–152, 155–163, 166, 168, 176–177, 186–187, 189–190
Flannagan, Shalane 108

gender nonconforming 94, 113–114, 155, 157, 166, 185

GPS 20, 32, 34–36, 85, 101, 104, 116–117, 132, 176, 179

Harley-Davidson 5–6, 11, 32–33, 51–52, 76, 77–78, 84–85, 90, 92, 171
Hoehn, Sheila 18, 24, 26, 70, 76–77, 120–121, 123, 140, 148, 150, 153, 157
Hoka Hey Motorcycle Challenge: challenge operators 12, 16, 20, 25, 34, 36, 42, 56, 66–67, 108, 132, 187–188; cheating 21, 104–105, 116–117; checkpoint 16, 20, 22, 32, 72, 88, 91, 101, 103, 105, 132, 167, 178; directions 12, 14, 16, 20–25, 30, 32–34, 52, 57, 80, 104–105, 117, 121–123, 132–133, 145, 164, 167, 177; logo 13, 15, 56, 61, 71, 77; prize money 16, 19–20, 35, 107; rules 17, 19, 21, 33–36, 104, 116–117, 156, 163; 2010 Challenge 34, 57, 65–68, 109; 2011 Challenge 34, 63; 2012 Challenge 35, 136; warrior woman 77–78, 111, 140, 171, 174, 176, 183
Hotchkilss, Effie 6

Iron Butt 4, 78, 119

Kendall, Tristica (T) 26, 70, 74–75, 120–121, 136, 148, 158, 165
Koo, Vera 130

Lakota 1, 15, 36, 52, 54–56, 58, 60–62, 64–65, 73, 78, 83, 134, 146, 187
Langley, Debra 26, 70, 83–84, 120, 125, 127 135, 149, 153–154, 157
Linden, Desiree 108
Londonderry, Annie 159

Mailloux, Eden 28, 30, 32, 70, 90–91, 108, 120, 126, 141, 149
marathon 12, 69, 107–108, 111, 133, 168
masculinity 1, 3, 7, 11–12, 37–42, 45–49, 51, 67, 75, 80, 95, 97, 110, 131, 134, 140, 152, 155–158, 163, 166, 168, 174, 176–177, 182–183, 189–190
Mason, Bryana 70, 80–81, 120, 122–123, 125, 149, 158, 160, 164

203

McKelvey, Kristin "Jersey Pearl" 57–58, 70, 79–81, 120, 123, 125, 135, 148
mother 73, 80, 151, 170–171, 177
motivation 74, 98, 106–118, 168, 172
motorcycle: clubs 4–5, 46–47, 50–51, 79, 135, 139; culture 4–5, 12, 37, 39–42, 44–45, 47–52, 54, 71, 87, 90, 133–134, 139, 150–151, 154, 161–162, 165, 172, 183–184, 187, 189–190

Newell, Sherie 18, 70, 91–92, 123–124, 127

O'Barr, Jeri 66–67

Patrick, Danica 39, 155
Pearson, Debby 70, 88–90, 117, 120, 122, 124, 148–149, 157, 157–158, 164
Pine Ridge 1, 15, 36, 54–57, 61, 63–65, 73, 78, 99, 107, 121, 129–130, 134, 187–188

Quinn, Kelly 18, 70, 82–83, 97, 120, 149, 153, 155, 157, 159, 164; *see also* Throttle Girl

Radcliffe, Paula 108
Robinson, Dot 6–8
Rose, Junie 18, 70–74, 81, 109, 122, 124–126, 135–136, 139, 148–149, 152–154, 158, 165

Seneca Nation 35–36, 188
Sons of Anarchy 47, 51

South Dakota 1, 15, 36, 54–55, 58, 60, 84, 93, 124, 133, 135
sport: center of 3, 37, 110, 190; endurance 107–108, 138, 171, 176; lifestyle 14, 26–27, 37–39, 108–109, 139, 162, 171, 185–186, 190
Stringfield, Bessie 7

Tail of the Dragon 33, 124
Throttle Girl 70, 81–82; *see also* Quinn, Kelly
Tulu, Deratu 108

Van Buren, Adeline 4
Van Buren, Augusta 4
Van Vlerah, Abby 14, 60, 70, 72, 82 92–97, 148, 153, 157, 188
Van Vlerah, Karen (Mom) 32, 58–59, 92–93, 147, 179–181
Van Vlerah, Jim (Dad) 12–14, 20–24, 30–32, 58, 61, 67, 78, 84, 85–86, 89, 92–94, 101, 112, 120, 126, 143, 147, 149, 167, 178–183

Wagner, Clara 6
whiteness 12, 38, 42, 49–52, 59, 67, 132–133

Yosemite 105, 117

www.ingramcontent.com/pod-product-compliance
Ingram Content Group UK Ltd.
Pitfield, Milton Keynes, MK11 3LW, UK
UKHW042005140426
5217IPUK00015B/988